THE CONTINENT OF
BLACK CONSCIOUSNESS

THE CONTINENT OF
BLACK CONSCIOUSNESS

*on the history of the African diaspora
from slavery to the present day*

Erna Brodber

New Beacon Books

First published 2003 by New Beacon Books Ltd
76 Stroud Green Road, London N4 3EN

© 2003 Erna Brodber

ISBN 1 873201 1 76

Printed by Woolnough Bookbinders, Irthingborough, Northants

CONTENTS

INTRODUCTION
Rupert Lewis

I have had the experience, on more than one occasion, of being invited to the Woodside community as speaker in Dr Brodber's Blackspace programme. Venues have ranged from her home, the community centre, the church, and the memorial called Daddy Rock where our forefathers and foremothers met to reason about their own business. Daddy Rock is situated on a steep hillside and in slavery times was covered with bush and was not easily accessible. These things combined to make it a good hideout for secret meetings by enslaved Africans in that community. It has now been recovered as one of the important sites for Emancipation 'reasonings' by Dr Brodber and the Woodside community. More importantly, as a result of her research, some of the villagers can trace their African ancestors back to the days of slavery and therefore family and community pasts have been fused in a new understanding of our story. This book provides the historical background to the experience of which Daddy Rock is a symbol.

In the foreword to *The Continent of Black Consciousness: on the history of the African diaspora from slavery to the present*, Erna Brodber tells us that the lectures which comprise the collection were "given in a series called the Seven Second Sunday Seminars. This series inaugurated what I hope will be the School for the Descendants of African's Enslaved in the New World housed here in the small rural village of Woodside in St Mary, Jamaica". What is this continent of black consciousness? It is a Pan-African construct based on the shared historical experience arising from the transatlantic slave trade, plantation slavery, slave revolts and post-emancipation construction.

The author has created an intellectual space for remembering and remaking self and she has built an important bridge between scholars and community that ought to be multiplied in rural and urban communities elsewhere in Africa and the African diaspora.

Over the years many courses have been taught at Blackspace to students visiting from overseas, including the Caribbean, as well as residents of the village of Woodside. There have been reasonings and reenactments around the anniversary of Emancipation from slavery in 1838. These reasonings take place over several days and those who stay the few days spend time in the homes of residents and fellowship with them. The reenactment of the reading of the Emancipation Proclamation, participating in religious activities around Emancipation, cap activities which would have included visiting the old coffee estate, its great house, the jail, the Flint River where our foreparents lived, and Daddy Rock. Emancipation songs and dances, and eating the kind of food that was available at the time ensure that the experience is not merely cerebral but also one of taste and touch. Most importantly it is a profound spiritual reconnection with the past and in certain ceremonies, marking the transition from slavery to personal freedom, tears flow freely from the eyes of participating descendants.

It is good that these lectures are now available for people anywhere to read, learn and do for their communities what she has done for her own. Very often research and publications by scholars on themes of immediate interest and benefit to our people do not reach them. When they do, participants from communities such as Woodside are not only highly appreciative but also ask when the next talk will take place. Our researchers and writers are the poorer for this lack of contact and valuable feedback. Very often this feedback takes the form of penetrating questions, which encourage new lines of enquiry.

Erna Brodber deals head-on with this issue, stating that her lectures are written "from a very personal point of view to emphasise the fact that though the issues they discuss are usually the subject of university courses, academia has no monopoly on them; they are matters which affect our daily lives. In addition, each of them tries to point us towards a path of social and psychological engineering".

She provides a rich comparative panorama of slavery, drawing on Orlando Patterson's *Slavery and Social Death* and his discussion of slavery in human history inclusive of slavery under the Greeks and during the early Roman Empire. She situates the modern enslavement of Africans in this context,

paying attention to its peculiarities. The post-slavery period is
also examined in a comparative framework of the Caribbean
and the United States, two areas of the 'Continent of Black
Consciousness' that are dealt with at length in these lectures.
She uses the word 'virulent' to describe the nature of slavery
experienced by Africans. Many fell victim during the
transatlantic voyage and the hardships of slavery. The many
ways that Africans resisted the virulence of this system in
cultural practices, in active and passive forms of rebellion, are
documented and interpreted.

The movements that emerged during and after slavery show
the roots of Pan-Africanism. The lecture 'Liberation Thought
and Action 1789-1900' discusses, among other topics, the
Haitian Revolution and maroon revolts, which were the
harbingers of modern Pan-Africanism. The maroon wars and
the historic Haitian Revolutions were highpoints of strategising
and demonstrated tremendous organisational skill and military
prowess against the most powerful armies in the world backed
by strong economies that owed so much to African slave labour.

This is followed by the 'The World the Freedman/Woman
Made'. The work of Marcus Garvey is discussed at length under
the topic 'Marcus Garvey and the Continent of Black
Consciousness'. His critics are engaged and the key
geographical points of the 'continent of black consciousness' are
given organisational expression through the Universal Negro
Improvement Association and African League. The traditions of
Pan-Africanism that Garvey built on are outlined. In addition
there is a follow-up discussion of C.L.R. James, George
Padmore, Claude McKay and others. These constitute a male
Pan-African tradition.

Brodber's fellow novelists Merle Hodge and Paule Marshall
represent the female Pan-African tradition of which she is an
integral part. The lecture entitled 'View from Juba's Head'
speaks to the present, using the novels *Crick Crack Monkey* by
Merle Hodge and Paule Marshall's *Praisesong for the Widow* to
see "whether these women's works indicate an intimacy with
the existence of Africa and its diaspora; whether they write out
of this consciousness; whether their works indicate that they are
not only born Juba, but feel Juba". Brodber explains that "[t]he
notion, 'Juba's head' ... allows us to posit the characteristics of

femaleness in Africa of the diaspora. In Bambara the word
'Juba' is more than a person's name. It refers to a hen who has
young children. Among the Wolof too, it is more than a female
name – it refers to tough-tough hair on the head. We have
chosen to assign the quality of mental toughness and nurturing
of her young to Juba and ask ourselves now, whether the black
women in these inventions of Hodge and Marshall are
portrayed as mentally tough-tough, as creatures who take care
of their young." These authors explore alienation from a wider
community through social mobility, economic advancement
and higher education and certainly in Paule Marshall's novel
reconnect to what the Guinea-Bissau philosopher and freedom
fighter, Amilcar Cabral, called 'a return to the source'. The book
ends appropriately with 'Writing your village history – the case
of Woodside'.

The Continent of Black Consciousness draws on historical
research, oral testimony, myths, fiction, and social science
research – all of which are areas in which the author has
laboured over a long and distinguished career as historian,
sociologist and novelist. Readers of this volume will benefit
from insights as to the way we were and the way we are now.
These lectures pose the question: What kind of world are we
constructing now? In 1999 the Daddy Rock Emancipation
anniversary discussion asked the question "If you knew in 1838
what you know now, how would you have advised us to
proceed?" There are no easy answers here as they involve the
future of the individual and his or her connection to local
community and through that to national and regional
community and the unavoidable redefining challenges of
globalisation of which the transatlantic slave trade and
plantation slavery were important building blocks.

Brodber provides not only the raw material but also the
analysis that will continue the process of mental emancipation
about which Garvey spoke in 1937 and Bob Marley sang in 1980
in 'Redemption Song'. Brodber can be placed in a line of
historians-as-activists, people such as W.E.B. Du Bois of the
United States, Eric Williams and C.L.R. James of Trinidad, Elsa
Goveia and Walter Rodney of Guyana, the pioneering gender
research of Lucille Mair, and the reclamation of the songs,
prayers and utterances of Yoruba speakers in post-

independence Trinidad by Maureen Warner-Lewis, reminding us of African survivals throughout the communities of the African diaspora and the sources of energy and renewal that these survivals represent.

What is distinctive about Brodber's work is the emphasis on learning from and with her natal community and returning to this community the knowledge and information about itself. It is an approach that can be followed by communities anywhere in the African diaspora and on the African continent itself. Out of this specificity of focus the general themes of slavery, liberation, reconstruction and redemption are worked through in a personally enriching way. Brodber challenges us to creative intellectual community leadership.

FOREWORD

In those days when we in Jamaica sat the Jamaica Local Examinations, we had to know about Toussaint L'Ouverture and about the 'six great Jamaicans'. Those were the days of the dual education system. One route of the system led from elementary school to training college and the lesser professions and the other, from prep school to high school and thence to university. The twain occasionally met when one of us elementary school children got a scholarship to high school. I was one of them. There ended my study of Jamaican or any other black history. University was little better but since I studied history there, I could later help myself to wider historical knowledge about my country and its people and those who most look like the majority of us.

Few of us who crossed over had or took this option, though all of us need this knowledge in order to make sense of our political situation. These lectures, called *The Continent of Black Consciousness*, are designed to fill this information and experience gap and to take us from First Jamaica Local Examinations and their equivalent throughout the British Empire, now Commonwealth, of which we are a part, through undergraduate to graduate seminars in Black History. The lectures were given in a series called 'The Seven Second Sunday Seminars'. This series inaugurated what I now hope will be the School for the Descendants of Africans Enslaved in the New World housed here in the small rural village of Woodside in St Mary, Jamaica. The further hope is that there will be continued meditation on the issues discussed at the seminars in private sessions by non-university seekers and that these informal sessions will take place in other geographic areas of Africa and the diaspora, a lack of knowledge of our historical condition being one of the commonalities we, in this area, share.

These lectures in *The Continent of Black Consciousness* are being made public in the hope that they will excite the private meditations and group colloquies, mentioned above, into being.

They have been written from a very personal point of view to emphasise the fact that though the issues they discuss are usually the subject of university courses, academia has no monopoly on them; they are matters which affect our daily lives. In addition, each of them tries to point us towards a path of social and psychological engineering. The first of these lectures, 'Comparative Slavery', makes the point that we of Africa were not the first or only people to be enslaved and it looks at how our experience differs from that of other enslaved groups. The second, aware that our forefathers did try to get themselves out of bondage, looks at 'Liberation Thought and Action 1789-1900'. The third, 'The World the Freedman/Woman Made', looks at how our people handled their freedom. We focus particularly on Jamaica.

The fourth of these essays posits a continent of black consciousness evolving from the days of slavery, and looks at Marcus Garvey within this context of black consciousness. It is called 'Marcus Garvey and the Continent of Black Consciousness'. The fifth essay called 'Afro-Caribbean Voices in the International Arena' looks at the way in which three of our African-Caribbean brothers – Claude McKay of Jamaica, and George Padmore and C.L.R. James of Trinidad – impacted the international scene in their day.

The sixth, 'View from Juba's Head', listens to the voices of the women. We see how two novelists – the African-Trinidadian Merle Hodge and the Barbadian African-American Paule Marshall – treat the concept of Africa and the diaspora in their fiction. We look only at Hodge's *Crick Crack Monkey* and Marshall's *Praisesong for the Widow*. The final essay is 'Writing Your Village History – the case of Woodside'. It is an invitation to the many of us cross-overs, who are looking at retirement and have *always* wanted to write the history of our family or wider group, to go ahead and do so, for every little bit of information about ourselves that we can find is vital to our communal self-knowledge. In this essay, I walk the reader through the process of writing my own village history, *The People of my Jamaican Village 1817-1948* published in 1999.

I wish to thank those people, most of whom originated from exciting Kingston, for motoring down the bad roads to Woodside to the 'Seven Second Sunday Seminars' to listen to my version of our business and to discuss solutions. I wish in particular to thank my sister Velma Pollard and my brother Clyde Brodber for the support they gave me in my venture into educational administration.

COMPARATIVE SLAVERY

1

My father grew up in what must have been a 'school boy' relationship with one Revd Carter, the English Anglican priest in charge of Blackstonedge church in St Ann, Jamaica. One of the things he told him, was that he should never let anyone make him feel inferior because of his ancestral history of slavery. Reason? Every ethnic group has been enslaved at some time or the other. My father could have told Revd. Carter the same thing: never let anyone make you feel inferior because your ancestral history has slave-ownership in it. Reason? Just about every ethnic group has been in slave owning at some time or the other. This is the lesson we learn from Orlando Patterson's very detailed study of slavery called *Slavery and Social Death* and on which our discussion draws heavily.[1] His work carries an appendix showing societies in which large scale slavery existed. Patterson lists societies in which slavery was an integral part of the particular society's social structure. To underline the verity of Revd Carter's statement to my father, I have reworked Patterson's list to show the geographic span of such societies and the historic span of the practice of slavery.

Countries in which there was slavery

Before Christ	Principally Greece and the Roman Empire
AD-1000	Korea, Italy, Spain, Iceland, Britain
AD 1000-1300	Ghana, Mali, Iraq
AD 1300-1500	Korea, Madeira, Songhai, Spain, Crete, Cyprus, Ghana, Mali
AD 1500-1700	Madeira, Canary Islands, Algiers, Ghana, Songhai, Hausaland, Senegambia, the Yoruba Empire, Panama City, Mexico, the Caribbean, South America and the USA South
AD 1700-1900	Algiers, Ghana, Songhai, Sudan, Hausaland, The Tuareg of the Sahara, Senegambia, Sierra Leone, Dahomey, the Yoruba Empire, the Vai,

	Temne, Ashanti and Gyaman kingdoms, Cameroon, Kongo, Angola, the Mataka chiefdoms of East Africa, Zimbabwe, Zanzibar, Mombasa, Mozambique, South Africa, Mauritius, the Seychelles, Thailand, Burma, South West China, the Caribbean and the Americas
AD 1900-	The Tuareg of the Sahara (until 1965), South West China (until 1940), Mozambique (until 1910), the Temne chiefdoms, the Vai paramount chiefs and Lozi state (the last three are in Africa)

The amended list above shows slavery to have been a central part of Grecian and Roman societies before the birth of Christ and that it existed in this way down to 1965 among the Tuareg of the Sahara, up until 1940 among the Chinese, until 1910 among the Koreans and among the people with whom slavery is associated in the minds of most, West Africans. Patterson's coverage and the amended list made from it, is global: the focus is neither on us whose slavery past is so close nor on the Jews of biblical times with whom our search in the Bible for right behaviour has put us in touch since our eyes were at our knees. This source – the Bible – tells us that like us, the Lord's so-called chosen people were slaves. It also tells us that they were slave holders as well. Leviticus, the ancient Jews' book of rules, laws, norms, states (Chapter 25 vs 44):

> Both thy male and female slaves, whom thou shalt have, *shall be* of the nations that are round about you; of them shall ye buy male and female slave.

Patterson's list of societies, in which large-scale slavery existed, societies he further defines as dependent on slavery, does not include the biblical Jews though he does mention that slavery existed among them. In the Leviticus, this Jewish book of rules, as we have seen, the Jews' God lays down the terms under which slavery is to be practiced, without a discussion of whether it should be practiced or not. It stands to reason that if slavery was not an integral part of the Jews' social structure it certainly was an important aspect of their lives to be so treated by their God. It seems then that the God of Israel, whom we adore, like the Gods of Romans, Greeks, Scandinavian, Icelanders among others, saw slavery as a natural part of social life. Slavery apparently had the sanction of many Gods.

Patterson's *Slavery and Social Death* also carries a chapter which, assisted by maps, deals historically with the slave trade. I paraphrase the data in these maps to ease our understanding of the slave trade in its universal context. The maps show areas from which slaves were taken and areas to which they were taken. There was the Indian Ocean slave trade in which ships sailed from Egypt to Northern Somalia expressly in search of slaves. This trade supposedly continued until the 19th century having been taken over by the Muslims with the rise of the might of Islam. The people of Mecca and Medina, the centre of Islam, simply went across the Red Sea for their captives. This captured population was taken to the Near and Middle East – today's Turkey, Syria, Iraq, Iran. Then there was the Black Sea and Mediterranean trade, which included areas around the Danube and St Petersburg. To satisfy Roman and Grecian demands this slave trade brought people from North East Europe, from North Africa, and from West Africa.

In the heart of Europe there was a trade – the Medieval European trade – in which Europeans – Danes, Swedes, the people of the British Isles – raided each others communities and enslaved each other. Some, Patterson tells us, were like the Africans to come later, both victims and traders. So Revd Carter's people really were slaves like the forebears of my father! Then there was the Trans-Saharan slave trade, mainly involving North Africa. There is no map showing the slave trading patterns of the people of the Far East, but we were told earlier of the Koreans and the Chinese having had a long history of managing slave societies. It appears that the enslaved here were natives who had fallen from grace.

Finally there was the Transatlantic slave trade, which is the one which took us here to Jamaica. This fissioned off from the Black Sea and Mediterranean trade, already discussed, and the Trans-Saharan trade. In this latter, people were taken from West and Central Africa as early as the 9th century to be sold as slaves in North Africa – Egypt, Morocco, Libya, Tunisia, Algeria – and the Middle and Far East. The earliest of us coming to this

part of the world, came through the part of the trade that
satisfied Spanish needs. This was the Black Sea and
Mediterranean trade. We later began to come directly from
Africa through the Trans-Saharan trade's Senegambia outlet.
This part of the trade was associated with the Portuguese.
Nearly every European country became involved after that, to
develop the greatest transfer of peoples in the shortest time –
the African diaspora. Note the areas from which these
Europeans transferred us to Jamaica and elsewhere in the so-
called New World. The principal areas are Senegambia (Senegal
on today's maps), Sierra Leone, the Gold Coast (today's Ghana),
the Bight of Benin (today's Nigeria) and Cameroon.

We can see from this review that in truth a wide cross section
of people of the globe have been slaves and have been in
societies in which their enslaved labour has been the engine of
development. The review shows too, as Revd Carter knew, that
it was not just us, the children of Ham, who were divinely
selected to be slaves. But was our slavery experience like that of
everybody else? Were all the other enslaved peoples also
carriers of wood and drawers of water to another racial group?
Did they too see their father's nakedness, were consequently
cursed and forced to serve their brothers perpetually as has
been said of us, taken out of Africa in the Atlantic slave trade?
These are questions we wish to discuss here. We will do this by
looking first of all at the slavery experience of our forefathers
here in Jamaica and comparing this with the experience of other
enslaved individuals and groups.

What did enslavement feel like to the Jamaican? Was this
common to all slaves? Listen to Mammy Edith of Lloyds in St
Thomas formerly of Elderslie, St Elizabeth in the southwest of
the island and Mrs Burke of Treadways, St Catherine in the
middle of the island. Mammy Edith, fat smooth skinned and
'high yellow' came from a grandmother whose grandmother
was an African. She reports in 1973:

> him sey when time him small a man tief him. One of him father
> friend see de man a gu wey wid him and de man say, "but mi nuh
> know dat pickney deh?" But him sey him heart was so full that
> him never answer, an de man tief him go sell him. Dat time dem a
> sell pickney like slave you know, slave ... im sey him heart so full
> dat him never answer for him know ... nuh mussi know sey well, a

tief de man tief him fe go sell him and thru him heart so full him nuh say nuttin. Dat time him a pickney. De man tief him a carry him go sell. Dat time dem sell people you know, in a slave. Mi great great grandmother was a African.[2]

Mrs Burke takes us from the experience of capture through to actual enslavement as she, in 1975, tells us what slavery was like for her forebears:

My grandmother used to tell me – she live 113 years – and she used to tell me that she was bought by the Old farmer Gyles. She is from the Guinea Coast in Africa and she was brought to Jamaica as a little girl. Very small, and with quite a few other slave girls and boys. And they came to this old General Gyles who bought them and bring them here ... Mi mother say, she say her name was ... Philisita Stryer. [Came] from the Guinea Coast in Africa. That's where she come from. And my mother used to say that there were some people around – black people, who were Gyles. She would say they were Gyles ... this one was so small that they couldn't tell their name, so they ... name them off themselves as Gyles but they are not really Gyles ... those are the black ones.

Mrs Burke's report continues concerning her grandmother:

She had different different children ... She had children as Francis, Dee, Laws and another name, but the last one was Francis. *That* she now, afterwards she marry to that. They didn't marry, they just go into these ... They [the slave masters] want strong, huge people, so then the big men, you know, they allow them to go in to healthy women. And my mother said that her grandmother said that she used to look after the mill where they pick the coffee. And when they pick the coffee now, she is the boss for around. And in the evening who pick the most coffee, but who pick the less, they flog them for it, you know.[3]

The social-psychological profile of enslavement in Jamaica, which these two reports portray, is drawn below:
- A sense of shock and hopelessness which came into the Jamaican slave system with the new slave.
- The loss of name.
- The subordination of the slave's personal feeling even to the master's eugenics plan.
- Rigid assignment of tasks and standards of completion

violently enforced by the master or his order.
* An effort to get slaves to give their sanction to the system by encouraging status ranking among them.
* Sexual relations between white master class and black slave, common knowledge, though not emphasised in these reports.

Was this the portrait of the experience of enslavement everywhere and under all circumstances? Was the portrait the same for my father's forebears and for Revd Carter's? Let us look at the circumstances attending slavery elsewhere to see the extent to which the experiences of Mammy Edith's ancestors and Mrs Burke's forebear are approximated. Let us begin with one aspect of this experience – the sense of shock and hopelessness – and see the extent to which God's chosen people in one of the clearest, earliest and most accessible biographies of emotions, felt as a result of slavery, fared.

Psalm 137, verses 1-4, of the Bible says:

> By the rivers of Babylon, there we sat down, yea, we wept when we remembered Zion.
> We hung our harps upon the willows in the midst thereof.
> For there they that carried us away captive *required of us* mirth *saying*, sing us *one* the songs of Zion.
> How shall we sing the Lord's song in a foreign land?
> [Scofield Reference Edition; emphasis mine]

According to biblical sources, Judah had been carried away by Babylon as a result of warfare. The people of Judah were taken together, thus "*we* sat down"; "*we* hung our harps"; "required from *us*"; "how can *we* sing". The king and the princes, the captain of the guards and the priests, the eunuch in charge of the men of the war, the principal scribe – the elite – were killed. Some of the poor were divided among the members of the invading army, some taken away in groups and some left to produce wine and to man the farms which were apparently colonised by the invaders according to the last book of Jeremiah. What is the emotional state of those carried away? No doubt sadness but certainly also relief to be spared the fate of the destroyed elite. And more relief still – "we" – social networks entered captivity; the enslaved could find active comfort in these.

Note here that not only is the social group carried over into captivity but the culture is too. The captives therefore had the comfort of their culture. We see that they were allowed to keep their songs and that they had their harps. And these, not just any song that they sing: this is the "Lord's song". And more, their captors want to hear their songs. Clearly these people have with them in captivity, even if they prefer not to share it with their captors, a religion which had the cognisance and respect of the conqueror. Compare this with the conditions attending the transfer from home to captivity of the little girl who was to be Mammy Edith's great great grandmother. She leaves home for captivity, alone. The child is numbed by this experience of solitary kidnapping, so numbed that she couldn't indicate to her father's friend that she was being stolen. Nor does she have the psychological benefit of thinking herself spared, for nobody as far as she knows has been killed; no-one else in her group has been taken away. She has been singled out for punishment with no one to ask why. No positive word precedes this solitary child about her culture. Her captors in the place to which she is brought, the factory on the coast of West Africa or Jamaica across the sea, see her religion as mumbo-jumbo and people who look like her as non-humanoid belonging to a line of apes. Sing? Religion? Who wants to hear her song? Does a soul-less monkey have a "Lord"? The Jamaicans' entry into enslavement did not share the pluses of those of the "Lord's" people.

God's people entered enslavement as a result of war. Capture of the vanquished like kidnapping of individuals was a way by which people were brought into slavery. Both were painful as the pathos in the psalms and in Mammy Edith's testimony quoted above, attest. Kidnapping by virtue of the isolation of the kidnapped seems to be the more psychologically painful of the two. Apart from these there have been other ways throughout the globe and throughout time for an individual to be introduced into slavery. Principal among these are: being given to others as tribute or tax-payment; handed over to others in lieu of an unpaid debt and not ransomed thereafter; exiled from the natal group and handed over to others as punishment; the abandonment and/or sale of children; self enslavement; inherited status. Let us look at each of these comparatively to meditate on the trauma involved for the individual. But first, let us return to capture as a result of war.

One may be vanquished and enslaved on one's own territory as in the case of the Tainos of the Caribbean and the other indigenous ethnic groups of the New World. Since such enslavement is normally the by-product of the outsider's desire to take away the material wealth of the vanquished, enslavement is as much an answer to the conqueror's question, 'What do we do with these people', as an answer to the question, 'with what labour do we develop these goods that we have taken away from these people'? Under these circumstances however, the conquerors' attempts at enslavement carry special difficulties and they have to be half-hearted; they usually kill these captives, as has been general throughout history and in all places, or sell them. Attempts to enslave the vanquished in their own territory, faces the fact that the vanquished have vital information which the conqueror doesn't have about the environment. They have their Gods and they have their friends and they have their family, at least to some extent. This puts them in a power position *vis à vis* the conqueror. Patterson's review of societies throughout the world and throughout time indicates that enslavement under these conditions has invariably met with failure. Referring to efforts to enslave a native population, he writes:

> There have been several noteworthy attempts at mass enslavement in the annals of slavery, all ending in failure. The most sustained and, not surprisingly, the most frightening, was the European attempt to enslave the Indian population of the Americas.4

The more usual way of entering into slavery through capture as the result of war was, as with Judah, being transported out of one's natal setting. Clear cases of capture, transportation and incorporation exist among the 'kin-based' societies of Africa, Greece in the 4th century before Christ, Rome in the 2nd century AD and the Islamic slave societies. In the 'kin-based' societies wealth is measured in terms of one's retinue: enslaved war captives become part of this kind of wealth, prized and often treated better than non-slaves. It was usual too for the descendants of such slaves to be incorporated into the clan as free persons. Hope existed in this case for your offspring.

In the case of Greece and Rome, captives were normally taken from the far extremes of their empires. A philosophy that the elite distinguished themselves in war and courtly behaviour and did no mundane work meant that there were niches at all levels of the society open to the vanquished, strangers in a society new to them but very familiar to their masters. These vanquished entered into a society whose ethics were already well established and which saw them not only as slaves but also as people who could be distinguished one from another by their occupational aptitudes. They were intellectual beings: this must have been a comforting thought to the captured, transported and enslaved. That there was work for you to do that you liked to do and that you could do well, could feed your self-esteem even in your sadness.

Similarly with Islam. Their jihad, their holy wars, declared all outsiders anywhere to be infidels who should be converted. Infidels could be taken home as slaves. The Koran like the Leviticus, though it did accept the fact of slavery, did not smile on the enslavement of one's own, did not smile on Muslims' enslavement of fellow Muslims. It follows that conversion could, if the spirit of the Koran was respected, change a slave's legal status. Clearly there was within the society a system of thought, which allowed the slave to see himself as a potential non-slave. That the manumission rate was high here, requiring more slaves and necessitating more wars to produce more war captives to be turned into slaves, is an indication that the transformation from slave to converted free did take place.

What is the mental state of the new slave kidnapped or vanquished in war? On arrival into his new society, he would look at what was happening to other slaves. If he were in a tribal African state, he would suffer the longings of the stranger but would be no worse off economically and probably even better treated than the non-elite around him. If he were a Greek slave entering Rome, as was once the order of Roman times, he would have seen his kind at work in a wide cross section of fields. The Romans acknowledged the superiority of the culture of the enslaved Greeks. They employed them in the executive as well as the administrative branches of government and in private homes as tutors. Skilled and literate, they came to and were allowed to dominate the urban industries as well as the arts, theatre and literature of Rome. The Greek entering slavery in Rome need not fear the cauterisation of his mental faculties. The same held true for slaves in Greece, masters being proud of the intelligence and skills of their slaves because this reflected positively on them. In Islam the slave could find himself in jobs with high social status. We know that the Mamluks in Egypt and the Janissaries in Turkey, foreign slaves, were essential to the administrative system of these countries.[5]

The young bewildered slave entering into Jamaican society, 70 per cent of whom, according to Patterson,[6] were after 1701 the subject of kidnappings, had no such example of possibility for his/her kind to cheer her/him. The only role he could play in this society was that of chattel slave and to this status he was assigned for perpetuity, whether he was prince, pauper, writer or master craftsman in his own land, though ofcourse given human nature there would be one or two omissions to this practice. The fruit of his loins and her womb shared this perpetuity so that this slave could not even hope that his children would see a change in occupational status. To make matters worse, he entered a society which was young and whose trendsetters were too often absent for rational ways of behaviour to emerge from their interaction with the social and physical environment in which he laboured and his master owned. There was no place here for observation, reason, morality to merge to create change. This was not the setting in which bewilderment could easily be turned to confident self-development. This was an unstable society with one clear goal – the making of money. The young bewildered slave entered a society, which defined its parts in terms of the market. In this market he was labour. Nothing more, as long as the system of values lasted.

Meirs and Kopytoff, in their discussion of the way one entered into the new society as a slave, underscore the range of occupational possibilities generally open to slaves in some societies.[7] They make the further point that modern Western slavery, of which we here are a part, was in this sense an anomaly. They graphically illustrate this:

> The great grandfather of the Russian poet Pushkin was an African slave acquired in France by Peter the Great, who ordered his marriage into a Russian noble family ... In the New World, however, almost all slaves entered the society as chattels of private

persons, acquired for political ends and further formal limitations on their ability were often imposed by society at large on the basis of race.[8]

Their volume's discussion of slavery in some parts of Africa gives slavery another non-Jamaican feature. Among the Senegambians of West Africa, according to Klein's study of the Wolof and Sereer reported in their work,

> a jaam [slave] was better off economically than a jamburr [freeman]...those who participated in the exercise of power ... consisted of the nobility, their jaam, and artisans ... most slaves actually lived in chiefly compounds ... the most important jaam were the *tyeddo*, slave warriors who did most of the fighting and the administering.[9]

The indication here is that a slave, by whatever process he leaves his natal home, need not live in a one-value system which excludes him from the experience of intellectual and spiritual development; he/she need not be bound to one role, nor does the word 'slave' necessarily translate into one occupational role. The New World/Jamaica case was different. Occupational mobility through the different layers of Jamaican society, and concomitant status change as a result of the application of one's intelligence, was not permitted to Mammy Edith's great great grandmother, was not permitted to our forefathers. Their intellectual ability and its potential growth were stymied in the kind of slavery to which we were exposed.

Most of us came here as a result of kidnapping. Are the circumstances and the related emotional profile the same for all people who have been thus enslaved? Africans arriving in Jamaica were not the only people to experience kidnapping. This was the principal way in which people were taken from their homes and enslaved. Whatever the society and in whatever geographic area, there were markets for human bodies. The need may be as in Greece and Rome, for people to fill all kinds of occupations; it could be for people to work on the farms in Korea and China and to help with the war effort in these places. The need could have been for attractive young men to satisfy the desires of older wealthy men as in some part of the history of Greece; it could be, as in West African societies, for the twin reasons of labour and the production of children; it could be for labourers on the sugar plantations in the Canary Islands or in Jamaica. Kidnapping could even feed a market specialising in the sale of slaves as was the case with the Indians of North West North America.

Slaves could be taken from one point and exchanged for another item or they could accompany and even be the burden bearers of other articles for sale, such as happened in the trade coming from Northwest Africa to the Mediterranean, where other prized articles for sale were elephants, ivory and hide. Though it did happen in 10th century Europe, it was unusual for the slave to be the sole article traded. In North Africa the mix, feeding the Black Sea and Mediterranean trade, was salt, grain, oil, sheep, camels, horses along with slaves; from Northeastern Africa it was wine, oil, grain, fruits, dates, perfumes, linen, ivory and paper; and from Northern Europe what came with the slaves into the states around the Black Sea and the Mediterranean Sea were grain, hide and horses. In the Bulgar-Volga area of North Europe, slaves came along with furs, wax and honey.

We were all that the traders visiting West Africa wished to take to Jamaica from Africa – human bodies capable of chopping, planting, lifting, capable of working at the behest of others. Thus there were large forts built on the west coast of Africa to store us and ships specially built for carrying large numbers of us as captives. It was on one of these that Mammy Edith's great great grandmother and Mrs Burke's grandmother came over to Jamaica, coming in Mrs Burke's case, from Guinea, both accompanied by the notion that we from Africa had nothing worth exchanging. That our colour, our hair, the shape of our bodies were so different from that of our captors, led easily to the notion that unlike other people we were unifunctional.

The horrors of the journey, called the Middle Passage, appear in the literature to be more harrowing than that of any other journey to the slave markets. Add then the feeling of numbness at being kidnapped to the distress of the Middle Passage and we ought to find very disoriented people stepping on these shores to be sold as chattels. Add to this the nature and the needs of the receiving society and their perception of our possibilities as limited, and we see that the forebears of Mammy Edith, Mrs Burke and our own, were incorporated on their entry into Jamaica into a situation which denied their humanity, and this unto perpetuity. Intellectual underdevelopment and genetic embarrassment were written into this welcome. A caste of black people bound to labouring tasks was the inevitable outcome of the life of the Jamaican slave. Not all slaves through time and clime shared our experience in its totality. Our experience of kidnap, transportation and life as a slave were surely more psychically disturbing than most!

The rationale behind enslavement could influence the treatment meted out to the enslaved and the degree of trauma consequently experienced by the enslaved. At a point in our lives we were kidnapped expressly for sale and bought and resold expressly for chattel slavery in perpetuity – a painful experience. Does the rationale behind the enslavement of all others, lead to our kind of experience? Let us go back to considering the ways in which individuals enter slavery, to ponder the psychic consequences for others. Being used as part of a tribute payment to another country by your own, is one of these ways.

A weak state is threatened by a stronger and to stave off attacks pays tribute in some material form to the other. Tribute often took the form of the slaves. Thus in the first century before the birth of Christ, Rome exacted tribute from its eastern provinces. The human being was the currency used to pay this tribute. A like situation eventuated in the existence of the Turkish janissaries. As mentioned above, this was an elite slave corp of Christian children in the Ottoman Empire offered or exacted as tribute. Some African countries on the Guinea Coast depended on this kind· of source for their slaves, developing a chain of clients, the weakest paying to the less weak, who in turn paid tribute to another, until the chain reaches a powerful state like the Oyo, who need neither buy nor hunt for slaves, for the train of vassals can satisfy their needs.

This system ofcourse encouraged the kidnapping of individuals who would now be turned into slaves. The Nubians are an extreme case in point. In their effort to pay tribute in slaves to Kushite Egypt they raided their southern neighbours, but they sometimes sent their own people as slaves to Egypt.

The psychological pain of kidnapping no doubt exists for the individual offered as a tribute. What differences in psychic consequence exist for those people passed over to another state as tribute, as against the experiences of Mammy Edith's great great grandmother and Mrs Burke's ancestor, lie in the treatment in the receiving state, an issue already discussed.

Indebtedness was another way in which people entered slavery. A person owing a debt and not being able to pay it could, in Levitican Israel, Ashantiland, early Greece and Rome, China and Vietnam, hand over a relative to his creditor as a pawn. Failure to ransom meant that the human pawn could be enslaved. The process of becoming a slave here is a slow one and seems less harrowing than being kidnapped or being captured in war and transported.

Then there was slavery as a form of punishment. Some of today's Ghanaians claim this as the grounds on which many of us were sold out of Ghana and into the Atlantic slave trade and brought to places like Jamaica. Our behaviour they claim was anti-social. What do you do with people who have thoroughly broken rules, laws, tradition? Imprison them and make them slaves of the state. This penal enslavement was the principal source of slaves in China. It operated to some extent all over the world – among the Ibos of West Africa, among the Northern South American Indians and ofcourse among the Europeans of recent times – remember the galley slaves in Victor Hugo's *Les Miserables*? To organise this kind of slavery – penal slavery – within your own territory takes effort and resources. How helpful if there is a way of selling these errant citizens out of the society rather than having to feed and take care of them, organise or kill them!

In societies where penal slavery existed, there would be lists of crimes for which the enslavement of a citizen was the prescribed punishment. Ofcourse where there was a market for slaves, a ruler might increase this list to suit himself. Patterson's comment on the practice in West Africa is so close to us that it is worth quoting verbatim here:

> In West Africa the list grew with the expansion of the Atlantic slave trade. A number of Africans who ended up on the shores of the Americas were tricked into slavery. A common practice was for several of the many wives of an unscrupulous chief to seduce

unwary young men, then accuse them of committing the capital offence of adultery with the wife of the chief.10

How does a youngman feel when a night of sexual pleasure takes him bound to the slave factory on the African coast, into the tightly packed ship and across the Atlantic, on to the auction block and then sent to cut cane in the heat of the Jamaican sun, fully aware that this will be his lifestyle forever as well as that of his progeny? Angry, I suppose. Even if he was guilty of a misdemeanour he must now feel very depressed. There must have been among the group of people, with whom Mammy Edith's and Mrs Burke's forebears had to live and work, some very angry and depressed people.

Another way of being enslaved was, for children, abandonment. In several societies, certain kinds of children were unwanted – twins, deformed children, children with birthmarks, children whose first tooth appeared in the upper jaw, children who were girls instead of boys, children whose parents were too poor to keep them. These would be exposed with the intention that they would die a natural death. Where there was a market for them, sale was of course the preferred way for the parents and of course the happier way for these children. Given the intention behind taking people into Jamaica, that is, for the purposes of enslavement, it is hardly likely that any of these fortunates came here.

Self-enslavement was another way of becoming a slave. China, Japan, Russian, Korea, Europe, the Kongo were places where this happened. Poverty was the main inducement to committing oneself to the service of another. This self-enslavement occurred too in cases where people were cut off, for whatever reason, from their kin group and sought the protection of some other. Not many of us would have been sold out of Africa for this reason, the self-enslaved fitting so well into the African cultural passion for a retinue of dependents.

The final form of entering into slavery is birth into slavery. This is universal to all slave systems and after 1807, when the slave trade was legally abolished, this was the principal way by which our people came into slavery in Jamaica. This slave, the creole slave, ought to have been the happiest of the sad lot in Jamaica for he experienced nothing but the life of the slave. The trauma of kidnap and/or capture he learns, if at all, second-hand. However that the stories of kidnap and capture have been handed down from their forebears to Mammy Edith and Mrs Burke among others, and preserved for more than a century indicates creole empathy with the nature of the incorporation of their ancestors into this society. The creole forebears of Mrs Burke and Mammy Edith would absorb the tellers' emotions with the tale, adding this abstract form to their own experience of slavery. Thus the emotions of the African transported into slavery would continue to be felt through generations unless something intervened to address the original pain. Generalised anger, without a specific referent, is likely to be part of the personality of generations of slaves and to continue, as there was not the kind of change which signified repentance on the part of those involved, concerning the original distress.

As we have seen, the nature of entry of the enslaved into the new society, is one thing; the nature of life in the system is another. In fact, it is conceivable that the life of a slave could be more attractive than life as a starving man. People have been known, as we see above, to have voluntarily put themselves and their children into slavery. We have seen too from our comparative examination, that Jamaicans and other Africans of the diaspora are likely to have been accompanied into slavery, to a greater extent than others, by a sense of shock and hopelessness. Let us now look into the practice of slavery to see whether the other features of Jamaican captivity are common to slavery experiences of people in other times and parts of the world, and whether they are prone to eventuate in the social psychological profile drawn by the experiences of the forebears of Mammy Edith and Mrs Burke.

None of the authorities on slavery, mentioned in this lecture, claim that the lot of the emperor's slaves in ancient Rome, who commanded the ships of the imperial fleet, or the Greeks, whose culture was so revered by their slave masters, or the eunuchs, put in charge of the king's household, were any less slaves than those who cut the canes here in Jamaica and wore the osnaburg. Patterson in discussing his notion that all kinds of slavery were social death, notes that in every place and in all times, the slave was systematically pulled apart from his personal past to become socially dead, a creature of his master.

Taking away or discounting his name and especially that name which links him to a group of people natally his own, was one of these ways. Thus Mrs Burke's ancestor has no name. It could have been coaxed out of her but that would have been to link her with an identity outside of the slave system. This was not the style of slavery. Nor did the manipulation of the slave's identity through naming stop at the entry into the society. It continued through to those born in the society.

Slaves were generally named not by and for those who made them genetically but by their masters, thus the "black Gyles" on the Treadways farm as in the evidence of Mrs Burke. In early slavery times, before the coming of Christian baptism in 1817, Jamaican slaves were not even allowed surnames. They carried one name plus sometimes a description such as Congo Jack. Several on the estate even had the same name, modified only by an adjective: Big Jane, Little Jane, as in the list below taken from Higman's *Slave Population and Economy 1807-1834* (Cambridge 1976):

Dick	Old Amelia	Hannah
Little Dick	Little Amelia	Little Hannah
Pompy	Phoeba	Hercules
Little Pompey	Caesar	London
Hamlet	Romulus	Polypus
Venus	Brutus	Cupid

(p. 270)

This treatment was by no means peculiar to Jamaica. In China, Pharoah's Egypt and the ancient Near East, slaves there too only had one name.[11] It was also the style internationally to give slaves insulting names.[12] A name found among the slaves of the Cameroons was translated "irritation"; in Burma female slaves were given sexually demeaning names[13] and here in Jamaica and North America, many were, to the amusement of those naming us, given the names of heroic Greek and Roman figures – Minerva, Homer, Jupiter, Juno, Cicero – as in the list above. The prized little slave of Lady Nugent, wife of the governor of Jamaica between 1801 and 1805, was Cupid and Cupid's mother was – you guessed it – Venus[14] and as we see above she was not the only person with a Venus and a Cupid though there is no evidence that those above were related.

Mrs Burke's forebear was mated with several different men to produce the best strain possible. Her sex partner was not her business; it was the business of Master Gyles who "allowed" certain men to mate with her. The separation of the choice of mates from those mating is by no means particular to slavery. In classical Indian and African societies mates were selected by parties other than the couple. The difference, however, is that in these cases the couple forms a new family or clan and the children are theirs even if shared with the original clan or with the extended family. This creative ability is not recognised in the system of slavery so that the children of the mating couple are not theirs but the property of the master. The children born of the many unions of Mrs Burke's ancestor were not hers or those of her mates but belonged to Mr Gyles and carried his name. This lady from Treadways, St Catherine, had no control over her body, had no control over the issue of her body, she was powerless, totally dominated by another.

The totality of the belonging of slave to master is one of the essential features of slavery everywhere, graphically demonstrated by the fact that in some cultures the master could, if he wished, kill his slave. This was so among South American Indians and among the Chinese. The Japanese slaves were killed to accompany high ranking people on their post-death journeys. Note too that, where the slave was killed by a third party, the compensation where it existed went to the master, for associated with this powerlessness was the notion that the slave had no honour. He therefore has no cause for retaliation against anyone. His master, not he, was the one insulted if there was ·negative behaviour towards him, and the master, not he, was the one who should be recompensed. By this token, Mrs Burke's forebear could not be raped; it was her master who was raped, if he chose to interpret a sexual incident, which involved her, as such. She lacked honour by virtue of being slave.

The notion that the slave lacked honour was everywhere and was everywhere maintained by stereotypes. Thus, though the Romans acknowledged the Greek culture to be superior, they managed to project images of the Greeks as preferring form to substance in their speech; having a propensity for inappropriate or excessive behaviour; being deceitful and having an aptitude for flattery; having a weakness for luxury and ostentation and devoid of honesty, faith and trustworthiness. We here have felt the stereotypes. Women like Mrs Burke's forebear were loose and oversexed anyway and probably invited the many men into intercourse with her!

In many slave systems, the completion of an assigned task and the way it should be completed need not be related to the capacity of the slave but rather to the master's needs and what he deems to be humanly possible. Punishment for performance below the standard set by the master was ever possible. Mrs Burke's ancestor's mates were punished for not carrying in as much coffee as the master felt, for whatever reason, could be carried in. The Jewish slaves under Pharoah were ordered to make x number of bricks in x time according to Pharoah's needs or risk punishment. Performing in accordance with the standards of the master and the associated punishment for failure to do so, is a general part of the institution of slavery. We find this too in the work forces in the free world.

An important distinction between rewarded and punished work in slavery as in freedom, lies in the severity of the punishment and the fit between capacity, vocational predisposition and task. A slave, who is a teacher and wants to be a teacher, is an administrator and wants to be that, a cane-cutter and wants to do that, applies himself creatively to his assigned tasks and need not be punished. Moreover, his well-done work is the major part of his reward. This constellation can only exist where there are several kinds of occupations available to the slave. The variety of vocations needed for the assignment of work according to aptitude did not exist for the Jamaican slave, though there are a couple cases in which slaves did some of the ciphering for their masters and where some slaves were in the armed forces. The British government, which ultimately controlled master and slave, had its own labour problems. It needed jobs for its middle managers, bookkeepers, overseers, clerks. The great bulk of the slave population was assigned to labouring tasks. Pity then, the

> little black girl [who] came to beg that I would take her with me. She was a remarkably thick-lipped and ugly, but intelligent child. She could say the Lord's Prayer perfectly, but could not tell how she had learnt it; both her father and mother are field negroes and neither of them can say their prayers.15

No chance, although she was literarily inclined, of being other than her parents were – field, and at best, domestic slave. Young as she was, she was aware of her innate capacities. She sought change; Lady Nugent, whom she asked to adopt her, did not oblige. Anger and resentment would be her companions as she grew older.

One of the problems facing the movers and shakers of societies, in which slavery is an integral part of the social system, is the possibility of unity among the enslaved. Such unity they fear could lead to defiance of the social order and ofcourse the power of the master, which itself is based on an acceptance of this order. Such unity could exist where the enslaved, as individuals, are conscious of their comparatively deprived condition, are conscious that there are others who share their condition and sentiment, and are willing to band themselves together on the basis of their shared sense of their condition. The response of the slave-holding group has been through time and space, to discourage social formations in the enslaved population that could lead to such solidarity.

Dispersion of slaves throughout the society is one answer: slaves do not meet by themselves long enough to reason and to create theories concerning their condition, which theories would lead to solidarity and eventually to group defiance. This dispersion could be social or geographic. Jamaican slave quarters were near to the great house, the master's quarters or within the purview of his telescope. Some slaves were even closer to the master, living in his household as in the case of the Greek slave, who tutored the master's children. This kind of dispersion, where some lived in the master's quarters, apart from keeping slaves away from each other, gives the slave the impression that he is as much a part of the family as a blood relation and enjoins him to place his loyalty here rather than with other slaves. A pointed example of this kind of dispersion, which results in what the literature calls 'fictive kinship', existed in the United States in 'Mammy', the slave woman, who was the fictive mother of the master's children – she wet-nursed them. A good deal of Southern American fiction dwells on this theme of partial incorporation and consequent separation from one's own, showing how psychologically divorced even from her own children these Mammies could become.

Another technique is occupational dispersion. Low stratum labour is divided into tasks. The enslaved are separated according to tasks and these tasks are ranked. The person doing the job with the highest ranking is given by the master, higher status than his fellows and given the feeling that he has been co-opted into the master's class and away from other slaves, though his job is intrinsically neither more physically nor intellectually demanding than theirs. With this psychological boost, such a slave, the master class hopes will want to maintain the system, for his prestige is tied to it. Mrs Burke's forebear seems to have been thrilled to be the boss of the coffee-weighing enterprise. She had fallen for this trick and as such was likely to have been so enthralled by her status that she is willing to report fellow slaves for not producing as much as they should. The slave tyeddo of the Wolof, outsider but elite, are unlikely to side with the lowly slave.

In Charles Town, in the east of the island, Lady Nugent, wife of the governor of Jamaica in 1801-1805, noted of the household of the coffee-growing master of the estate, Sherriff:

> This house is perfectly in Creole style. A number of negroes, men, women, and children, running and lying about, in all parts of it.[16]

Again in Seville in St Ann, the middle of the island, she notes:

> I could not help laughing, as we entered the hall at Seville, to see a dozen black heads popped up, for the negroes in the Creole houses sleep always on the floors, in the passages, galleries etc.[17]

Mrs Nugent does not use the world 'slave' to refer to people. The term 'negro' subsumes the meaning 'slave'. According to her observation, slaves in Jamaica were dispersed even throughout the great house. The image conjured from these references is of slaves, lying about like dogs, comfortable, even petted but definitely of a different order than their masters. Could people dispersed and incorporated into the master's household in this way, coalesce in a revulsion of their status? This kind of dispersion coupled with the practice of restricting them to one occupational category and then creating ranks within that category as the case of Mrs Burke's forebear shows, discouraged the development of solidarity among the enslaved.

A related strategy was to incorporate slaves into a religious ideology, which justifies their enslavement and makes obedience to the master a route to salvation. This could not happen to the Biblical Jews for not only had they taken their harps and their songs with them into captivity, they had taken their religion, which inspired and would inspire their songs, their culture. Individual kidnappings made it difficult for whole cultures to be transferred from Africa to Jamaica. We were thus structurally placed to accept a religious philosophy, which sanctioned our enslavement. Lady Nugent in 1801-1805 had a ball teaching her "blackies" her catechism, the theological understanding of the British people, teaching them her prayers and getting them christened into a variation of the Christian religion, which saw black people as the children of Ham, assigned perpetually to being carriers of wood and drawers of water to other racial and ethnic groups.

That our slavery was from generation to generation and was held in place by a deeply entrenched and increasingly profitable international economic system, meant that the cultural understanding that we were divinely selected for slavery became a firm part of the belief system of the slaves themselves. According to Patterson in only 25 per cent of cases, over time and space, has it been possible to differentiate the enslaved and the slave-holders by skin colour. Our kind of slavery fell in this 25 per cent. In the larger number of slave systems, the enslaved are forced to carry distinguishing marks – shaved hair, different styles of dress. These can be discarded. In our case, our pigmentation and hair type were the distinguishing marks and these could not be discarded. That these our distinguishing features were natural made it easy for all concerned to believe that we were divinely selected for something and that that something was to serve others. Compared to other slave systems manumissions here in Jamaica were few. This meant a perception of us from generation to generation as distinct and set apart for the tasks we were seen to be doing and the role assigned to us – manual labour as slaves. Our physical features became our dungeons.

Sexual relationships between the master and his female slaves exist in all slave societies. How the society treats the child of these unions can affect the possibilities for other slaves and ultimately for the shape of the slave system. In some instances, the issue of such unions legally inherit the status of their fathers and are born-free. Within these societies then automatic mobility out of the status of slave existed. This was not the case in Jamaica. Slave masters did have loving relationships with their enslaved mistresses and even manumitted their children and left large behests for them but these acts of manumission were individual ones requiring the case by case intervention of the law. Sexual relations between a slave woman and her master in Jamaica and its outcome were therefore here, unless specifically sanctioned by the law, outside of the purview of the law. The notion of illegitimacy attended these children. The majority remained slaves, no legal sub-class being called into being by their existence. The manumitted like the others carried with them the stigma of social illegitimacy. A brown face told one story: disapproved sexual connection. This was an embarrassing unpleasant burden to take into the free world.

Lady Nugent writes with respect to her visit to Hope estate in October of 1801:

> The overseer's *cherie amie*, and no man here is without one, is a tall black woman, well made, with a very flat nose, and a skin of ebony, highly polished and shining. She shewed me her three yellow children, and said with some ostentation, she would soon have another. The marked attention of the other women, plainly proved her to be the favourite Sultana of this vulgar, ugly, Scotch Sultan, who is about fifty, clumsy, ill made and dirty.[18]

No change of status was brought to the slave woman and her children *vis à vis* the larger society by her sexual liaison with the master class but there was status change within the slave society. She and her group gave her a higher ranking by virtue of her sexual connection. The assignment of a ranking, not originating in the group, undermines group control, group confidence, group solidarity and eventually, the efficacy of the group. Thus while miscegenation increased the master's labour power, it decreased the psychological strength of the group of enslaved persons. In this too, the function which miscegenation played in the life of the enslaved, we tended to be different from others.

We come now to our final understanding. What do we now know about being a slave, an experience in the past of my black father and of Revd Carter, his white mentor? Our examination of slavery through the ages and over the globe has brought us to the understanding that there are experiences, which we share with others who have been enslaved. These experiences are the creations of those interested in enslaving others whether these enslavers be Romans, Greeks, British, Korean, New World Indian, African or any other group. To make a human being into a slave, the enslaver has to reduce him, in Orlando Patterson's terminology, to 'social death'. This design involves: making him into an outsider in the society in which he lives; defining him as powerless within that social system; treating him as one without honour; presenting him within the society in terms of negative stereotypes; keeping him isolated from his kind by a partial integration into the master's group.

Legal instruments direct the enslaved into this state of social death and in time he begins to feel: that he is an outsider in the society in which he lives; that he has no power to change the system from within; that he and his kind are genetically less honourable than his master and his kind; that the stereotyped picture of himself that has been circulated in the society in which he lives, is the true picture of himself; that there is nothing to be gained from bonding with his kind.

These are the characteristics of slavery anywhere. It seems to me though that our version of it was particularly virulent given the way in which we were pulled out of Africa and how we were incorporated into the receiving society and given the phenotypical distinctions between the master group and the enslaved group. Black skin and woolly hair, where the master has white skin and straight hair, could so easily be interpreted to mean "born to be slave", especially when passages in the Bible, the celebrated compendium of the word of God, the final authority, could be bent to suit this view. And it was a curse and a state, which had no in-built end: it was handed down from generation to generation. The issue for us today, though, is one of self-perception. The master may draw pictures of us, but do we believe those pictures? Did we/do we see ourselves as socially dead, as doomed to enslavement, as constitutionally the outsider, as without honour and therefore without the capacity to assume responsibility for our actions?

October 1996

LIBERATION THOUGHT & ACTION 1789-1900

2

I have chosen to use the date 1789, as the upper point at which to look at black liberation movements in this series of lectures. 1789 resounds in modern history as the beginning of the end of the old order of inherited privileges and the beginning of the acceptance of the notion that all men have the inalienable right to work towards being rewarded with the world's goods. This was the year in which the States General, or the National Representative Assembly of France, met for the first time since 1614 and was captured by the commoners who through a combination of chance, skill, and manipulation of the aristocracy's fear of the Paris mob, subsequently forced them to surrender some of their rights, to accept the primacy of a National Assembly and to accept a Declaration of Rights. This coup led to a broadening of the political process so that the least of the country's citizens were allowed to participate in that social system. It also led to the broadcast internationally of the notion that each man is equal to the other and equally deserving of liberty to pursue happiness. The slogan 'liberty, equality, fraternity' is associated with this French event.

The pre-revolutionary French state had seen itself as organised in terms of status groups called estates. The social and political change with which the date 1789 is associated, occurred amidst meetings of the representatives of each estate, amidst diplomatic initiatives between groups, confrontations between groups and violence between groups. The need for change of its status position was seen and worked for most assiduously by the commoners, called the third estate, a group dominated by lawyers. The struggle they set in motion was one in which groups known and felt to belong to the same social system grappled with each other to create something new, to create a new social order. The blacks of the New World had reason like the French third estate to desire change but, as we discussed in the last lecture, unlike this French group, they were

seen by the other groups within their society to be outsiders in
the social system to which they gave their labour. The path to
liberty could not be, for the slave, intergroup action of any kind
towards the creation of a new social order, for slavery had
given him a perception of himself like unto that held of him by
his master. It had taught him not only that he was an outsider
but that he had no power to change the system from within and
had generally taught his freed and coloured brothers that there
was nothing to be gained from bonding with him. The path
defined for his liberty, for the liberty of the black enslaved
person, was that of pushing the system from his location on the
outside. The path defined for him was that he should before
this, spend some time in finding the people who belonged to his
group and that he establish bonds with them before he began
the pushing. In this lecture we will look at which of our
forefathers had taken which path and why.

Slavery ended in the New World before 1900, the nether
boundary of this discussion. We are here dealing then, with
'black people', Africans of the diaspora, not just enslaved
people nor the period of slavery. We need to understand, in any
case, that even during the period of slavery there were among
our forefathers in this part of the world free men as well as
slaves. Did the free black think of 'freedom' in the same terms
as the enslaved men? Our black forefathers were not all of the
same shade – contrasts among them having been created
through sexual intercourse with whites, their masters among
others. We do, know that although there was no hard and fast
rule about it, mixed children in the Caribbean, with fathers
among the master race/class, generally had a status position
that differed from that of the slaves. The works of Ira Berlin and
Orlando Patterson indicate that in the South of the USA, an area
which concerns this discussion, the position of the free(d) man,
black or white, *vis à vis* white society, was little better than that
of the slaves.[1] Did miscegenated people's view of the road to
freedom differ with geographic space? This discussion looks at
liberation thought and action in the light of the variety of kinds
of blacks and of geographic regions in which we lived here in
the New World. We look at the situation of our forefathers in
Haiti, Jamaica and the USA. But first a note on the dynamics of
group consciousness and the experience of one kind of black

people in the diaspora.

The perception that certain individuals are more like each other than any others is one of the ways in which people come to be thought to belong to the same group. The relative status of those making the judgement is important to whether the individuals perceived to belong together eventually become a group. White women were in Jamaica in the days of slavery an important status group. They perceived mulatto women to be a group. They assigned power to them, considering their own welfare to be threatened by them as their voice below indicates:

> It is extraordinary to witness the immediate effect that the climate and habit of living in this country have upon the mind and manners of Europeans ... In the upper ranks, they become indolent and inactive, regardless of every thing but eating drinking, and indulging themselves, and are almost entirely under the dominion of their mulatto favourites.[2]

So says Lady Nugent the wife of the governor of Jamaica between April 1801 and September 1805. She clearly sees mulatto women as having a powerful influence over high ranking men in Jamaican society. Other white women share her perception, a fact she also commits to her diary:

> The ladies told me strange stories of the influence of the black and yellow women, and Mrs Bullock called them serpents.[3]

Mrs Bullock and her group had reason to categorise the mulatto females among our forefathers as a group and a frightening one: they felt their sting.

> A large party at second breakfast, and all the conversation about a sad affair that has just taken place. A Mr Irvine, in a fit of jealousy, having murdered one of his servants. It seems the favourite was a brown lady; and to, [sic] mend the matter, Mr Irvine is a married man, and his unfortunate wife has been long nearly broken hearted, as his attachment to this *lady* has occasioned his treating her often with the greatest cruelty.[4]

White women in Jamaica in the early part of the 19th century and perhaps before and after, clearly saw certain black women as a group with a distinguishable kind of behaviour. Their white men gave them cause to think so.

> Poor foolish Captain Johnson is in great distress, about an ugly
> mulatto favourite, who has been accused of theft. General N [the
> governor] will give all the good advice he can; but *cui bono*?[5]

It is also clear that white men were sentimentally involved with
this kind of black woman and that this kind of black woman
was sending ripples through the peace of a group of persons
well-placed within the social system.

It is essential to group formation – and one which ought to be
so close that it can consciously work for and achieve political
change – that the people in the group see themselves as, and
behave as a group. That Mr Irvine is so emotionally involved
with one of these 'serpents' that he kills her lover in a jealous fit
and that Captain Johnson is publicly distressed about his "ugly"
lady is not evidence that these our foremothers perceived of
themselves as a group within the social system, is no evidence
that they had political power within the Jamaican social system
or even were more than the outsiders that their enslaved
parents were. What power they had was individualised, was
contingent upon each one's relationship with one man and
lasted, if as much, until his death. Such relationships neither
spoke of liberation nor eventuated by themselves into liberation
of the group.

A universal feature of slavery is the slave-master's effort to
isolate the slave from his kind by a partial integration into his
group. Taking a black woman as mistress separated her from
her kind. Our question here is not whether there is genuine
affection between slave and master or whether the relationship
was crassly developed with ulterior motives; the issue is, what
the relationship does to the liberation process. And the answer
is that the connection of the mulatto woman with the white man
is likely to retard the development of the bonds necessary to the
kind of group cohesion which can inveigh against the system,
for double loyalty ensues for the black in the affair, unless like
Delilah she is clear about her political motives and has a
politically conscious group supporting her. It is logical that
there would be a debilitating confusion at the psychic level for
those blacks involved in these affairs. Freedmen in the
Caribbean, and in particular mulattos, were faced with this
debilitating confusion which stymied bonding with their
blacker brothers.

In any case, whites had skilfully written safeguards into the system to prevent their sexual and romantic passions from eventuating into social change. In Jamaica between 1792 and 1838, 80 per cent of freedmen were mulattos, given their freedom by their fathers, but they were not let into white society, for there were laws promulgated by the whites, which specifically limited their freedom, which confined them to the city, confined them to certain jobs and to wearing certain clothes (a blue cross on your shoulder if you have no land and less than ten slaves).[6] The white society in its legal treatment of mulattos, to borrow from Gad Heuman quoted above, obviously saw them as outsiders, yet several of them were given large inheritances by their fathers. 'Said' fathers, such as Governor Manchester, we learn from Gad Heuman could, despite these gifts, perpetuate and apparently believe myths concerning the "timidity and lack of resolution"[7] of these people who carried their genes in their veins.

By their edicts as well as by their perception of them, the freed mulatto among the black population was an outsider in the social system. This outsider/insider status, more pronounced than among the enslaved population, kept freed mulattos 'between black and white', a buffer status which crystalised in the 1830s with the repeal of most limitations against them. This repeal was done with the expressed motive of keeping the freedmen, a dominantly mulatto group, from wanting to and from establishing the kinds of bonds with slaves that could have political significance. The freed mulattos seemed to have acquiesced. The biblical Moses had been in a position similar to theirs. Two roads lay before him. He could choose to be with the lowly Jews or with the ruling Egyptians. There was no Moses here in Jamaica during slavery, choosing to relate to one set and spear-heading a liberation movement, in which blacks and browns coalesced, although together they were by far the greatest number of people in the island. Let us see now whether skin colour was a deterrent to group consciousness in all the areas in which our forefathers lived.

Successful liberation action here in the New World began in Haiti. The behaviour of Haiti was what inspired the British government to repeal limitations on the grounds of colour in its territories, including Jamaica. Still, even there, it was not a coalition of black and brown, slave and freedmen, which produced the liberation movement that so frightened Britain. This Haiti was established as a slave society before Jamaica. The usual miscegenation had therefore had an earlier history there and consequently Haiti had a fairly large mulatto population. Haiti had in the 18th century about 20 times as many slaves as it had whites. Like elsewhere these slaves were seen as socially dead, as outsiders. Their coloureds, like some Jamaican ones, were comparatively wealthy and had come by their wealth by the same process as in Jamaica. Like their Jamaican counterpart, they were the greatest proportion of free blacks.

As in Jamaica too, coloureds/mulattos were partially outside of the dominant social system, distinguished from whites here by attire – their women could not wear their hair in curls – and by the fact that they could not wear side arms. As in Jamaica too the two sets of genetically related blacks, the enslaved and the freed, most of whom were mulattos, were socially apart, the mulattos having bought the standard line emerging from the slavery experience, that there is nothing to be gained from alliances with the slave, the blacks. The French government which had ultimate responsibility for Haiti in much the same way as Britain had responsibility for Jamaica, now in its revolutionary phase, responded favourably to pleas from both the whites and the mulattos for freedom, liberty and fraternity. For the whites the need was liberty to be part of the French National Assembly; for the mulattos, it was freedom from social and political discrimination. The grant of this latter freedom meant the whites' opening the society's door to the free coloureds. The whites were not about to do this.

The black enslaved population had not sought liberty from the French National Assembly and had sent it no emissary. In its clairvoyance it must have seen Napoleon trying to get them back into slavery, as he did try to do shortly after he gained power; must have known that the country for which it laboured was the wealthiest sugar producing area in the world and that the trade in its kind of person was what kept it, as with most of the New World and Western Europe, afloat. The slave population must have seen that the kindest interpretation of 'liberty, equality and fraternity' would have to continue to see them as outsiders fit only for the hewing of wood and the drawing of water. They had had a history of revolt; they were thus already bonded and politicised. While the free coloureds and the whites wrangled about admitting the former into the social system, the blacks, like the wolf, blew the house down.

In August 1791, signalled by drum beats, the black-skinned enslaved population of the north of Haiti, set fire to canefields, to houses and murdered the white inhabitants. Within two months, they had killed 2000 whites and had destroyed 180 sugar plantations and 900 coffee and indigo settlements. They had given a social system, which had treated them as outsiders, a sound battering.[8] They had lost about 10,000 of their brethren in the battles. C.L.R. James writes in *The Black Jacobins* with pride of their bravery in combat:[9] they obviously knew that for outsiders, it was freedom or death and that the way to liberty was through physical attack of the system, not the dialogue of the French estates. By 1800 the Haitian blacks – with some help from the French Revolutionary Army, a unit estranged from the old Haitian social system and those supporting it, and with goodwill from John Adams of the United States – had defeated the English and the Spanish and decimated the mulattos who as slave owners themselves had resisted the liberation of enslaved blacks. The liberating action of these slaves, most of whom were unmixed, ended slavery in Haiti.

As we learnt in the last lecture, a central tenet of successful enslavement of another is to give that other the feeling that there is no other with authority over him except the master. This understanding is expressed in the presentation of the Martinican, Moreau de Saint-Mery, in his opposition to the granting of citizenship rights to the free coloureds. Parry and Sherlock quote him as saying:

> For if once our slaves suspect that there is a power other than their masters which holds the final disposition of their fate; if they once see that the mulattos have successfully invoked this power and by its aid have become our equals – then France must renounce all hope of preserving her colony.[10]

The three way negotiations between France, the Haitian whites and the Haitian mulattos had indeed shown the Haitian blacks that ultimate power did not lay with their masters. This would have strengthened their resolve, but not produced it, for the

Haitian blacks had launched attacks on the system before. The statement was more *à propos* for the international world of great powers. The successes of the Haitian slaves forced them to consider what new steps to take now that slaves knew that there was another temporal power besides their masters and now that slaves knew that they could take over a country. The leaders of the French National Assembly took the line of least resistance: they legitimised what was already a *fait accompli*, at least for the blacks in the north of Haiti – they officially emancipated Haiti's slaves. Britain made her statement to her blacks in Jamaica and elsewhere by supporting the ex-slave owners, though this was not her only reason for choosing this side of the fray.

According to Parry and Sherlock[11] it was the Jamaican system, not the Haitian, that was expected to collapse under an outside push from its slaves. Orlando Patterson's *Sociology of Slavery* supports this thesis.[12] According to him, there were more rebellions of slaves in Jamaica than in any other contemporary area, not to mention other forms of resistance to slavery such as malingering, the creation of satirical verse aimed at the authorities, running away, suicide and poisonings. Before the success of the Haitian slaves, the Spanish-owned slaves in Jamaica, today called the maroons, had engaged the English steadily between 1655 and 1670. In 1673, 300 slaves from the Gold Coast murdered their master and 13 other whites in St Ann. They later formed a maroon settlement (Leeward). In 1678, slaves on an estate in St Catherine killed their mistress and wounded their master. A few were killed but the majority escaped to the hills. In 1685-1686 slaves on Grey's estate originally from Madagascar revolted. Some were seized, some surrendered and the rest bolted to the hinterlands. In 1690, 400 slaves from Sutton's estate in Clarendon killed the overseer, torched the plantation and fled to the interior of the parish. Many of these eventually joined up with the Leeward maroons. Another set in St Elizabeth killed the wife and children of their master and fled too to the interior to join up eventually with Leeward maroons. Conflicts occurred between these maroon groups and the whites through to the signing of the first treaty between them in 1739.

1760 is the date of one of the most serious slave revolts in the

New World. This was Tacky's rebellion in St Mary. In the course of the rebellion, which involved thousands of slaves, 60 whites were killed and between 300-400 slaves either killed or lost to suicide. In 1765 another revolt broke out prematurely on 17 estates. The year after, there was one in Westmoreland and in 1769 there was a plan to burn the city of Kingston. In 1776 there were revolts in Hanover and St James and in the very next year there was the discovery of another large scale one which was to have involved the massacre of whites. Another plot was discovered in 1784. With such a history, it is not surprising that Jamaica had been the place where the successful slave uprising was expected to be. The relevant question for us here, is why it didn't. Why didn't those people located on the outside of the system, already with revolt on their minds, succeed in overturning the system? Most of the revolts mentioned above were spearheaded by newly arrived blacks coming from the Akan-speaking regions of West Africa, where they were accustomed to military organisation. In their origins lay their determination, but here also lay one problem: antipathy among new and creole slaves, based on ancient hostilities between tribes, which they brought with them into Jamaica. There is no clear evidence that these prejudices among slaves did not exist among the Haitians. In fact, not all Haitian slaves had fought with the rebel slaves, Parry and Sherlock tell us.[13] In the south the white planters had armed their slaves and they had fought on their side. One of the crucial variables seems to be the state of the social system. The slave society, which the Haitian rebels stormed, was one in psychological disarray, split by the masters' varying positions over the ideas of 'liberty, fraternity and equality'. These ideas had not infected the British in Jamaica. There are historians, Patterson being the major one, who would even claim that ideas were not a part of the baggage of the Jamaican whites.[14]

Another important variable, militating against the success of violent liberation movements of the enslaved population in Jamaica after 1740, was the Anglo/Maroon treaty by which the maroons helped the British to capture and return rebels. It was their might and their skill in guerrilla warfare that cornered Tacky in 1760. That a black organised opposition existed decreed success to mean prior agreement with them. What had.

enslaved blacks to offer maroons that was better than the treaty
signed with the British, by which they were guaranteed
freedom to establish their own government, land on which to
grow crops and rear livestock to feed themselves and a bounty
for all rebels returned? Success for the enslaved would have
meant a two-pronged attack. There is no evidence that rebels
during slavery, tried to settle the maroon part of the equation or
that they tried to eliminate inter-tribe hostility as a balance to
the maroons. The diplomatic initiative seems to have been
missing from these attempts at physical liberation.

The existence of the maroons and their history is likely to
have affected the liberation process of the Jamaican slaves in
another way. The maroons had eventually negotiated the terms
of their freedom with the British and were from time to time in
colloquy with them. This must have left the creole slaves with
the impression that there was some possibility of another group
of blacks negotiating their freedom from them. The coming of
the missionaries and their talk of salvation would also have sent
the message that change of the system by the players in the
system would redound to the eventual liberation of the
enslaved outsider, especially as these missionaries were of the
same ethnic stock as their masters.

Nevertheless Jamaican slaves still resisted enslavement, and
violently too, after the Haitian revolution. The evidence is
mostly of plots discovered before they were put in force. The
clearest evidence of actual physical resistance occurred firstly in
1808 when 33 Chamba slaves and again Coromantee slaves –
i.e. slaves from the Akan-speaking regions of West Africa,
recruited to the West India regiment – mutinied and killed two
of their officers while being drilled. Half of them were killed in
action and the others executed. Another occurred between 1823
and 1824 in Hanover. The leader, this time an Ibo, committed
suicide. As we can see, the incidence of post-1784 attempts at
physical liberation were less than before. We can guess at a
number of possible causes:

- There was greater militancy among the whites still
  frightened by the Haitian debacle. And with Britain
  engaged in war with the French Revolutionary army – for
  the Caribbean was frequently the theatre in which these
  European hostilities were played out – blacks expected that

a significant armed force was nearby.

- With the end of the slave trade in 1807 fewer Africans, new to enslavement and therefore disgruntled and eager to rebel were coming into the country.

- By now there was a greater degree of creolisation and with this, a greater degree of accommodation to the status of outsider. By this time too the system of rewards meant to placate the outsider would have been transferred to and internalised into his system as positive. The outsider/ insider position would be less cognitively dissonant.

- The end of the slave trade, the amelioration acts of 1823, end of discrimination against free coloureds and blacks – changes legislated by a power outside of themselves – might have lulled enslaved blacks into a wait and see stance. That members of the inside group, missionaries and abolitionists, were championing their cause would have confirmed them in this position.

How do we then explain one of the greatest revolts in the New World, the 1831 rebellion in the west of island, which involved five parishes and thousands of slaves? We know from Kamau Brathwaite's *Wars of Respect* this was a different kind of liberation move.[15] It was not like Tacky's or like that of Haitians, intended to replace the government. It began as a strike, a withdrawal of labour until certain working conditions were met. Beneath this determination to stop working until conditions were improved lay another voice it seems which added: we intend to show the whites that the enslaved now perceive of themselves as equal to them and as such are demanding a place within the system, are demanding negotiations as equals. This voice called forth more people than Sam Sharp, its leader, was expecting. This, as British commentators of the time realised, was not the voice of a 'slave' but of a person who happened to be enslaved.

An uprising of thousands in which only 14 on the enemy side are killed truly does not sound as if a bloody Haitian-type liberation was intended. Note that Sam Sharp was a Baptist deacon and many of his followers were church-going Christians, not of the Native Baptist church alone but of that affiliated to the English Baptists. As such they could not fail to feel that they were a part of an international religious and

political organisation. As such they were now no longer slaves –
fatherless, kinless beings; they were now children of God,
members of the worldwide religious organisation, the English
Baptist church and members of the British Empire. They were
no longer only the creatures of their masters, standing on the
outside; they were inside of something; they belonged to a
being other than and greater than their masters. These children
of God had only to make a stand and their father would do the
rest, if the British Parliament and the church did not. The British
Parliament acted. Three years later there was an Abolition Act.
Liberation had come to the enslaved Jamaicans, who now
perceived of themselves as equals in a Christian kingdom, more
by an act of faith in their right to be regarded as an equal, than
an act of war. The push was from within the kingdom of Christ
of which the Jamaican social system was a part, if a satanic one.

The goals of liberation clearly had to be changed after
Emancipation in 1838. Blacks were given at Emancipation from
the hand of the highest authority in the land the "blessings and
privileges of freedom", but that they were to remain landless
labourers was no secret.

> If ever the black population of the West Indies should become
> squatters on waste land or mere cultivators of provision grounds
> instead of labourers for hire, then slavery and the slave trade
> would have received the last and greatest encouragement which it
> was in the power of man to bestow.[16]

This was the view, as aired in the House of Commons, that Peel
the Prime Minister of Britain had in 1841 of our possibilities. We
were to be a caste of labourers. The Jamaican black, given no
land at Emancipation with which to begin to make himself
other than a labourer, would have to spend some energy in
finding a way of liberating himself from the perception that he
was only free to be a hewer of wood and drawer of water, from
efforts to make him part of an occupational caste, customarily
disvalued. He tried to change this situation by diplomacy and
petition, techniques usually used in inter-group negotiations
within a social system. But such manipulations did not work.
Good Queen Victoria had responded to the plea for land by the
people of St Ann with the message that they should go back to
work for the estate, making it clear by innuendo that you are

inside but inside as a lower caste. It would have to be pushing again if there was to be change. Bogle pushed in Morant Bay in 1865 with the result that the system was changed but not necessarily in the interest of blacks for representative government was withdrawn.

Despite the hardships, as Swithin Wilmot's several works show, some ex-slaves had managed to get enough property after Emancipation to become part of the voting public and were returning candidates sympathetic to their cause to the House of Representatives.[17] This growth of black political power within the system was now put on hold. The governor of Jamaica, Musgrave, in 1879 felt moved to point out the fallacy in the view that the only contribution the African-Jamaican population could make to the national good was labouring on the estates. He pointed out that these freedmen and sons of freedmen were supporting themselves as peasants and at the same time bearing the brunt of the taxes in the country. But the contrary view persisted and we find J.R. Williams, the new superintendent of schools at the beginning of the new century, seeing his job as making

> active and efficient and available the labour of a population of nearly 800,000 of mostly very poor people.[18]

The liberation of the black population from the stereotypes concerning its possibility and place within the society in which it laboured, remained in 1900 to be attained, as did tight bonds between blacks of various shades and economic circumstances.

The alignment of factors was stacked differently for the slaves and other blacks in the USA, and their liberation movements took forms different from that of the Caribbean peoples of Jamaica and Haiti. When we look at Donald L. Robinson's *Slavery in the Structure of American Politics* we see that for the states of Delaware, Maryland, the district of Columbia, Virginia, North Carolina, South Carolina and Georgia, areas in which slavery was practiced, between 1790 and 1820 only in South Carolina were slaves more than 50 per cent of the population.[19] In Haiti they were nearly 20 times as many as whites and in Jamaica they were nearly ten times as many. Robinson points out too that most blacks, at least 90 per cent, were between 1790 and 1820 slaves.

Blacks were in the slave-owning states of the USA a minority
group. Plantations were smaller units. Unlike in Jamaica, the
master and his family lived here and could in subtle as well
more obvious ways police his farm and demonstrate his
personal power over his slaves and with close neighbours, insist
that slaves behave in accordance with the slave laws. The
technique of keeping beings in a state of slavery by treating
them as outsiders while giving them tasks which made them
feel like insiders, worked very well here. Mammy, the outsider
in *Gone with the Wind*, virtually ran the household. And who
were the wet nurses?

In these societies too, unlike those of the Caribbean, there
were relatively large working class white populations. Slaves
and black freemen were therefore outsiders to a great many
people including those poor whites whose only claim to status
was that they were ethnically insiders. Blacks and especially
those freed, often needed protection from this kind of white
who was impelled by his sense of his own inferiority within his
ethnic group, to demonstrate his inside status by harassing
blacks. Such protection had to come from the master or, in the
case of freemen, influential whites. This bound him to whites.
The black American then, very bound to whites, had little of
himself left to himself to make common cause with his own
brothers.

There was miscegenation in the USA as there was everywhere
else. In the USA however there was no group of mulattos with
the potential that those in Haiti had. Roman Catholic Haiti and
Anglican Jamaica did not take the Biblical rules against
fornication as seriously as did Puritan North America. Unlike in
Jamaica, where according to Lucille Mathurin, "white women
came, saw and fled"[20] the American women lived there and
with her husband made a small contained social system,
household group. Cohabitation with black women was not as
necessary as it was in Jamaica. To engage in this, made an
American master not only a fornicating sinner in his God's sight
but a sinner against his wife and their small household group,
the most basic cell in the larger social system.

The American mulatto produced by this master thus carried a
heavier burden than his Caribbean cousin. He was not only a
black, an outsider and of a minority ethnic group but he was the

incarnation of sin. Understandably he was given no special place on the outside as was the case for his kind in the Caribbean. A free black man was a contradiction in terms in the thinking of the Southern whites. It was happier to see the back of him. This feeling applied as well to the mulatto who carried whites genes. If he was freed, like other freed blacks he faced exile from his state. In 1808 Virginia, Maryland, Delaware and Kentucky passed laws to keep manumitted blacks out of their states. We can see then that whether they wished to or not, the chances of freed blacks, mulatto or otherwise being able by their own revolt, as in Haiti, to open the way for black revolution or to assist it by joining it, were for the most part very slim. But these special conditions laid the groundwork for the development of group consciousness, bonding blacks of all colours and all economic circumstances together.

We must not think that the strictures on them stopped American blacks in the South from making attempts to liberate themselves physically from slavery. There was one attempt in Charleston, South Carolina in 1720 and another in 1739. There was the Prosser rebellion in Henrico County, Virginia, on August 30th 1800. Scores of slaves were arrested and 35 executed. Heavy rains had stopped this plan from being more than a plot. In the same year there was Vesey's attempt in South Carolina. There were attempts also in Louisiana and Georgia and in August 1831, again in Virginia, Nat Turner's rebellion. This is the most significant and measurable of the USA revolts; Nat Turner and his followers actually killed 60 whites including his master and his family before the state and the federal troops intervened. Later in the 1830s there were uprisings in Georgia and in the 1840s there were attempts in Alabama, Louisiana and Mississippi and in 1853 one in New Orleans and another in North Carolina in 1856. These outbreaks were relatively few in number and, compared to Jamaica and Haiti, mild, and made little impression on the status of enslaved blacks in the USA.

Violence was only one way: there were other paths to liberation. Out of their special conditions North American blacks paved for themselves liberation goals which involved first, integration into the existing society as equal members and second, withdrawal from the social system but as a distinct group, a society within a society. These were goals articulated in their written philosophies as well as their active behaviour. These thoughts and actions were located in the North where there were free blacks of all hues, the Caribbean colour distinctions being less respected here. An offshoot of this kind of thought and action, as our examination of liberation postures and actions in the USA will show, is a literature devoted to the idea of black liberation.

Black slavery in the USA began in the state of Virginia where, unlike in Jamaica and Haiti, it crept into the society as the social condition of the black man, gradually. The first black workers had been bondsmen, who like bondsmen of other ethnic groups there, became landowners at the end of their contract. By 1667 a distinction was made between bondsmen coming into the state by land and those coming in by sea. Those coming in by sea were to be slaves. Twenty years later all non-Christians were declared to be slaves as well, and since there was an embargo on preaching to slaves and on preaching slaves, any African coming in by sea, which is how the slave ships travelled, was *ipso facto* a slave. The majority of the delegates framing the American constitution in 1787 supported the slave trade. They declared it to be legitimate for 20 more years. With the expansion of cotton as big business in the South and the need for labourers, slavery become seen as a pre-requisite of economic success and so, by the beginning of the 19th century, when there was the black ex-slave Toussaint L'Ouverture directing the government of Haiti close by, the blacks of the USA South were more rooted in their position as outsiders in the societies in which they laboured than ever before. Slave laws legislated them into this position; their minority numbers made it easy for these laws to be observed.

While slavery was taking deep root in the South, it was losing ground in the North. Pennsylvania, Massachusetts, Connecticut, Rhode Island, New York and New Jersey had outlawed slavery by 1804. Blacks in the North were now inside the system. They gave it their intellectual strength and established a tradition of black intellectual capacity – Phillis Wheatley with her poetry in the 1770s, Onesimus with his small pox inoculations and Banneker, mathematician and astronomer, with his surveying and laying out of the district of Columbia. These free blacks, now mainly in the North, were three times as many by the end of the 18th century as were slaves in the country. Their inclusion into the main stream of the society and their proportion relative to the enslaved, was greater than it had been for freemen in Jamaica or Haiti during their slavery days. These blacks could even vote! Between 1807-1837 the tables were turned on them, however. New Jersey, Connecticut, New York, Rhode Island and Pennsylvania, in the wake of the increasing power of a white working class jealous of jobs, passed laws discriminating against blacks. Neither Haiti nor Jamaica had had during slavery or after, a working class of white people who could influence the liberation initiatives of blacks and so it was that by 1838, when the blacks in Jamaica were moving into the society as a vote-less people, the American black was demoted to the Jamaican's status and worse.

Political advancement within the Jamaican society up to 1865 was possible, difficult but possible. The franchise was related to property holding, not race or colour. Thus the ex-slave blacks who had managed to acquire property could vote for and influence the choice of elected members of the ruling House of Representatives. As we shall see in later meditations, a small body of articulate blacks was in this way making a block in this House. With his demotion, this move was not possible for the American black. Further Liberation, in the Jamaican case, now meant getting as much wealth as those established on the inside had; in the American case it meant convincing those on the inside that you were intrinsically equal, that their God had made you and made you equal to them, a battle Sam Sharp had fought and won in 1831. It was an effort, which the American had to be conduct under the fire of the enemy's use of the law.

The fugitive slave law of 1850 – second to one promulgated in 1793 by which enslaved blacks were denied a jury trial in federal courts, their testimony declared inadmissible and the unsworn testimony of an absent and alleged owner could be used against them – by making it possible for even free blacks to be captured and taken to slavery in the South, further depressed the status of black populations everywhere in the USA. The Dred Scot decision pushed them firmly to the outside of the system. By this Supreme Court ruling, no black man had rights that a white man need respect.

Blacks in the North had, as slaves there, experienced a kind of liberty, which translated into the end of their enslavement. This emancipation was nonetheless no grant; northern blacks had fought violently for it. New York City in 1712 was the scene of one such effort and there was another in Manhattan in 1741. Northern blacks had fought too in the revolutionary war along with whites, with the understanding that they would be rewarded with their freedom. The learned erudite black leaders of the 1850s and 1860s, many born free of fathers who had been part of these liberation efforts, knew that a different kind of struggle was now mandated, that violence would get them nowhere. The liberation movement now took two main strands – first the non-physical fight for freedom of the enslaved and second petitions based on reasoned arguments for civil rights. These fissioned into other strategies. A key variable concerning which strand or version of which strand was most popular among blacks was the involvement of whites in it.

The underground railway was associated with non-physical liberation of the enslaved. This was black dominated. Names such as Sojourner Truth, David Walker, Martin Delaney, Frederick Douglass and, ofcourse, Harriet Tubman, were associated with it. They guided slaves to freedom in the free states of the North and into the British territory, Canada, where slavery was disallowed. The abolition movement was white dominated. It too was interested in the emancipation of slaves. Their interest was not so much in the welfare of black people but in the righteousness of the nation. It was immoral, they felt, to keep men in bondage and they sought to convince Americans of this by oratory and literature. At their public meetings black refugees were presented and their intelligence touted. Their books, some ghost-written, some written by themselves, were sold.

One unintended consequence of this version of liberation was the development of a liberation literature. Ideas could be passed from one part of the blacks' world to another, to become the foundation for further discussion and clarification, and to become the basis for revolutionary action. This was more a USA development, than Haitian or Jamaican, and decidedly the action of free black Americans residing in the North. One of the most prolific of these writers was Frederick Douglass. He was the blackman most associated with the white dominated abolition movement. Apart from authoring several books,

Douglass also ran a newspaper. Another significant black literati venting his spleen on paper for contemporaries and posterity was David Walker whose *Appeal to the Coloured Citizens of the World* had made its debut in 1829 and created a stir which put him in physical danger.[21]

White domination of the abolition movement, the most public of the struggles for black liberation, had its reaction among blacks. Black thinkers now found it necessary to make the point that their discrimination was as a race and that the elevation of that race had to be, and be seen to be, dependent on their efforts. Consequently they turned their attention to the development of black institutions. Implicit here is the statement that we are racially distinct but we ought still to be equal. Out of this thinking and action came, from 1816, the establishment of the African Methodist Episcopalian church as a national body. The Baptists too split off to establish black congregations. Now too there were black schools and there were black conventions. The black conventions of the 1840s and 1850s emphasised the reform of the black character by blacks. This should be done through a tightening of the bonds of racial unity, through the cultivation of thrift and education in trades and through blacks' insistence that each be of morally sound character. On this road lay racial respectability and wealth, the thinking went.

Delegates to these conventions, mainly wealthy black businessmen, repeatedly asserted that they were American citizens and as such should have equal rights with all other citizens. They meant their reforms of and policing of themselves to be seen as evidence that they were worthy of inclusion into the white dominated social system. They did not intend this action to be seen as a desire for, or to eventuate into an argument for, a separate black state within the larger state. But the demand for inclusion is meaningless unless those who control the system are willing to grant this demand. The conventions did not take the black American very far on the road to an equal place within the system but they did feed into and enlarge the notion that liberation would come through self-help, strong character and racial solidarity. These notions were the harbingers of Pan-Africanism, a philosophy whose central motif is that there is something called a black race and that liberation of the enslaved and the children of the enslaved people of the New World depends on solidarity within this group. The notion has elements of separatism in it.

There were those who saw liberation as separation and this in its ultimate form, emigration. Diametrically opposed to this position, at first, were such as Frederick Douglass, who saw separation as a temporary tactic with the potential of bringing together in great numbers those people convinced of the need for change of the system. This was a retreat to coalesce and more effectively beat against the doors of the system. Douglass favoured dispersion of blacks among whites and attacks on the system from within its institutions. One should, for instance, stand in the aisles of discriminating churches and embarrass the membership into admitting you into full citizenship rather than go off to found one's own church. Even he, however, was led by 1860 to acknowledge the nonsense of wanting to bang from within, when no-one would let you in. He and his kind began to see withdrawal as a route to liberation.

Emigration had been on the agenda of liberation routes since 1808 when Paul Cuffee, a black Boston merchant, made his first trip to Sierra Leone to make plans for black American emigration. Cuffee was moved by the 1787 definition of the free black man, such as he, as three-fifths of a person and the notion that the African continent, from which he and his likes came, was a heathen, dark land. He predicated migration of black Americans to Africa as a way to get them out of a land in which they would always be the outsider, as well as a way of making Africa a place of which Africans abroad could be proud. Total emigration out of Egypt as with the biblical Israelites was not in his imagining. These sentiments attended the emigration movements to Africa up to Bishop Turner's plans of the late 19th and early 20th centuries.

The problem with the back-to-Africa movement for many free black Americans was the involvement of white people in it. On his return to the USA, Cuffee gave his help to the founders of the American Colonisation Society, founded in 1816 by a group of white liberals. It was they who began the movement of black Americans to Liberia. Some free blacks saw this as a plot to put them further outside of a rich society, which they had helped to make so. The charge had some grounds, as among the first emigrants were people who had been manumitted with the understanding that they would begin their free lives in Liberia. Lack of response to their case for civil rights within the USA social system led many of the free black American literati to accept the notion of liberation through emigration, some settling the issue of white involvement by calling themselves civilisationists, thus distinguishing themselves from colonisers, a label which the whites accepted.

In 1858 a group of prominent New York blacks founded the African Civilization Society for missionary and colonisation work. Others made their peace with the white outfit. Among these were the Harvard-trained physician, Martin Delany, and the Cambridge-trained episcopal minister, Alexander Crummel. Out of this impetus towards emigration to Africa came a liberation ideology: blacks had made a contribution to world civilisation in the past; to destroy the slave trade, to redeem and to christianise Africa from whence they had come, would bring her back to her glory, one which would reflect on Africans abroad, change the perception of them in the white world, raise black consciousness and lead eventually to the grant of civil rights and a place within the American social system. Frederick Douglass, though accepting the argument that the struggle for civil rights from within had been futile, could not countenance the expenditure of so much energy on Africa. He turned his eyes to Haiti. With the development of emigration as a route to liberation, we get a reaffirmation of the notions of self-help, racial solidarity and betterment of the race and extension of the boundaries of 'outside' to include Africa and the Caribbean. Pan-Africanism was about to be born.

The drive towards the redemption of Africa which we see in the black American emancipation/liberation movements, has been called Ethiopianism. "Ethiopia shall soon stretch forth her hands unto God" said the Bible.[22] That the blacks of the diaspora should help her to do so was a central and theological part of the reasoning associated with liberation-by-going-back-to Africa. This back-to Africa movement was for the most part a northern pre-Emancipation thought and act. It was held in abeyance by the civil war years of the 1860s when that equal place within the USA system, which was considered by all to be the desideratum, seemed near. There were signs that this had come with the reconstruction years of the 1870s, but by 1877 the North had withdrawn its protection from the blacks of the South and out went the newly established institutions by which blacks were made equal and hoped to remain equal.

Where the effort to keep the black population in Jamaica in peonage had been left to market forces, in the USA South this was done by law, as well as by custom. Negative stereotyping by cartoons, films, books, lectures, was supplemented by scientific arguments about the inferiority of the Negro. All this in a setting in which the black is a minority ethnic group. The echoes could be heard in the North. Now a new set of people sought liberation by physically distancing themselves from the USA state. The letters to the colonising societies seeking information concerning going to Africa, poured in from the South. It is the rural poor who were now saving their money to access liberation through settlement in Africa. This new move had less of the missionising rhetoric about it, though clerics such as Henry Turner, a bishop of the African Methodist Episcopalian church, was a prime mover in this effort and the *Horsa* and the *Lauredo* – carriers under Turner's initiative – did take blacks to Liberia.

The interest in missionising Africa, in helping her to stretch forth her hands unto God, was something felt by Caribbean people, Jamaicans included, as well as black Americans. On February 7th 1843, 12 married couples, three unmarried people and eight children left Jamaica and arrived in Akropong, Ghana, on June 18th of the same year. They had answered the call of the Moravian missionaries in Jamaica to minister in Africa. They were to stay for five years and to return to Jamaica at the end of their stay if they wished to. These Jamaicans went:

> not for any outward advantage which they hoped to get but from the true love they had for the Lord and also to witness to the Grace of God not only to the white man, but also to the blackman. Their only prayer was that the eyes of the blacks whom they regarded as their brothers may be opened to see Jesus as the Saviour of the world.23

These Jamaican blacks, liberated into the Christian faith and seeing Africans as their brothers, went to spread the joy to them. Their inclusion of Africa into their concerns came out of a mindset that was less interested in civilisation, colonisation and flight from the land to which they had been brought as slaves than that of their American brothers. That they both saw the development of Africans as part of their business is however the significant point. And here our review ends.

We have been reviewing the period 1789-1900, looking at the nature and kinds of liberation thought and action which emerged from the minds of the Africans of the diaspora over this period of time, a period which involves enslavement as well as official emancipation. We have used three geographically distinct areas – Haiti, Jamaica and the USA – and noted that in each of these the African population was distinguishable in terms of legal status (free or enslaved) and in terms of colour (black-skinned or mixed). The review noted that our forefathers throughout this period sought liberation through violent overthrow of the system which enslaved them and through flight out of the system. There were those who realised that thrown into a society which defined them as incapable of being other than servants, liberation also had to mean an attack on the perception that they and others had of their possibilities. Throughout this period, along with violent overthrow of the system and flight out of white dominated societies, our forefathers in all the areas and among all the colours as well as throughout the times of slavery and of freedom worked at a change of perception.

One or other technique was used more frequently in the time of slavery than in the time of freedom; more among the mixed than the pure bloods; more among the enslaved than the free; more in one territory than in the others. Different situations evidently called for different responses. We here are the late 20th century Africans of the diaspora. How is our time different from that of our forefathers? How are our selves different from their selves? Do we, their great grandchildren, need liberation and, if so, what programmes do our situation require? These are questions on which our history asks us to meditate.

November 1996

THE WORLD THE FREEDMAN/WOMAN MADE 3

Queen Victoria gi wi free
Gi wi free, gi wi free
Queen Victoria gi wi free
This is the year
Of Jubilee[1]

the freed slaves had sung.

The process of 'giving free' had been set in motion before the good queen ascended the throne. It was in the "3rd and 4th" year of the reign of William IV in 1834 that the "act for the abolition of slavery throughout the British Colonies" was passed. Please take note of the sub-titles. It was not just an act for the abolition of slavery, it was an act "for promoting the Industry of the manumitted slaves, and for compensating the Persons hitherto entitled to the services of such slaves".[2] These 'persons' throughout the British West Indies, were to be compensated to the tune of £20,000. 'Such slaves', on August 1st 1834 were to be made into apprentices rather than slaves. In this state, they served their former master in an 'as slave' role for $40^1/_2$ hours per week and for the rest of the time, practiced freedom. In this part-free state, African-Jamaicans were to have stayed for seven years. The hope that they would be rid of the interference of the British government in the running of their affairs made the Jamaica Assembly follow Nevis, St Kitts, Montserrat, the Virgin Islands and Barbados and in June of 1838 decide to end apprenticeship from August 1st 1838. After this date we were officially free.

To understand the environment in which the now free African-Jamaican had to build a life, it is wise to look some more into the process by which freedom came to him officially. Freedom was a gift from the British government which, true to biblical terms can be said to have redeemed us for £20,000. The British were the ultimate political power in Jamaica and could intervene in the running of the colony. Theoretically they could have intervened at any time and imposed 'freedom'. That they did so in 1834 is due to several factors, one of these being Sam Sharp's rebellion of 1831, discussed in the last lecture. Sharp's rebellion was widely discussed in Britain and brought the issue of British involvement in what some saw as an inhumane institution to a head. Sharp's rebellion, as we have seen, was not that of the new 'nagar', who could be expected to be less rebellious with time. It was not that of the lower end of slaves, who with ameliorated conditions could be expected to be satisfied. This was a revolt of the upper reaches of the slave system, of people many of whom and certainly most of its leaders, had never had a lash on their backs.

Sharp was a driver on the Croyden estate and a respected Baptist leader whose master allowed him to travel freely. George Taylor was a saddler and a Baptist deacon who also was allowed to travel; Tharp was a driver, Charles Campbell a carpenter and Thomas Dove a literate headman.[3] The British working class, beginning to be seen and heard at that time, could identify with such men, who like them were artisans and Christians. British intellectuals were reformist and getting more so. Harsh reprisals and the dignity with which the rebels accepted hanging, projected them as upright men defending ideals, men in search of freedom and willing to help themselves to it. The intellectuals' anti-slavery fervour was increased. This sentiment percolated throughout Britain and several petitions were sent to the House of Commons, where there was already a strong anti-slavery faction. Had the sugar and coffee interests been of as much economic and military value to British, as they had been during the struggles with Napoleon in the 1790s to 1815, sentiment might have been set aside. But it was not.

Even the more pure capitalists, who had been pro-slavery before, were now changing their position. The feeling amongst them was that there were more men like Sharp and his fellow conspirators among the Jamaican slaves and that men like those no longer had the mentality of slaves, would not work well in a slave economy and would before long destroy it. They now felt that the foundations on which the Jamaican economy were built was in decay and the whole edifice in danger. A different approach to labour was indicated. The arguments and

sentiments of the various British factions left the Jamaicans,
with their old slave system, isolated. They, however, did not
seem to appreciate that the tide of public opinion was against
their way of life, that there was a new ideology in ascendancy,
which required that individuals be freed from arbitrary power
and that men like Sharp, Tharp, Taylor, Dove and Campbell
were no longer seen in intellectual quarters as Long's fleecy
animals but as Christian artisans, who should be helped
towards self-discipline and individual responsibility.[4]

Instead of reforming their system, the Jamaican plantocracy
continued to maltreat a people who, contrary to their
prophesies concerning reprisals, had killed no one on August
1st 1834, the day of abolition. This behaviour continued to
isolate them and to force the British government to disregard
their laws and to intervene directly to protect apprentices, the
quasi-free, from abuse. Their current governor, Lionel Smith,
had said of their local governing body:

> It is impossible for anyone to answer for the conduct of the House
> of Assembly. Many are there in the island who would be delighted
> to get up an insurrection for the pleasure of destroying the negroes
> and the missionaries. They are, in fact, mad.[5]

To prevent further interference from Britain in their internal
affairs the Jamaican assembly opted for total emancipation. In
this social-psychological climate, with the ill-will of their former
masters towards them for forcing them into a new kind of
labour system, and with tensions between the local assembly
and Britain about this, the newly freed people – the cause of
dissension in the family – sat down to build an independent life
among people, who for centuries had only seen them as
extensions of themselves.

The freed African-Jamaican had been given no compensation
money. Their ex-masters who ruled the land were annoyed by
the fact of their new status, were not sure how to handle
relationships with them, and were not likely to stretch out a
hand to them individually or politically. On the contrary they
could be expected to be positively hostile. They could expect no
material help from Britain for was not self-discipline and
responsibility the other side of the freedom which British public
opinion had wished for them? And what notion of freedom for

African-Jamaicans did those, who legislated this opinion into fact, have? A clue lies in the title of the Abolition Act ...'for promoting the industry of the manumitted slave'. Freedom meant freedom to work; the idea of a prescribed social space in which this freedom and freedom to work were to take place, persisted in the mind of the local elite as well as in the mind of their betters in Britain. Let us look at the Emancipation Proclamation read in public places on the eve of August 1st 1838.

It reads, *inter alia*

> By the Queen
> A Proclamation
> Whereas an act has been passed by the Legislature of this our Island of Jamaica for terminating the system of apprenticeship on the first day of August next, and thereby granting the Blessings and Privileges of unrestricted freedom to all classes of the inhabitants and whereas it is incumbent on all the inhabitants of this our island to testify their grateful sense of this Divine favor [*sic*], we do therefore by and with the advice of our privy Council of this our said island, *direct and point* that Wednesday the said first day of August next be observed in all churches and chapels as a day of General Thanksgiving to the Almighty God for these His Mercies and of humble intercession for his continued blessing and protection on this most important occasion, and we do hereby call upon persons of all classes within this our said island to observe the said first day of August next *with the same reverence and respect which is observed and due on the sabbath.* [emphasis mine][6]

This was the Proclamation of 1838 declaring full freedom. It "direct[ed] and point[ed]" how the freedman should celebrate his freedom. African-Jamaican celebration of freedom was to be contained within the confines of a particular cultural system represented by the Christian church. Similar strictures were placed on his crafting of his free life as we see in the title of the Abolition Act.

Thomas C. Holt summarises more succinctly, than I can, the context within which African-Jamaicans were to build their world as per the intentions of those who designed the legal parameters of his freedom.

They would be free, but only after being re-socialised to accept the internal discipline that ensured the survival of the existing order. They would be free to bargain in the marketplace but not free to ignore the market. They would be free to pursue their own self-interest but not free to reject the cultural conditioning that defined what that self-interest should be. They would have opportunities for social mobility, but only after they learnt their proper place.[7]

The "Industry" called for in the Abolition Act of 1834 presented no problem for the freedman. In the two years between full emancipation and mid-1840, 2074 freedmen had got themselves freeholds.[8] Five years later ten times as many, being 20,724, had done so too. This means that seven years after full emancipation about 21 per cent of freedmen had made themselves into peasants. Their lots were small as lots went in Jamaica: they were under 20 acres. Along with the growth in the number of freeholds went a growth in the number of towns. Lands had come into the freedman's hands through the decline of coffee and sugar estates. The area in which I live is a case in point. By 1848 plantations in the South St Mary – North Catherine areas had ceased production.[9] The Palmetto Grove estate declared itself no longer able to grow sugar cane profitably and the coffee estates of Woodside, RockSpring, Smailfield, Louisiana, Richmond Hill, Stapleton, Waterton went out of agro industry. Windsor Castle had by 1843 cut up 252 acres to be sold to former slaves.[10] None of these lots was bigger than seven acres. Petersfield[11] which shares a border with Woodside had begun earlier and Palmetto Grove consistently sold out its periphery into little one and three acre plots after 1846.[12] Land transfers into the hands of freedmen continued into the 1850s, freedmen buying into sub-division, buying as individuals and as a corporate entity: "the negroes of William Kelly" "holed and patented" three pieces of canelands in Fort Stewart, St Mary.[13]

During slavery planters had found it economical to have their enslaved workers plant foodstuff to feed themselves. Thus they had been given provision grounds. A law of 1792[14] stipulated that they be given a day off every fortnight, except in crop time, when other plans had to be made concerning their free time. This time they had used to attend to their gardens. They were also due every Sunday. This became the day on which they went to the markets to sell their surplus. These Sunday markets became a traditional meeting place, but more importantly, part of an economic institution created, and to the extent that one can speak of "control" in a slave society, controlled by the enslaved. Though everything a slave owned belonged by law to his master, it was rare that a master required of him/her the returns from his grounds and his sales. A law of 1826[15] gave the slave legal right to his property, although it was still possible for the master through the Supreme Court to seize whatever he had that was valued at more than £20. There were several things he should not possess, according to the law, but the only ones about which the Jamaican planters were consistently adamant was the owning of a horse and a gun.

As a slave then, the freedman had known money and had known how to conduct business, so much so that Diana Wilson and Jestina Sewell could in 1836-1837 have bought the unexpired term of their bondage for £35 each from the Woodside estate.[16] Obviously the freedman came out of slavery with enough money to buy land which was going at about £3 an acre in the 1840s.[17] One could even buy a cow: Mrs Beatrice Williams' grandmother, a St James freedwoman[18] was the first woman to own a cow in that parish. You could obviously add dairy farming to your other skills as a farmer to answer the charge of the Abolition Act that you be industrious. The planters' needs facilitated this 'industry', forcing some to make lands available to the freed people: some among them told themselves that selling lands to the potential workers would create a nucleus of labour available to them; there were others who simply needed the money. There were others who rented and leased for the same purposes as those who sold. The lands sold were usually the hilly backlands.

On these lands the freedmen planted ground provisions for home supplies and for the internal market. Free people living in the towns had been their customers. With the mass of their own people no longer supplied with essentials by the master there would now be a larger market and quite likely a wider range of goods – a market for fish and meat and clothes for instance. Speculating as well as higglering would now be in the freed person's menu. The speculating dealt with non-ground provisions, with goods that were likely to be imported and implied a relationship with merchants in the towns. The freedmen planted what they had planted for their masters; they planted coffee; they planted sugar cane and processed it. This peasant agriculture-cum-marketing system in time fed into the American fruit market with its interest in coffee and later in bananas and oranges. By the mid 1840s, less than ten years after full freedom, the establishment had to note that its grant of freedom had produced a distinct class of people. They found a new name for us. The literature now referred to us as the `small settler'. The development of a black peasantry did not please local white planter interest; nor did it please the British government, which had initiated its freedom. An economic interest of your own did not allow you to be at the beck and call of another, and this was precisely what was felt to be needed, if the "promotion of the industry" of the ex-slave was to maintain the plantation system – as the British architects of freedom had intended. The freedman, on the other hand, was steadily moving outside of the confines of the system in which a class of people gave their labour to another in a total way, accompanied in this move by the anger of the planter class. It was the planters now who by the late 1840s were in danger of being isolated. The storm clouds had been there from the apprenticeship period.

Those people who had championed the abolition of slavery in 1834 had made all children six-years of age and under free immediately. They had expected that these children, with their parents still in partial slavery, would have been around to continue in the 'pickney' gang doing a little light weeding, tending to the mules and helping to manure the fields, chores which took little energy but were important and which had traditionally been done by children. The parents of these freed children had a different view of their freedom. One estate in St Thomas, which had had 50 children of work age in 1834, had only 16 left by 1836.[19] It is thought that the enslaved sent their freed children off to relatives in the towns. Some estates tried to get around this by offering the education parents saw as the route to social mobility for their children. On the Blue Mountain and Greenwall estates in the St Andrew hills parents did allow children under six to be formed into gangs in return for an hour and half of education per day. Lucky Valley estate in North St Catherine was another one such: 14 of the 21 children resident went to school under such arrangements. These children at

Lucky Valley, in return for their schooling, reared provisions at the back of the school. In some places to have one's children out of the clutches of the estate was better than education. A school in Kellits kept by the bookkeeper could only attract two of the 90 children. In 1835 apprentices in parts of St David and St Mary refused to allow their children to work in the fields even when free education and allowances were offered.

Women's labour was another issue. Women had borne the brunt of the labouring tasks on estates. It was they, according to Holt, who were the most vociferous in their protection of their free time during the apprenticeship period. Children had, on estates during slavery, been taken care of by old women while their mothers went back to work. The apprentice and the freewoman now wanted to take on to herself the care of her children. It appears, from the evidence of African-Jamaicans born in the early 20th century,[20] that the freed and freewomen were now, with full freedom, moving into a specialised part of the internal marketing system – the planting of women's crops, legumes and vegetables, into such agro-industries as the preparation of coconut oil, sugar head and other sweet meats and were concentrating on taking the produce, which men grew and which they turned into edibles, to the markets. It appears that they were in the process of building an alternative form of making a living. With women and children unexpectedly out of the labour market the planters were faced with a new creation – the blackman in his castle with his own small social system of wife and children, over whom he presided; a woman with a source of livelihood that had no association with them except possibly as landlord. Their ex-slaves' castles even had names just as theirs had. Here in my Woodside, St Mary, by the 1870s there was Happy Content, Poorman's Corner, Primrose Cottage.

In many cases the freedman still needed the wages offered by the estate and he was willing to work on it but only when such work did not interfere with his system and only to the extent that he could incorporate it into his system. That he should have a system at all, amazed plantation interests. Not only was it not part of the projected design: the ex-master could not understand the choices his ex-slaves made. How could they be willing to spend their energy on back-breaking backlands

instead of accepting regular work on the estate with its regular
pay? This was what a free market was about. Normal people
wanted material things immediately and took wage-earning
jobs to get them. This was the going theory of human
behaviour. Further amazement for the planter lay in the
existence of cases in which the freedman struck for higher
wages and walked off the estates after their demands were met.
More amazing were the existence of cases in which he wittingly
accepted work on estates paying lower wages than those
offered on other estates. Planters, like slave owners all over the
world and all through time, as we saw in our first lecture, knew
slaves to be without honour. It was difficult for them to
appreciate that such people could be moved by feelings of self-
worth and could choose to distance themselves from a
relationship which had hurt by degrading them, was likely to
do so again, and from a situation, to handle which at close
range they had as yet devised no strategies.

In the last lecture we saw the lament of Peel, the Prime
Minister of Great Britain when the fact of the freedman's
tendency towards autonomy was brought to his attention. It
bears restating:

> If ever the black population of the West Indies should become
> squatters on waste land or mere cultivators of provision grounds
> instead of labourers for hire, then slavery and the slave trade
> would have received the last and greatest encouragement which it
> was in the power of man to bestow.[21]

This sounds very much as if social mayhem was all this mind,
so important to the welfare of the British Empire, could see as
the necessary consequence of the determination of the ex-slaves
towards autonomy. If social mayhem is seen as a change in the
way black people made themselves available to estate labour,
then he was right. And the statistics did show that the estates
were less productive after Emancipation. When we look closer
to home we see how disturbing this move of former estate
workers towards autonomy was for the local planters and how
threatening it must consequently have been. Thomas Price of
Worthy Park, whom Holt calls one of the "more liberal
planters",[22] had, like so many of his peers, blamed the failure of
plantations on the lack of labour. He was asked by a

parliamentary committee in 1847 to clarify what he meant by a shortage of labour. An enquirer asked: "What you want is this, that at any moment when it suits your convenience you may be able to put your hand upon the labourer". He replied: "Undoubtedly. You could not have expressed my meaning better". Clearly the freedman's creation of a peasant society and the planter's maintenance of a plantation society were on a collision course. Animosity between the two classes, between the two colours was inevitable.

Estates continued to fail and close, and by this act, take themselves out of the network of the freedmen. Freed people who would have lived close by and given their occasional service to the estates now sought land, often by squatting, further away from the estates. The society is now distinguishing itself into two cultures, soon to be antagonistic towards each other. The African-Jamaican is no longer under the eye of his ex-master as he was before. The latter, brought up with African slaves as part of his landscape, cannot get them out of his head, and must now imagine instead, what they are doing. Imagination is like the ganja weed; it magnifies what you think and feel. Thinking within the ex-master's mind must have gone like this: blacks, I know, do not work unless I prod them, therefore if they are not working on my estate, they must be lazing about. The myth of the lazy negro was born. Again. This is a savage taken from cannibalistic Africa and made by my association half civilised. If he is not around me, he cannot imitate me and must be regressing into Africanisms and such barbarities. Ergo, blacks have regressed culturally since Emancipation. How can I relate to this lazy savage? Lack of a determination of the emerging classes to relate to each other in good faith and respect, was now a part of the psychological environment in which the freedman began to create his new life. The white perception of what was being created with freedom, was shared to a considerable extent by the coloureds among the elite, who considered themselves to be a class apart from both whites and blacks. They made their separation very clear in the discussions following the 1865 Morant Bay riot/rebellion.

Official action in the British political system was led by consensus between the Crown, the Lords and the Commons.

The process of arriving at this consensus frequently involved vociferous recalcitrance. So it was in the legislative system in Jamaica. But where there were three orders in Britain, the Jamaican system faced more than that. It faced its own configuration as well as that of Britain. There was constant bickering between sides of the House and between the House of Assembly and the Privy Council and governor. Then there were the differences between the governor and the Colonial Office, and between the Colonial Office and the range of British institutions, which made up Parliament. The freedmen became another constituency; none of the old order saw him as part of themselves. The position of Mr Osborn, a coloured man, in the debate on the bill to surrrender the constitution after the Morant Bay incident, is very revealing. It is reported below as published by the journalist covering the debate. Osborn's position was

> that he would take every constitutional means to oppose the progress of the bill. He felt persuaded that he would not succeed; but representing as he did the three races[23]

The reporter's comment was that by "three races" he was referring to whites, blacks and coloureds and that, as a coloured man, he represented all three. Represented, but still not part of the black population. Samuel Constantine Burke, another coloured man, had this to say:

> Why should the class to which I belong be deprived of their right of free expression of opinion? What have they done that they should be disenfranchised? Is it because of the wicked insurrection by the negroes of St Thomas in the East that a class of men who have ever been most loyal and conservative – who have by their honest industry acquired property equal in proportion to their white fellow subjects[24]

Coloured he was, and clearly not of the class of "negroes". The freedmen, most of whom were black-skinned, like the cheese, stood alone. They saw good Queen Victoria, the head of all of this kingdom, as their supporter and petitions to her, their political instrument.

Petition was one thing; their deliberations and actions in the streets and on the estates left no one in doubt about the freedmen's concerns. The people in the west of Jamaica were very active in defining and broadcasting the position. Here in the west, sugar estates dominated the economic culture. There was little land available for the free African-Jamaican to move out of interaction with his former masters and build himself into an independent peasant. There was no choice here but to face the establishment and bargain for a new place consistent with freedom. In several instances their ministers fronted for them. We find however Hanoverians rejecting the one shilling and eight pence per day that the Presbyterian and the Wesleyan ministers had argued for them and joining the Baptists in their strike for two shillings and six pence per day.[25] Their strike lasted for three weeks. They were eventually convinced to accept the one shilling and eight pence but added their proviso that they work on a task basis and that they take no task which required them to work past midday. A set of issues between planters and workers was that of accommodation and the estates' demand that women be in the work force. At Point estate in Hanover, one of the largest in the parish then, workers withheld their labour during the crop season until these two issues were resolved. Finally, John Davis Armstrong, James Clayton and David Dehaney, the workers' leaders, called off the strike when the estate's attorney agreed to their proposal that their cottages and provision grounds be rented to them for a fixed period and that women be excluded from labour contracts, and that the women work on the estates if and when they chose.

The behaviour of the workers in the west of the island, described above, indicates that there was here among the freedmen a personality which had faith in its right to a just return for its labour, and a faith in its capacity to argue its case and demand its rights. This was not just a western-Jamaica personality. Look at the behaviour of the people of Bushy Park estate, of the parish of St Dorothy's, now called St Catherine,[26] immediately after Emancipation. The governor himself had to beg them to accept one shilling per day for their labour and beg them to pay two shillings out of this per week for use of their houses and provision grounds. The response to the governor was thank you very much with respect, sir, but not for less than one shilling and six pence. This was the rate at which this same

labour had been priced, when in the dying days of slavery
African-Jamaicans had sought to manumit themselves. The ex-
slaves' assertiveness and their ability to locate themselves
conceptually within the economic system is as clear as a bell in
the words of William Allen, a labourer on the Virgin Valley
estate in St James, as he addressed an audience of labourers at
the Salter's Hill Baptist church in the face of the planters' 1841
attempt to counter falling sugar prices by a reduction in
labourers' wages.

> De Busha dem all hab tive to six horse; dem lib well, nyam belly
> full; lib na good house; we lib na hut ... We pay half a dollar rent,
> den dem wa gib we shilling a day. Tell me now how much lef fa
> you when week out? No half a dollar lef fi you? Den wha fe buy
> fish? Den wha fe gib paason? ... De Busha get ten shilling a day;
> dem want to rob we ... Oono will take one shilling a day? ... Well
> den, tick out fe good pay and see if dem no blige and bound fee
> gee wha we ax a day.[27]

Along with seeing himself as a person with a precious
commodity, for which he should demand a just return in the
market, one who was willing to combine with his peers towards
this end, the freedman also saw himself as the guardian of the
precious commodity of freedom and was willing to combine to
preserve this. Many were the confrontations with the police
who dared to intervene in their celebrations of their freedom.
And on more than one occasion there was active resistance to a
perceived threat to return them into slavery through a state-
association with the USA and with Cuba, areas in which slavery
was still being practiced.[28] Calls to action in the many civil
disturbances in which they were involved, more often than not
were framed in an us versus the white and brown people.
Freedman like Willam Allen with no chance of being a peasant
had developed a perception of himself as being of the class
called worker, and of the race of blacks, and he saw himself as
not just a black-skinned worker but quite justly as a person
under siege. He responded accordingly.

The freedman's consequent assertiveness and resistance to
white power, spilled from the area of industrial relations even
into the Baptist church, that institution which had been closest
to the enslaved African-Jamaican. A conflict, which developed

in the Spanish Town church between 1842 and 1850, saw a part of the congregation seizing the chapel, with the justification that it belonged to them, who had contributed towards its building and maintenance, and that the church be run consonant with its democratic posture[29] and they accordingly be allowed to chose their pastors. Their animus was against the white incumbent minister, Phillippo, who had allegedly portrayed them negatively in his recently published book, *Jamaica, its past and present state* (1843). Some black deacons broke off to establish the Independent Baptist church in Spanish Town. They went with Phillippo's opponent, a white minister. The time still remained to be when they could find a cadre of black ministers from which to make a choice. Such expressions of resistance found their way into the attention of the relevant formal structures. The Baptist church in Jamaica knew of the controversy and took sides in the argument; the church in Britain knew of it and apparently took no action.

As it was for the sacred, so it was for the secular. The freedman saw to it that his opposition was heard and noticed by the political establishment. The action of the freedman in the tollgate riots in Westmoreland in 1859 and the response of the establishment is a case in point. To expand its coffers, the government of Jamaica, noticing the increased commercial activity among the newly emancipated people, fell upon the idea of having tollgates established along popular highways and requiring people to pay as they passed along these highways. There were riots instead of tolls. So forceful was the freedman's action towards the plan and so loud his actionist and other arguments that the House of Assembly heard, took note and the tollgates were, within six years, a thing of the past.[30]

The freedman's resistance was not simply resistance against the establishment; it was resistance against what he saw as injustice meted out to him. Cooperation with the establishment where justice existed was not ruled out. Indeed there was in the mind of the freedman, a sense of possible reciprocity by which he could have been encouraged to modify his demands where he saw his interests as linked to the interests of others. Benjamin Robertson, an ex-slave and now a fisherman, knew in 1847 that the economic depression on the estate, fathered by the Sugar

Duties Act of 1846, was responsible for his having to seek markets further away from home for his catch.[31] And Richard Nelster, a labourer, is attributed with the remark that if no money were made on the estate no one could live, for if a carpenter sells a chair or a table, the man who buys it must get the money from the estate.[32] Clearly there was in the freedman an understanding that the fortunes of the worker and the master were intertwined. Here lay the potential for inter-class and inter-colour/race dialogue. It would have to develop through the building of a black block in the House of Assembly, presenting black ideas and a consequent black position. This was about to begin. Black ideas and responses were melding into a political position; formal political representation was about to join civil disobedience and petitions to the Queen. The immigration issue offers itself as a case.

As strong as the planters were in their belief that the freedman's life began and ended with working for them, so did the freedman feel that the planters should have jobs for him to do as and when he needed them and at a price that he liked. His refusal to work in the way the planters wished had led to plans for the immigration of workers. Several of the few, who entertained an involvement with the formal political process, presented a class position towards this bill. New black electors such as those St Mary voters, egged on by the Baptist minister, Revd Day, returned a representative to the House of Assembly on an anti-immigration platform.[33] They were incidentally supported by George William Gordon,[34] one of their few coloured supporters. A start for the black electors, if a small one, towards adding electoral politics to their armoury. A small step. In 1838 males, whose property was worth six pounds or who paid 30 pounds in rent or three pounds in direct taxes, could vote. There were at least 20,000 black freeholders who qualified, but only 2199 were registered in 1839.[35] The figures did not get much higher into the 1860s. The black political instrument of choice remained the petition to the Queen.

Convinced that unused land reverted to the Crown, to the Queen who was the Crown, and that the good Queen wanted them to be self-supporting peasants, the freedman, and the free people who would by then have been in their thirties, continued to distance themselves from the way in which the plantation owners wanted to "promote their industry". When there was no more land available for sale to them, they squatted on and sought to gain legal control of unused lands rather than accept the remuneration offered by their ex-masters. By the 1850s, therefore, there were many landless, workless freedmen ready to petition the Queen for help in accessing lands. The Baptists supported their position and helped them with their petitions. The response to a petition from the 'poor' people of St Ann was the famous Queen's letter dated June 1865, reflecting Peel's 1840s statement concerning the labour of the African-Jamaican and its relationship to the upkeep of a plantation society:

> the prosperity of the labouring classes as well as all other classes, depends in Jamaica and in other countries on their working for wages, not uncertainly or capriciously but steadily and continuously, at the times when their labour is wanted; and that if they would use this industry, and thereby render the plantations productive, they would enable the planters to pay them higher wages[36]

Ofcourse the letter was not written by the Queen but neither was the Emancipation Declaration. They refused to believe that she had written such an unkind missive and continued to petition. Thus the Morant Bay rebellion and thus the love and the hope in the Queen continued into other generations.

A small group of new electors understood that power was possible through electoral politics, and intended to make access to political power through the legislature part of black life. Between 1837 and 1865, new black landowners made up 46 to 63 per cent of the voters in the parishes, then called St Thomas in the East, St Thomas in the Vale, St John and Vere.[37] They and those for whom they voted held a recognisable position as supporters of the governor, the representative of the Queen. Their position was quite distinct from that of the planters' Planter Party, which battled with the governor and the Colonial Office for economic concession, and different from the coloureds' Town Party, which was interested in more power to the local legislatures. It was a rare and noticeable occasion when blacks voted against the governor and with another group, as happened in 1853. Then elements of all three voted for limits to be put on the governor's spending. The majority of freedmen however kept themselves as individuals, outside of the electoral process. As a group black active acceptance of the formal political process was limited.

The partialness of their involvement in the plantation system and in the formal political process, is reflected in the freedmen and freemen's use of the publicly accepted cultural institutions. They used them at times when they made sense to their system of needs. Brathwaite in *Wars of Respect*, intimates that Sam Sharp had not really been an English Baptist, but had used their organisation, with its class system and units spread over a wide area, for his own politico-religious ends; that he was in fact a Native Baptist, a black (with the help of USA blacks) creation.[38] Bogle was an outright Native Baptist helping those who went before him in this faith, to bend Christianity into a more relevant and African-Jamaican mode. It is a good guess that their peculiar history pushed African-Jamaicans, at this time, towards developing their own institutions rather than towards contemplating participation in the formal political system.

The opportunity to build themselves a culture had been there before now: there were sizeable numbers of blacks living together and left, in dealings with each other, to their own devices. Even on a coffee estate such as Woodside, the number of slaves averaged 153 between 1811 and 1832.[39] The population would be larger on a sugar estate for they were larger than coffee estates. Among such a large group of all-black people there would naturally be inter-black activities and sentiments, which had nothing to do with whites. Blacks would have loved and hated and taken revenge as all other people do. I have not seen the data that indicates that, like Solomon or Moses, the masters were so involved in the private sorrow and joys of his people that he held court to settle personal problems and differences among and between them. In his inability to see the enslaved as total human beings and in his fear of gatherings of his bonded people, whom he saw as inhuman, the master failed to operate as, and to be seen as, a caring arbiter of justice. Differences had to be settled privately and within systems devised by the enslaved.

Most West African societies had a notion of man as a duality, having a tangible self and another, sometimes called the shadow. It is this intangible self that is the most powerful. The intangible self is ofcourse unseen. The unseen is the most powerful and capable of inflicting greater punishment. The idea of the unseen hand on its avenging path fits well into a situation where discord has to be settled privately and unobtrusively, yet effectively. The notion that there was something called *Obeye*, an unseen power within persons singled out by the Almighty to be given special spiritual gifts, had travelled with the Africans to Jamaica. The gifted could conceivably send his power secretly and obtrusively to avenge effectively. The obeahman or woman became part of the justice system. With distrust of, unfamiliarity with, and geographic distance from the courts, this way of getting justice was popular among African-Jamaicans, now more on their own with emancipation. Not being publicly admitted, this system could not be streamlined and controlled.

Obeah is about avenging. In the hands of tricksters it could wreak havoc. There were laws in the domain, controlled by the planters, against obeah, but given obeah's necessarily secretive character, these laws were ineffectual. A spiritually-based antidote had to be applied to it. Myal was that antidote. In contrast to obeah, myal was a group-based force and therefore more public. It was myal that the white society saw. Its anti-obeah activity, which involved marches to cotton trees to pull out obeah, and its drumming and the spirit possession, must have seemed like savage madness to those who didn't understand the need to clean a sub-section of the society in which the practice of obeye had got into the hands of the immoral.

Myal began to be observed in 1842 when groups of these cleaners, delivering themselves in Christian terminology, said they were sent by God to release souls bound by obeah men and buried under cotton trees.[40] How could people who had burnt their witches, who still held to the notion of a distinction between cleric and laity and the notion that God reached the laity through the clergy, take this? A people who had never heard of the Chinese cure based upon the energy field, whose Freud was not yet born? A black system of understanding and consequent behaviour confronted the white establishment. They saw the behaviour of the freedman and freemen as a sign that the black population had regressed into behaviour they did not understand, and behaviour that they did not understand, was wrong behaviour.

With their withdrawal from the estates, with hard times and no access to a socio-economic theory which better explained their situation, both obeah and myal thrived among the freedmen as central parts of their understanding of their reality. Creolised African rituals, such as these, had existed on estates during slavery but to a lesser extent. They had been witnessed by whites, some of whom mentioned them in their writings. They had obviously been seen as opera. With the end of slavery these same rites, no longer performed by 'our' people, whose behaviour could amuse us because we could control it, became frightening signs of degradation. Says special magistrate Fyfe in 1854 of ancestor rites, which are likely to have been practiced in slavery

> whilst they will lavish pounds on a funeral, they grudge a shilling for the medicine that might avert it. Disease entails trouble, death is followed by merriment and feasting.[41]

Fyfe served in St Mary, St George, Metcalfe and possibly St David. Others of his class agreed with him. The magistrate for Trelawny added that "Their march back to barbarism has been rapid and successful".[42] Some saw the hope for change in the education of the African-Jamaican from early in his infancy.

Obeah might have been a relatively pure African import. Myal was fashioned out of the mix of good African witchcraft and Christianity. The freedman had again taken what he needed from the master's culture and recreated it to suit his purposes. He did the same thing with education. Augier and Gordon say of the Negro Education grant of 1835:

> It was not an ambitious scheme so much as a way of teaching the people Christian religion so that they should wish to accept the position in life in which they found themselves.[43]

The purpose of the gift of education was again made clear in the 1850s when a democracy, in which Jamaican blacks were the majority, loomed its ugly head. In 1847 the Colonial Office had urged the Jamaican Assembly to adopt a literacy qualification for voting. A strategy of deceit is in mind. Says the Colonial

Office:

> The political object ought to be kept entirely out of sight & the
> promot'n of educat'n by making it a means of obtaining the
> franchise, alone insisted upon.44

The real and political motive for this offer of education was to
purge blacks from the register of voters. It was to be disguised
as an effort to encourage education. In the usual tussle between
the Jamaica Assembly and the Colonial Office, the Assembly
refused this suggestion and another such in 1851 failed to pass.

The notion of using education to control black Jamaicans was
not new. The schools that had existed, and which were run by
the churches were established for the civilisation of the
freedman's children and through these ultimately the whole
black community. Parents saw the book and the access to what
was in it, as agencies of the liberation of their children from a
dependency on estate labour, into another kind of industry.
They patronised the school established by the churches without
necessarily accepting the faith of the churches. Here, very early,
was the game of deceit played by both sides on the issue of
education. The deceit accompanying the gift of education,
whether from the government or the church, and guessed at no
doubt by the freedman, taught him that the establishment's
offerings were quite often tricks to limit his freedom and that he
should respond by limiting his involvement with these
programmes to what he could get from them. One, who by the
very nature of slavery as we discussed in the first lecture, was
an outsider in the society in which he resided was encouraged
by post slavery conditions to develop a mindset, which plucked
what he could reach from his position on the outside from the
establishment, rather than participate fully in the production of
the goods to be distributed. He was outside grabbing from the
inside. This plucking and grabbing could be violent, as the
people of St Mary and its environs taught them in 1849.

It had been felt in some quarters that the need for money
would force the freedman back on to the estates. Taxes levied
on him were therefore high. William Knibb notes this in
speaking to a public meeting in England in 1845 of the "animus
of these men",45 the ex-master class, in reducing the duties on
the lumber used for making puncheons, hogshead and hoops

and raising it on white pine and pitch pine. The pre-emancipation duty on staves had been 12 shillings; by 1845, it was four shillings. The duty on hoops had been four shillings; it was now one shilling. The duty on white pine and pitch pine had been four shillings; it was now eight shillings for white pine and 12 shillings for pitch pine. All this now that the freedman had bought land and was ready to build using white pine and pitch pine. This and other taxes had the workers of Goshen estate and the Guy's Hill settlers nearby beat Richard Riggs, the tax collector. When police approached to arrest the perpetrators, they heard the sounds of horns blowing and found themselves facing about 500 men and women from neighbouring districts and even some maroons.[46] This 1849 act of these St Mary's freedmen went down in history as the "tax revolt". Paul Bogle's 1865 action in St Thomas made this look like child's play. A governor had refused to allow the freedmen their preferred form of political action – a petition to the Queen. A stubborn vestry, the parish's government, had refused them a hearing. Instead there were shots which killed some of them. In return, a custos, 18 volunteer soldiers, a police officer and six civilians including a minister of religion and a black-skinned vestryman were killed. The official reprisals were so tremendous that the governor was subsequently charged with wrongful action. Such was the state of "animus" between the freedman and the establishment.

Despite the "animus" between the classes and between their outlook and behaviour, progress invariably meant in the freedman's mind as it had in the coloureds, as we see in Burke's statement above, getting as close to Euro-Jamaican behaviour as was possible. The object of autonomy from the estates in any case, was not so much a conscious plan to establish an alternative ethic as to find a respectable place within Queen Victoria's family. The successful in this effort became the new black middle class, beginning as small proprietors but steadily amassing more lands and more facility along with the Euro-Jamaican culture. Their women had as steadily managed to get out of estate labour. Their children, like the parents of Amy Bailey went to the teacher training colleges where they met white socialisers: they were the teachers, one of the few professions open to people of their colour.

A consequence for the African-Jamaican women of their move out of estate employment had been that they fell out of the range of landowning, except in cases where land was given as a gift. None of the 16 persons getting the one and two-acre plots of Palmetto Grove's land in 1846 was a woman.[47] Only three of the 49 allotments in 1843-44 of Windsor Castle land went to women. The pattern persisted:[48] only Jane McKenzie and Peggy Stewart were among the 39 persons who controlled land in the greater Woodside area of St Mary in 1869-1870.[49] The imbalance was not as stark in 1880-1882: 22 names were female and 70 of 100 were unmistakably male.[50] Women as well as men were given provision grounds during slavery and they presumably worked these plots. If the data for the greater Woodside area reflects that of the rest of Jamaica, the free woman seems to be moving away from control of the means of economic production and the freed people seem – at this point in their history – to be introducing patriarchy into their world, part of the trappings of the new middle class.

This apparent move towards patriarchy was quite in line with the then popular brand of Christianity and the' associated propriety. Legislations in 1833 had made the job of island curate in the Anglican church, the established church, attractive. The number of these clerics had also increased. Their influence was felt among the apprentices in an area such as Woodside, as well as among the freedmen. Before them had been the Baptists who had helped the freedman to buy lands in groups and to settle in villages. Church took up a great deal of the energy of some freedmen; it had also taken a great deal of his money. The several old churches throughout Jamaica are a testament to the commitment of the freedman to a Christian life style. It, in return, had given him his earliest skills at reading and had put into his hands and his head knowledge of the Bible. With this knowledge some had built integrated arguments supporting an anti-slavery position. A man cannot serve two masters, a Christian dictum, is reported to have been the saying among the Baptist deacons in the western part of the island who, in 1831, had made themselves the subject of talk along with abolitionists and other kindred spirits.[51]

The Christian ethic is likely to have depressed the status of the black woman. In these churches there were deacons, no deaconesses. During slavery high-status work-related jobs had indeed gone to men. They were the drivers and they boiled the sugar, but the housekeeper-cum-mistress had had its status too. The women could and did produce coloured children, who often enjoyed a higher status than their black brothers and brought some material and social improvements to the conditions of their seduced mothers. Church with its dicta against fornication and adultery took this away and emancipation subverted claims of rape and raised questions about complicity, since freedom to resist the master was at least theoretically possible. The upright freed and free woman lost an avenue to power. The notion of the socially and economically powerful male became part of the culture of the new black middle class. Some black women reverted to or continued to do estate work of the slavery days, dropping manure, dropping salt, weeding and hoeing. They kept their autonomy, but it was now without the legal protection of the estate's master and carried its own problems.

The world the freedman made, then included a creolised religion with aspects of Europe and Africa mixed together to produce something new. It was a world which prized the knowledge contained in the whiteman's books, which saw the home as the nuclear unit and saw a man working at his own business as a central part of it. Women ideally worked around the home at special jobs and went to the markets at weekends. The political head of all of this, was the Queen of England. Access to her was through petition and/or through the ministers of the Christian church and the governor. The freedman operated in an environment whose hostility was not concretely spelt out. It did not ask him to wear special clothes or to get out of the way when others passed. It did not ask him to and did not bridle a tongue, which in man or woman was as willing and eager to let itself be heard as those tongues in the legislature, but the freeman and freedman knew that there were those who coveted his freedom and that techniques, such as increased taxes, were the weapons used to return him to a plantation type relationship in which he was the bonded worker. He was under siege. His struggle was to free himself from this. Paul Bogle went too far. The Morant Rebellion, an incident associated with pleas for land on which to base autonomy, played into the hands of white Jamaican power, which used Crown Colony government to turn back the small black bid for electoral power and a place in the legislature and, according to Satchell, through land reforms moved Jamaica from plots back into plantations.[52] The children of these freed people, the first generation of freemen, could now neither hitch their autonomy upon land nor upon political power.

Those African-Jamaicans born after 1838 would be, at the time when Crown Colony government was declared in 1866, very close to 30 and mid-adulthood. Those freed in 1834 would be middle-aged. What could they create? Their fathers and mothers had handed them the mind set and way of proceeding described above. What were the boundaries set for them by the establishment and within which they had to work? Between 1869 and 1900 the government in a new land policy, recovered 33,000 acres of land from squatters.[53] The sons of the freedmen would now have to buy or lease or rent if they wanted access to these lands. By 1880 the government had recovered 123,000 acres from persons who had not been paying quit rent. Ninety-seven percent of these recovered lands were sold to 81 persons. With the government's streamlining of the country's real estate, the island's lands were legitimised in the hands of the few, who could manage a plantation-style economy, hardly the descendent of the freedman, who had made himself into a peasant by the purchase of small acreages of lands or by squatting and had had, from its produce, to support a family. The African-Jamaican, born in 1838 and in his thirties, the prime of his life, in 1866 had very little new land available for him to buy and little if any to get from his parents.

In a growing arrangement between peasants, local middlemen and American traders, a banana industry was developed. In 1868 Captain George Busch took his first load of bananas from Oracabessa through two merchants, Peter Moodies and Edward Sutherland, who encouraged freedmen and their children in St Mary and Portland to supply them with this fruit. Banana joined the list of agricultural products which the Jamaican blacks were sending to the USA. The profitability of banana cultivation and export leaked out. By 1882, John Pringle, recruited into Jamaica by the government as a physician, had taken over 1793 acres of the Hopewell estate, formerly owned by the Grants and formerly in sugar.[54] He turned this into bananas and expanded within St Mary. Other owners, usually white, followed him. The large acreages bought from government and bought privately were going into a revived sugar industry and into banana-growing plantation style, a kind of industry which was very jealous of the peasants' production and naturally sought to keep lands out of their hands. Pringle for instance is said to have refused to lease any of his land to peasants for he did not want them to compete with him.[55] It was the same sort of thing in St Elizabeth, where large land owners were making headway with the logwood industry.

Without lands, the sons of the freedmen turned with less ambiguity to wage labour. Those who had had skills did a multiplicity of things, one of which was quite often farming. Within the black population born in 1838 and the years immediately after, which we could call the first generation of persons born free people, were peasants such as the grandparents of Mr J.N. Fearon of Kellits, Clarendon. Mr Fearon was born in 1894.[56] His grandparents must have lived in the tail end of slavery. By the end of this century, they had had a property under 20 acres on which they had planted coffee and sugar cane. These they milled for re-sale. At the same time, grandfather was the village carpenter and grandmother was the village seamstress – they were making their living from farming as well as other skills. Occupational multiplicity became established as a black Jamaican way to making a living. Other popular trades added to farming were tinsmithery, butchery, shoe-making, hat-making, wheelwrighting.[57]

The shift between occupations is mirrored in a geographical shift. For those who had neither land nor skills, wage earning lay in the estates and often the necessity to move from estate to estate. There were those who lived and worked on the estate as in the days of slavery; there were the very many who opted for or had to opt for seasonal work. Moving from estate to estate and from parish to parish became by 1900 another part of the style of making a living of the first generation of freemen. By 1882, another destination had been firmly established, another bellows-like shift. The shifting has always been. Higglering, the oldest of the professions, had involved finding the best market and spending the weekends there. Estate labour now involved finding the best wage earning estate job and spending some months there. The new shift, that to outside of the island, could keep the African-Jamaican away from home for years. Between 1882 and 1884, the adventurous children of the freedman were among the 32,958 persons leaving Jamaica for Central America and among the 14,962, returning.[58] They had been going and coming since 1850 when they worked on the Panama Railway.[59]

Backing and forthing, to and from Jamaica, was not new to the society. It was the style of the planters for years. At the death of her husband in 1800, Mrs Frances Neilson of Woodside, St Mary, had left his business in the hands of a relative and returned to England to come back to Woodside, ten years later, when her son and heir attained majority and his skill in surgery. With their move to Central America, the African-Jamaican of the first generation of freemen put in place for their kind a peculiar external movement. This they did as a response to the problem of making a living. The movement involved temporary residence in areas located outside of the country. A Jamaican diaspora, which dallied between outside and the 'rock', came into being. Their backing and forthing was distinctly different from that of Mrs Neilson: she dallied within the British Empire; they dallied without. In her dallying, she was manipulating the system in which she lived. Their movements took them outside of the system and outside of learning how to cope with it. There were ofcourse immediate positives to the freeman's action. With his movement there came into being new produce markets for peasants. Those of Hanover sold their yams to their countrymen working and living in Colon. Migrants did not intend to stay in the lands to which they went: they rarely travelled as a family group of parents and children and rarely kept all the children with the family. This meant another negative, the break-up of the family unit. Thus Mammy Edith of St Thomas, born at the turn of the century, did go with her parents to Limon but was sent back at age three and never saw them again.

Another related negative of this dallying from Jamaica to Colon, from Manchester to the sugar estates in St Elizabeth, was its effect upon the learning of interactive skills. It is in the small family group that people learn through frequent interaction with major players how to relate successfully with others, how to settle differences and how to combine for what they hope to achieve, how to handle social and emotional commitment. Such a setting could not exist for those in perpetual motion. The result was that one whom slavery had designated the outsider, whom immediate post slavery conditions had continued to make into an outsider, was by the end of the 19th century an outsider physically outside of the country and its political and social activities, and also outside of the small group in which he ought to be developing skills for dealing with his social and political environment. Home was a place to which he went on vacations; at home he was not a participant: he was a tourist.

The freedmen had developed a peasant society; had established at the public level a religious culture; had made civil disobedience and petitions to the Queen into a political tool. As slaves they had been outside of the system; as freedmen they were still outside but were forcing themselves into the system. Their children, the first generation laid the foundations for seeking employment outside of the island. What effect would this have on an effort to move from the outside of the home system into the system itself?

Dallying is still a part of our culture. We, the new generation, dally to England, to America, to Canada, to anywhere that will have us. What effect does this have on the process of building consensus within the polity we call Jamaica?

December 1996

MARCUS GARVEY & THE CONTINENT OF BLACK CONSCIOUSNESS 4

I know now that my mother was black conscious. I learnt from her that there were people black like me, in Africa, who had built a glorious civilisation. She didn't use those words but what else could it be, if, as she told us, they had made golden chairs and not just golden chairs but ones which the British government covetted and stole? She had learnt of Africa from her father who had seen service in the Ashanti or Boer war, she wasn't sure which. He died when she was nine, the eldest of six children plus one to come. How much could he have told her in nine years or less? Perhaps she embellished. She had books in the house which told us of heroes. Alongside Drake and Hawkins and the Norsemen sat Toussaint L'Ouverture. I therefore knew of Haiti from early and knew it as a place which had people as heroic as those anywhere in the world. I basked in Haiti's glory and in that of my gold-working forebears. My mother had made me feel that I was part of a black continent whose boundaries were extended beyond seas.

It was through the government of Jamaica and its prescribed reading book that I met the largest concentration of English-speaking blacks, the African-American. Knowledge of them came to me via the *Royal Reader*'s Uncle Tom and Topsy. They were not real people. Tom had my colour but he wore pants which stopped at his knee. That was unreal. And Topsy. Those white eyes, those plaits sticking off from her head and that perpetual grin was no black girl I had ever seen in the mirror or any other place. Tom and Topsy were from no place. I dismissed them. Perhaps denied them. Black America remained a blank but not so white America. I got a lock of Little Miss Eva's hair and I wept when she passed. Little Miss Eva died but Simon Legree remained. I was to meet him several more times, as before, through the medium of the printed word.

In the early 1950s I saw a big picture of Billy Eckstine leaning on the outside wall of the Bank of Nova Scotia on Harbour St in

Kingston. This African-American and I knew our place. We were on the outside of that institution. But this, my companion, frightened me. His hair was so straight and slick, he was the ventriloquist doll that I had seen at a fair. I couldn't walk back pass that picture. Then there was Nat King Cole, similarly slicked. Again not real. 100 per cent of the black Americans I knew were caricatures. The one my sister and I followed on East St, so amazed to see a black man in a sailor's uniform, chased us, giving me no opportunity to connect with the real McKoy. The connection with black America came through the music.

Later in the 1950s, I was to realise that all those songs which I loved so well were sung by black Americans, and when the Platters made the movie screen, me and all my friends were that female singer in their group. At university here in the West Indies, in the absence of a specialist option in West Indian history and the chance to know more about myself, I chose to try to find out about the lady in the Platters, if and how she was related to me. The reconstruction period in the South of the USA became my special paper for my honours history degree. Here I met Simon Legree again, this time lynching people who looked like me. I determined never to enter that country. But I did, because information I wanted was there and because I met some white Americans who did not seem to want to eat me. There I met Marcus Garvey.

Garvey was not totally new to me. My father in his effort to sell the PNP to a neighbour brought this man to dinner one night. Our neighbour's effort to match my father's glowing tribute to Norman Manley, the leader of that party, had him saying incessantly: "Marcus Garvey said he came ten years too late". That Marcus Garvey had mentioned Manley at all was what in my neighbour's eyes made Manley anything. My father let this reference fall flat upon the ground, which meant for me that what my neighbour had said had little value and Marcus Garvey likewise. At high school in Kingston I saw the first sculptured bust I have ever seen – it was a bust of Marcus Garvey. Didn't God say somewhere that making a graven image was a sin? I could not look at this truncated man. Somewhere in an exchange in the 1960s in which Bert Ollman, the campus leftist, called the Queen an unusual name – Mrs

Elizabeth Mountbatten – angering the journalist Morris Cargill, who had just finished claiming to be more Jamaican than most, having been here since 1655, I heard a word about Garvey. It was brown-skinned Leslie Alexander, shyly talking about his aunt who would not let him play with black boys and about his determination to bring home the body of Marcus Garvey. The Garvey of this timid intervention was a long dead corpse. My Jamaican glimpse of Garvey was of a truncated deadman.

In the black America of the late 1960s that I entered, Marcus Garvey was the life of the party. I heard how Garvey had mobilised "us" African-Americans, how Nkrumah of Ghana revered the man; how the colours of the Ghanaian flag were the colours of Marcus Garvey's organisation and how his economic programmes went further than the current black power mode: it was black power linked to green power. In Seattle where I was, there were books on Garvey sold on the pavement, even books written by Jamaicans. It was there that I met Adolph Edwards' study of the Garvey movement. Edwards was an age mate, a peer and a fellow Jamaican and I had never seen his work in any bookshop in Jamaica. It shook me that here in America, contrary to where I was coming from, was an image of Garvey, so potent that my American brothers and sisters, the heart of the black power movement, were saying that we should go back to his works for guidance. There were some, who were angry with the man. Look at the mismanagement in Africa and he wanted to take us there! None was questioning whether this man, whom I knew to be a Jamaican, had the right to devise programmes for Americans; no one was even calling him a Jamaican. He was just Marcus Garvey, a man belonging to black people.

The appropriation of Garvey by the African-Americans told me that whatever else I was, I was also part of a consciousness shared by the African-American, part of a family that included them. The relationship between African-Americans and I was now more than the fantasy of being a singing female Platter: I was by association with Garvey a celebrated part of the family. I did recall hearing one of my migrant Jamaican cousins saying that black Americans were unhappy with our attitude; that they thought we felt ourselves be higher on the totem pole than they and felt it their business to cut us down by reminding us that we were no more than King George's slaves. But family members do quarrel so that was nothing and remained so until I read Harold Cruse. His *The Crisis of the Negro Intellectual* makes no effort to hide his vexation with the West Indians of the 1920s when Garvey was in the USA, and even with today's West Indians.[1]

Cruse takes on W.A. Domingo a contemporary of Garvey who, like him, was a Jamaican resident in the USA and very involved with the politicisation of black people there. Listen to the anger of Cruse in the 1960s concerning a secret document which Domingo wrote and which was revealed in the 1920s. Domingo had claimed, according to Cruse, that the American negro could not be relied on to carry the socialist programme to its ultimate destination because

> every medium of negro thought functions in the interest of capital ... being of slave origins and depending on tips to a large degree ... tips take on a magnified importance in the eyes of the tip receiver.[2]

Domingo continues, according to Cruse:

> All [the] foregoing influences exerted upon Negroes have tended to make the race docile and full of respect for wealth and authority, while creating an immense gulf between white and black workers

Abandoning any attempt at reasoned refutation of these charges against the personality of the American negro, Cruse launches into Domingo and the West Indian with such verve that I felt, on reading him, that I was personally the butt of his anger:

> But what about his own West Indian country men? Were they not of slave origins? Did they not come to the United States and take jobs with tips and were not most of them glad for the tips? Were they not as docile in the West Indies and full of respect for British wealth and authority – especially the upper- and lower- middle class and even the "peasants".

He spends a whole other page in cursing me:

> once a West Indian gets to the United States he becomes critical of Negroes being exploited because they "don't understand

business". To get out from under the double yoke of British colonialism and alien traders, the West Indian emigrates. Socialist revolutionaries such as Domingo did not fight British colonialism in the islands. It was necessary first to go to America and learn such advanced thought from the Russian Jews. After learning it, it took on the nature of something philosophically transcendent. It was right because it was white; it was essentially pure because it was Western and thus advanced. For Domingo it was so pure, wholesome, and inviolate it had to be defended against American black subversion and desecration.

This 'tracing' made me blush. It didn't feel, as the African-Americans say today, "family". Moreover, said Cruse "an undercurrent of bias on the part of both groups exists to this day". This was a hard blow for one like me who feels that the future of black people lies in cooperation between the several groups of us within Africa and the diaspora.

Domingo's supercilious comment and Cruse's tracing made me wonder if there had ever been a family feeling between his people and mine.[3] It made me wonder: if West Indians in Garvey's day felt about African-Americans as Domingo did and, if Cruse's forebears felt about West Indians as he did, how did Garvey manage to launch from this point the largest movement of black people that the world has ever seen and how did his memory manage to survive with such centrality into the 1960s black power colloquies? What is the truth of the past? Was Cruse distorting? Was I and other outspoken black-conscious West Indians in the USA who thought that with African-Americans we had a history and a future of joint action, just deluded, interfering outsiders or had we the right to speak up as family members should do? I was thus forced to examine African-American/African-West Indian relations to see for myself, first, whether there was a continent of black consciousness in which several parts of the African diaspora were joined psychologically, the ancestor of our 1960s experience, and second, what was the social-psychological environment in which Garvey did his work while he was in the USA.

Cruse 'traces' another West Indian, Cyril Briggs, also a contemporary of Garvey who, like him and like Domingo, had designs on the political sentiments of black people in the USA of the 1920s. Briggs had been part of a black secret society called the African Blood Brotherhood. Of his programme, Cruse writes, bringing Garvey's reputation into the quarrel:

> Not a single innovation that Briggs et al formulated in the African Blood Brotherhood was actually new. Every "Back to Africa", "separate state", "emigration" programme that Briggs experimented with had been anticipated back in the nineteenth century beginning with Martin R. Delaney's work ... Every Pan-Africanist trend of the twentieth century, including Garvey's had its root in nineteenth century American Negro trends.

Cruse seeks to strip Garvey of the claim of originality. We did see however in our session on Black Liberation Thought and Action that 'back to Africa' movements, discussions about a separate state for blacks as a solution to the race problem in the USA, did take place and that there was not only talk of emigration but actual emigration. Wherein lay Garvey's originality? This was another question I had to ponder and answer. Where Cruse in the 1960s sought to question Garvey's originality of mind, Chandler Owen, an African-American contemporary of Garvey who like him had a programme which he wished to sell to blacks in the 1920s, sought to diminish Garvey's reputed popularity. He called Garvey's movement a "British West Indian Association" which "does not have the following even of ignorant American negroes".[4]

This is the fourth lecture in the series on Africa and the Diaspora and I have therefore the burden of examining the historical data. To look for a feeling of family within the several parts of the African diaspora. Did it really exist? To note the nature of the relationship between African-Americans and African-West Indians (British West Indians) while Garvey was in the USA. Was there a family feeling then? Did African-Americans separate themselves from the British Caribbean people, leaving them to follow Garvey by themselves. To note the educational background of Garvey's followers of whatever national background. Were they "ignorant"? We have also to see whether Garvey's programme was all derived and what if anything he brought to the sum of black history. Let us look first of all at some of the individuals associated with Garvey's movement to see whether there are any persons born in the

USA among them (African-Americans) and if we find any to see whether they can be called "ignorant".

The Universal Negro Improvement Association was the name of Garvey's organisation. We begin with names of persons found in the footnotes of Robert Hill's *Marcus Garvey and the UNIA Papers*.[5] In this collection of papers relating to Garvey and his UNIA, considered to be the most comprehensive, Hill is able from time to time to note the birth places of people mentioned in these papers. The names Pope Barrow Billups, Reverdy Cassius Ransom, Ida B. Wells, Henrietta Vinton Davis, Jeremiah M. Certain, James Walker Hood Eason, Clarence Benjamin Curley and Adam Clayton Powell, give the lie to Chandler Owen's assertion concerning the presence of American negroes in Garvey's movement. Further introduction to these people, establishes that not only were they born in America, they were not "ignorant".

Billups was born in Athens, Georgia, was a lawyer and was elected to the New York State legislature in 1924. He was elected second vice-president of the UNIA in 1918. Ransom was an outspoken sympathiser of Garvey and his organisation. Born in Flushing, Ohio and educated at Wilberforce University seminary, he was in charge of the Bethel branch of the African Methodist Episcolian Church in New York and between 1912 and 1924 edited the AME's Church Review. In this newspaper he wrote positively about Garvey's movement and ideas, and even addressed one of Garvey's mass meeting in 1918. Ida B. Wells was one of the first persons to welcome Garvey to political life in the USA. She was a journalist owning a newspaper and a foremost voice in the anti-lynching campaign. She was elected to represent the UNIA at the peace conference in Versailles at the end of the First World War. Henrietta Vinton Davis was born in Baltimore, Maryland and taught at home and in Louisiana. Davis was a dramatist with her own dramatic company in Chicago and as such she travelled widely even visiting Jamaica. She became associated with the UNIA in 1919, being in that year one of the original directors of the Black Star Line, the movement's shipping interest. She later assumed several other high-ranking positions and was sent by Garvey in 1924 to Liberia to make final agreement for lands in that country.

James Walker Hood Eason was a clergyman who was very
prominent in the Garvey movement. This, the UNIA's first
chaplain-general and later its elected "leader of American
Negroes", was born in North Carolina and prepared for the
ministry at Hood Theological College. Eason was a casualty of
the movement, shot by its supporter in New Orleans in 1923.
Clarence Curley was born in Memphis, Tennessee. He had a
law degree from Howard University, an MBA from New York
University, and was vice-president of an industrial school in
Virginia. He was also a business instructor at a school in New
York City, an inspector of Alabama Life Insurance Co and
controller of the North Carolina Life Insurance Co in Durham.
Curley was the general accountant and secretary of the Black
Star Line. Adam Clayton Powell Sr. was a another clergyman
who was a strong supporter of Garvey. He was of the Baptist
faith and was born in Franklin County, Virginia. These men and
women, born in the United States, were professionals with
graduate degrees and certainly educationally on a par with, if
not above, Chandler Owen. From other sources we know that
the well-established journalists John Edward Bruce, T. Thomas
Fortune and William Ferris were African-Americans who
supported Garvey as contributors and editors of his
newspapers.[6] Ferris had the kind of pedigree that ought to have
silenced Owen – he was a graduate of Harvard and Yale.

Jeannette Smith-Irvin's research published as *Marcus Garvey's
Footsoldiers – UNIA*[7] introduces us to some other African-
American Garveyites. Thomas W. Harvey was born in Georgia
and belonged to a uniformed rank in one of the organisation's
Philadelphia branches while Garvey was in the United States.
Ruth Smith was born in Alabama but joined the movement in
Detroit. Harvey and Smith joined the UNIA in the 1920s. In the
early 1970s when Smith-Irvin interviewed them, they were still
members of the UNIA. There is no data on their educational
background. Nor do we know the educational background of
Queen Mother Moore, born in 1898 and still a life member of
the UNIA in 1972. We do know that she was born in the USA,
in New Iberia, Louisiana.[8] The same goes for Madam de Mena,
one of the UNIA's international organisers, who was born in
New Orleans, Louisiana.[9]

From Tony Martin's *Race First* we are able to see the points in the USA where there were UNIA units.[10] There were branches of the UNIA in 38 states, the most populous being Louisiana with 74, Virginia with 48, North Carolina with 47, Pennsylvania with 45, West Virginia with 44, Mississippi with 44, Ohio with 39, Arkansas with 38, Florida with 32, New Jersey with 31, Oklahoma with 28, Georgia with 26, South Carolina with 24, Illinois with 23, Missouri with 21, California with 16 and New York with 16. Michigan, Alabama, Connecticut, Maryland, Tennessee, Texas, Kansas, Massachusetts, Arizona, Colorado, Delaware, Washington, the District of Columbia, Iowa, Rhode Island, Nebraska, Oregon, Utah and Wisconsin had between one and 14 branches. Emory Tolbert's figures are higher – 75 for Louisiana, 50 for Virginia, 48 for North Carolina, 45 each for West Virginia and Pennsylvania and 41 for Mississippi.[11]

The population breakdown for the USA in 1920 gives Louisiana 700,257 negroes.[12] It separates 'negroes' into black, mulatto and West Indian. Of this figure, only 1225 are listed as West Indians. Who were the people in the 74 branches of the UNIA in Louisiana? The members must have been more than the 1225 West Indians. The figure for negroes went up in 1930 to 713,874 while that for West Indians went down to to 680. If Charles Lionel James, one time UNIA commissioner for the states of Kansas, Arkansas and Ohio and first assistant president general of the organisation, is right, each branch/division had between 150 and 1000 people. Who was in the 74 branches of the UNIA in Louisiana? The same question can be asked of Virginia. Here there were in 1920 690,017 negroes of whom 399 were West Indians. Hardly enough to fill 48 branches. In 1930 the negro population in Virginia went down to 650,165, only 295 of whom were West Indians.

The same population proportions were true of other states. There were not enough West Indians to fill all the UNIA branches. Let us look at the areas of high West Indian density. The highest concentrations of West Indians were in New York where there were 28,288 in 1920, and 64,466 in 1930. The figure for other negroes was in 1920, 198,483 and in 1930, 412,814. We were more than a fifth of the New York population between 1920 and 1930 and could only manage 16 UNIA units, though these were exceptionally large. The second largest concentration of West Indians was in Florida where there were 19,171 of us in

1920 and 18,543 in 1930. However there was a much lower ratio of West Indians to other negroes than in New York, with 329,487 negroes in 1920 and 431,828 in 1930. The showing in terms of UNIA branches was more respectable. There were 32.

It is not possible to say whether the members of the UNIA branches were 'ignorant' as Owen claimed, or were "the lowest kind of negro"[13] as Du Bois, a contemporary with the distinction of having been trained at Harvard, claimed. But we certainly can say that it is highly improbable that the people in the many units of Garvey's UNIA were West Indians. They had to be overwhelmingly African-American. The claim that Garvey's was a British West Indian movement was specious. Please note that the census figures for West Indians, at least in the year 1930 includes Cubans.

Owen might be more accurate if his reference to Garveyism as a British West Indian phenomenon was meant to be applied to British West Indians living outside of the USA. There were UNIA branches in non-British West Indian territories as far afield as Australia and South West Africa. British West Indians are prone to migration and to seeing their migration as temporary stays from home. As workers sharing a definition of themselves as strangers, they are likely to bond into a distinct group with interests different from those of the general population. A philosophy igniting one, is likely to ignite many of them. British West Indians went in droves to Cuba, Panama and Costa Rica. It is quite possible that Garveyism flourished exclusively among these West Indian migrants in those countries outside of the USA.

Cuba heads the list of non-British West Indian territories hosting UNIA branches. It had 52. Then comes Panama. Fourth is Costa Rica. Cuba and Costa Rica are non-English-speaking areas. Garvey's newsletters were translated into several languages. The native population could have had access to the ideas of the UNIA and could have joined if they saw fit. Without more information, however, we cannot be sure that there were none but British West Indians in these branches. The existence of the 30 branches in Trinidad leaves us with no doubt of British West Indian suzerainty, nor does that of the 11 in Jamaica. Nevertheless, together these areas plus the others outside of the USA, have less branches than those in the USA.

According to Tony Martin, there were 725 UNIA branches in the USA and 271 outside.[14] The UNIA and Garveyism was clearly centred in the USA probably with a majority of USA citizens as its base and this base had satellites all over the world.

Nor were those known to be West Indians inside and outside of the USA all "ignorant" people. Eric D. Walrond (Guyana/ Jamaica), a well-known figure in the Harlem Renaissance, stayed close for some time as did his peers, the Jamaicans, Claude McKay and Domingo, and the Nevitian, Briggs, who had been associated with Garvey and his work initially. You couldn't call Arnold L. Crawford of Jamaica an ignoramus. He hailed from Manchester, migrated to Brooklyn, New York, and established himself in his own trucking and furniture business.[15] Hucheshwar G. Mudgal was an Indian who migrated to Trinidad and after that to the USA. He had a master's degree from Columbia University, was said to be a PhD candidate and was an editor of one of Garvey's newspapers.[16] Certainly no ignoramus. John Charles Zampty was also a respectable man, a Trinidadian, he had attended St Mary's College, the college of Panama and was a qualified mechanic.[17] And Julian, the Trinidad-born ace flyer, hardly an "ignorant" fellow, counted himself among the Garveyites.[18]

Perhaps all West Indians in the USA were in Garvey's movement and Owen's comment therefore justified. Quite the contrary. In fact, the African-American political elite's continual association of all British West Indians with Garvey and Garveyism was one of the issues which brought an African-American/British West Indian split in the socialist group in Harlem, the acknowledged capital of the black world in the 1920s. It is with great pride that Domingo for instance later distances himself from Garvey. Cruse quotes him as saying:

> Who are the bitterest and most persistent opponents of Garvey? Aren't they West Indians like Cyril V. Briggs, R.B. Moore, Frank Crosswaith, Thomas Potter and myself – who caused his arrest and. indictment? West Indians: Grey, Warner, Briggs and Orr![19]

It was his West Indian peers who established the West Indian Protective Society of America to effect Garvey's downfall. It

was they as much as any other group of people, who wanted to
see him jailed. Clearly Garvey and the Garvey movement was
not a closure of ranks – West Indian versus African-American.
There were West Indians as well as African-Americans who
detested his programme; there were British West Indians as
well as African-Americans in the USA who followed him. There
was in the Garvey movement in the USA, people born in the
British West Indies and people born in the USA. What is true
and clear is that narrow nationalism, while Garvey was in the
USA, gave way to a great extent to the larger sense of self as
blackman, "race-men" as was the popular epithet then.

We come now to the major charge against Garvey and his
memory –

> Every Pan-Africanist trend of the twentieth century including
> Garvey's had its root in nineteenth century American negro
> trends.[20]

Cruse does not define Pan-Africanism though he is sure that it
began with the African-American Martin Delaney, whose
lifetime spans the period 1812-1885. P. Olisanwuche Esedebe
(1982) offers a very comprehensive definition derived from his
study of the philosopy and ideas of those called Pan-Africanists
between 1776 and 1963. Pan-Africanism, according to him, is a

> political and cultural phenomenon which regards Africa, Africans
> and African descendants abroad as a unit. It seeks to regenerate
> and unify Africa and promote feelings of oneness among the
> people of the African world. It glorifies the African past and
> inculcates pride in African values.[21]

Esedebe's discussion elsewhere in his work quoted above and
called *Pan-Africanism – the idea and movement 1776-1963* makes
skin colour a crucial part of the definition. Integral to this
definition but implicit to it, is the notion that action has a larger
base than any one territory. Ideas and philosophies often give
birth to – and are expected to give birth to – action. Integral to
the actionist aspect of Pan-Africanism are two forms of
behaviour – cooperation and incorporation. The first refers to
joint action and the second to the act of making one's self at
home in a part of the African diaspora in which one was not

born. We will continue by looking at action in terms of these two forms of behaviour as well as at ideas and philosophy, in the effort to show that Pan-Africanism was neither a 19th century phenomenon nor began with African-Americans.

Prince Hall, a Barbadian born about 1748, left home and settled in Boston, USA.[22] Assuming that he was at home, he prepared himself for leadership of *his* people by becoming a property owner and a methodist preacher, making his church a space in which people discussed and formulated programmes for change in their position. Hall subsequently established the first lodge – secret society – for black people. His African Lodge No. 1 came into being in 1776. By 1880 this secret fraternity was in 15 states. The lodge bonded blacks together for social, political and economic action. Hall also established schools for free blacks in the Massachussetts area and through his agitation contributed to the demise of slavery in Massachusetts. Another West Indian, the Jamaican Peter Ogden, obviously assuming that he too was at home, organised another lodge, this time in New York City. This was the Odd Fellows Lodge for Negroes, it too functioned, like Hall's lodge, as a bonding devise.[23]

John Russwurm in 1827 graduated from an American college and established his own newspaper.[24] This was a first for a black person in the USA. Russwurm was born in Jamaica, he teamed up on his newspaper with Samuel E. Cornish, an African-American. Their first editorial makes no distinctions according to place of birth. The corporation cum cooperation is obvious:

> We wish to plead our cause. Too long have others spoken for us ... there are many in society who exercise towards us benevolent feeling; still (with sorrow we confess it) ... Our vices and our degradation are ever arrayed against us, but our virtues are passed unnoticed[25]

"Our cause", "our virtues", "our vices", "our degradation", and concerted action: publishing together a newspaper to speak for "us". This is family. Common feeling and common action. Russwurm and Cornish are determined to speak not for Jamaicans or for African-Americans but for an "us" which is not just themselves but a wider group of which they see themselves to be a part – "any person of color".[26] Russwurm's world eventually extended beyond Jamaica and the USA. In 1829 he went off to Liberia, began another newspaper there, served as superintendent of schools and finally as governor of the Maryland colony there.

Here comes Cruse's Delaney. Martin Delaney was an extraordinarily talented man who combined the practice of medicine with the literary arts and scientific exploration.[27] He was at one time in the USA army. Delaney did spend a great deal of his life in championing the cause of African-Americans, most of whom during his life time were still enslaved, but like Russwurm he also felt himself to be a part of a larger body of people. His continent was larger than the USA, thus he led in 1859 the first exploratory party from African-America to Nigeria for scientific study and towards the settlement of peoples of the diaspora there. With this party was Robert Campbell, a Jamaican who had made his home in the USA and worked as director of the Scientific Department of the Institute for Colored Youth in Philadelphia. Campbell, after this mission, recorded his intention to make praxis of sentiment and take his family back to live in Nigeria.

Delaney's action as we now see, was neither peculiarly African-American or peculiarly 19th century. His action celebrated a wider period and a wider geographic area. His Pan-Africanism, to which Cruse refers, was part of a behaviour that spanned time and place and expanded space, and like Russwurm and Cornish his personal behaviour was in accordance with the Pan-Africanist stance of cooperation and incorporation. And this action did not end with him. Several West Indians and African-Americans parallel to him and Russwurm and Campbell incorporated themselves into Africa and there cooperated with each other and with native Africans, two of the most distinguished being the Danish West Indian, Edward Wilmot Blyden, and the African-American, Alexander Crummel, both ministers of religion and both teaching at the same University in Liberia. It is noteworthy that Blyden, a prolific writer and speaker urging the peoples of the diaspora to see Africa in positive terms, found his way to Africa in the USA, where he had come to be trained, and that he was very often in the USA on speaking tours. Blyden's world was thus in a very real sense geographically and sentimentally, the extended space, Africa and the diaspora. Blyden's exegis on Philip, the Ethiopian Eunuch, his published arguments that Africa should be for the Africans at home and abroad and his depiction of Africa as the place "where the gods" loved to dwell, are foundation pillars of Pan-African thought.[28] He wrote and lived in the 19th century, was certainly not African-American, nor did he do his work solely in African-America.

The cooperation between Russwurm and Cornish, and perhaps also to a lesser extent between Delaney and Campbell, the shared identity and feelings to which we have drawn attention were by no means peculiar to them. Cooperation and incorporation were written into the historical experience of people of the African diaspora from the earliest times. Slavery had moved them from identification with a small social unit to identification with a continent. Those who had the powers to define them legally and publicly in the world to which they were brought, did not see Pappaw and Mandingo; they saw African. As we saw in the first lecture, it was possible for an enslaved person to be a high government official under other systems, but it was not so in the world to which Africans were brought. We who came from Africa to be enslaved in the New World all came in as chattel slaves, all negroes, nagos, nagers, niggers, all subjected in all parts of the New World to the same kind of treatment. Given this state of affairs, there would be among us a similarity of outlook, the foundation stones of sentiment, political and otherwise.

The opportunity for face to face meetings facilitated the knowledge that there was a shared identity, heightening the feeling of shared identity. Close ties between the master class of the USA and the West Indies before the USA Declaration of Independence in 1776 facilitated this learning: these people travelled with their slaves. Slaves from one part of the world could note and acknowledge their commonalities. Out of this grew concerted cross-country black action. George Liele a slave came to Jamaica from Georgia in the late 18th century with his master, bringing with him the Christian word according to the Baptist sects. And it was enslaved African-Barbadians, who with enslaved African-Americans, established the rice and cotton industry in the Carolinas. The resulting commonalities have yet, as far as I know, to be unearthed but in Jamaica – a land which the Guinness book of records hails for having so many churches, we cannot doubt the African-American connection.

Cross-country black cooperation, as we have seen in the case of Haiti, spanned language areas as well as governments. As we noted in the second lecture, the Jamaican-born Boukman and the Kittian-born Christophe were central to the military success of the Haitian revolution and Haitians and their behaviour became, as would be expected, a model of resistance within the African-American consciousness. Haiti also became seen and accepted as a possible home for African-Americans. It was in this direction rather than Africa that James Theodore Holly, African-American episcopalian priest, made his extension out of the USA in the 1850s. Confirmed in and sharing the Pan-African notion that unity of people of African descent was central to the advance of any individual or set, this cleric saw Haiti and Haitians as the rallying cry.

The joy of the black peoples of the British West Indies was the joy of the black people of the USA. To quote Nancy Prince, an African-American, who with her husband had served in the royal house in Russia, "after the Emancipation in the West Indies, [I] was bent upon going to Jamaica".[29] Kindred feeling had moved Nancy to seek to investigate for herself word that their emancipation had brought no good for black people. She arrived in 1840 and deciding to join the effort to make emancipation real in this part of the African diaspora, went back home to collect money to establish a girls' school in Jamaica. This was Nancy's way. Other African-Americans stayed at home in the USA and celebrated August 1st, Emancipation Day, with the people of the British West Indies. People from Baltimore traditionally went to Philadelphia to do this to the consternation of one Revd John Miflin Brown of the Bethel Church, who in 1859 gave pen to his feeling that given their state of poverty the people were spending too much money on this celebration.[30] Ofcourse African-Americans did come from both Baltimore and Philadelphia to settle and work in Jamaica.

Ann Plato, an African-American born of Connecticut, a teacher in the black Zion School there, was one of those who apparently felt a sense of empathy with West Indians. She was moved to pen a poem between 1840 and 1865 entitled 'To the First of August' and wrote in her last stanza.

> Then let us celebrate the day
> And lay the thought to heart
> And teach the rising race the way
> That they may not depart[31]

Political issues were rare in Ann's work: she was apparently very moved to racial empathy by this particular event happening in the British West Indian part of the diaspora.[32]

George Liele, still a slave when he came to Jamaica, had little choice, given his status, in his incorporation into this society. Nevertheless it is a tribute to Pan-African action that while here he felt himself to be so much at home, and was so accepted by Jamaicans, that he was able to lay the foundations of Christian instruction in this country.[33] There were several other African-American itinerant preachers, who felt like Liele and were treated like Liele. George Lewis was one. Brought from the USA to Jamaica by his American-born mistress he was hired out as a peddler. In this station he preached in Clarendon, Manchester and St Elizabeth. George Gibb was another. An ex-slave from America, he preached in Portland, St Mary, and northern St Catherine (St Thomas-in-the-Vale). Moses Baker unlike the others was a freeman from the USA who, according to Shirley Gordon, came to Jamaica of his own accord and incorporated himself to the point where he could assist Liele in bringing what they thought was salvation to their Jamaican brothers and sisters. Baker's presence in Jamaica in the late 18th century ante-dates Mrs Nancy Prince. The behaviour of these two is evidence that there were African-Americans, who with choice to do and to feel otherwise, saw British West Indian blacks as their responsibility and acted accordingly. The behaviour continued into the 20th century. Henrietta Vinton Davis, already mentioned, continued in Nancy Prince's tradition.[34] In 1912 she took over the management of Kingston's Covent Garden Theatre, established in Jamaica a branch of the African-American benevolent society, the Loyal Knights and Ladies of Malachite, and thinking to build a school for girls went off and found the funds to do so.

Emotions continued to flow in the 19th century after

Emancipation here, between British West Indian people and the African-Americans. Phillips, a Trinidadian black, went to England and Scotland to study, returned to Trinidad in 1849 and headed back for London in 1851.[35] There hearing about the Fugitive Slave Act of 1850, which threatened the freedom of the many who had fled from the slavery of the South to the North and made there a new life for themselves, he wrote a romance to instruct African-Americans on how to respond to this legislation. Phillips had never been to the USA nor Plato to the British Caribbean: the literary arts carried their sentiments. The word, now a part of the experience of Africans of the diaspora, was able to bond together a different kind of person than the face to face efforts of the itinerant preachers, who were less skilled in literacy. These literary arts had been brought to them in their respective parts of the African diaspora by Christianity, the non-conformist part of which, in particular, was in sympathy with the black cause. These religious organisations constituted an institution operating in ways similar to the triangular trade. The latter in its economic thrust and philosophy had brought people from the continent of Africa to the New World where it moulded them into a people sharing life-style, sentiments and eventually an identity. It made them into Africans. The former followed its geographic path but making these people, now with a common identity, into people sharing a literature-based religion. Using the written word, the Christian's Bible, the African of the diaspora evolved a peculiar theosophy, Ethiopianism, which was to be one of the pillars of all black nationalist movements thereafter. "Ethiopia shall soon stretch forth her hands unto God".[36] The Danish-African, Blyden, was only one of those word-based philosophers who wove this verse into a theory.

From as early as 1797, Prince Hall the Barbadian-born blackman had used this verse in commenting on the success of the Haitians whom he called "African brothers ... in the French West Indies".[37] The phrase continued through the years to link the diaspora consciously to Africa. The link was not merely philosophical nor the property of those who wrote philosophical statements. Nancy Prince on May 18th 1841, attended a Baptist missionary meeting at the Queen Street chapel in Kingston, Jamaica. The attendance was large and several ministers spoke of the importance of sending the gospel to Africa. The ministers were white and coloured and they applauded the congregation for giving £100 to this enterprise. At other meetings on June 22nd and 23rd, this time of only African-Jamaican ministers, the message was re-iterated, a resolution passed and the membership left determined to be "macaroon-hunters" for the African ministry.[38] African-Jamaicans' interest in the spiritual welfare of mainland Africans had been manifesting itself in this way since the 1820s when in their churches they had instituted a special collection called "throwing up for the Guinea country".[39] The Baptists were not the only denomination interested in their African brothers. In 1843, the Congregationalists sent African-Jamaican families to save souls in Africa.[40]

Nor did this happen in Jamaica alone. Throughout the British West Indies, Africans of the diaspora were making the trip back to Africa out of concern for the soul of their families. In 1865 a shipload of 346 Barbadians migrated to Liberia through the USA.[41] Before that a West Indian Church Association had been launched there to return persons of African origin to Africa. It was from this point and through this agency that the Kittitian John Duport[42] went to do missionary work in what is now Guinea in 1855. In time, the saving of souls converges with the need for social space, to make Africa a part of the conceptual framework of African-Americans as well as African-Britons. It was this conjunction of sentiment and practicality that in the 19th century created the ricochet called Liberia and Sierra Leone: the African diaspora was doubling back to Africa. Bishop Turner towards the end of the 19th century made this ricochet into a permanent circle by taking African-Americans as settlers to Africa and by establishing the African Methodist Episcopalian church in parts of Africa, in South Africa and in the Caribbean – Guyana, Jamaica and probably other areas. European designs on Africa, this time the intention being to create colonies, further heightened sentiments about Africa in diasporic communities. This was where my grandfather and other African-Jamaicans of his time dipped into the stream, passing on the feeling through my mother to me. In ways such as this, by the early 20th century, Africa became firmly established as a point in the continent of black sentiment and became bound in a new way to its diaspora. It had become an alternate home of choice, a heaven – the place where the gods love to be, an icon. Black literature has many references to it.

Not much is known of the sentiments of Africans towards Africans of the diaspora at this time. Did they feel that they were an active part of the family or did they feel that they were passive matter to be saved, whose economy was to be set right by people whose grandparents had been sent/taken out of their lands? Chief Sam's life gives us some clues.[43] A native of the Gold Coast, Christianity claimed him like his cousins in the USA and the British West Indies. Economic issues also attracted him. Out of cocoa buying and selling he was able to finance himself to travel to the USA where he intended to involve himself in Christian matters and in trading. Sam was taken care of by his church brethren and subsequently advertised himself as one who could help African-Americans to find agricultural lands for settlement in Africa. White racism and its attendant horrors after the end of the reconstruction period in the South in the last quarter of the 19th century, had stimulated in many African-Americans the urge towards westward migration. Oklahoma was one of the major states in which they settled, establishing there all-black townships.

Life could not have been very pleasant in Oklahoma for these migrants from the South for it was from this source that several of the would-be migrants, flocking to Bishop Turner's late 19th century programme, came.[44] The limited success of the Bishop's to-Africa programme did not quench these fires: the people of Oklahoma were among the first to respond to the call of Chief Sam, the mainland African. His call brought back the excitement of the days of Bishop Turner to their emigration clubs. Chief Sam's existence in history signifies African-Americans' willingness to cooperate with and depend on Africans, for there were none of them on Chief Sam's board of directors.[45] Instead Sam's Trading Company had Africans from the Gold Coast and from Liberia as its directors. These mainland Africans had the support of the West African intellectual and economic elite interested in racial and economic independence from European colonisers. One newspaper described Chief Sam's scheme as "the great scheme for building up the blackman's country by the blackman".[46] By 1914, Chief

Sam's ship the *Liberia* had sailed for Africa, and clearly Africans had arrived as an active part of the family, part of the continent of black consciousness.

The ships taking their baubles from Lancashire and Yorkshire to the West Coast of Africa in the age of slavery, and swopping these for bound natives, left more Africans in the USA in completion of their triangular circuit than in any other part of the English-speaking world. White power in the USA did not care to make shade distinctions so that even those half breeds that they made were called 'black' and left to identify with Africans and Africa. This made the black population even larger. By 1808 Americans above the Mason-Dixon line no longer wanted slavery in their states. A consequence of this position was that by the beginning of the 19th century the USA also had the largest concentration of free black people in the English-speaking New World. Even if these had wanted to distance themselves from their brothers in the slave states they couldn't for they themselves were not accepted in the body politic. What to do with the free negroes was a constant problem which, with the emancipation of the enslaved in the South became the massive 'negro question'. It was a question that the free blacks had long taken on. Some had argued for emigration and followed through; there had been those who felt that a separate state within the USA was the thing; there were those who thought social integration into the white groups and culture was the answer.

One of the commonalities in most of the arguments of these free blacks was the acceptance that black-skinned people were a distinct racial group with roots in Africa. Race became for African-Americans as for other Americans, not just a theoretical construct; it was a fact of social, political and eventually psychological life. Any black person thinking in racial categories could feel intellectually comfortable in the USA. There were black businesses, black schools, black churches, a black philosophy. By the time Garvey reached there in 1916, the USA and Harlem, New York, in particular, was undoubtedly the black capital of the world. In the black family, the USA was the big brother providing models for the others, Marcus Garvey included. He first went there to sit at the feet of his big brother Booker T. Washington, the educationalist who had the ear of the president of the USA. Garvey followed the trend in incorporation and cooperation that had been earlier established at the several points of the African diaspora and in Africa, operating as we have shown, not just in the USA but throughout the African diaspora.[47]

Garvey must have been aware of the programmes and theories of the black nationalists who preceded him. Love was his mentor and Love had been in touch with Blyden and with Crummel among others.[48] Garvey was also very aware that there were collectivities of black conscious people throughout the world. He had been among them in the Caribbean islands, in Latin and Central America and Europe and in England, he had been with and heard of black conscious people in Africa. All this before he arrived in the USA to see Booker T. Washington. He was aware that African-America was the most advanced politically of these collectivities and admitted it verbally and scribally. He wrote:

> In the last ten years I have given my time to the study of the condition of the Negro, here, there, and everywhere, and I have come to realise that he is still the object of degradation and pity the world over, in the sense that he has no status socially, nationally, or commercially (with a modicum of exception in the United States of America).[49]

And again:

> The honest prejudice of the South was sufficiently evident to give the Negro of America the real start – the start with a race consciousness, which I am convinced is responsible for the state of development already reached by that race.[50]

He had said to them:

> The acme of the American Negro enterprise is not yet reached. You want more stores, more banks and bigger enterprises. I hope that your powerful Negro press and the conscientious elements among your leaders will continue to inspire you to achieve.[51]

On the boat home from Britain in 1914 Garvey cogitates on the findings established by his research, the finding that there was a universal blackman; that everywhere he was without a government, without a flag, without an army and despised by others for this lack; everywhere he was aware of this lack and the attendant negative feeling that others had for him. Garvey saw that these blackmen described a family, needing to know and plan with each other, needing to move on to the status of nation. They described a continent of sentiment needing now to make itself into a government. Garvey vowed to make these men into a nation. This was a resolve that pre-dated his visit to the USA and remained unchanged with his visit there. Garvey acknowledged the relative advance of the African-Americans but insisted that they were still a part of the family needing to be melded with West Indians, Africans and the blackman, wherever he was to be found, into a nation.

A. Phillip Randolph, an African-American and a major trade union figure in Garvey's day had said:

> If Mr Garvey is seriously interested in establishing a Negro Nation, why doesn't he begin with Jamaica, West Indies (not Jamaica, Long Island)[52]

For Garvey, as for the long line of Pan-Africanists, who had served in other's birth places, blackmen and their ameliorative action belonged and was justifiable wherever there were black people. Jamaica, New York was Jamaica, West Indies. In this Garvey was part of a Pan-African trend begun well before the 19th century.

Wherein lies Garvey's originality? In 1914 Garvey stepped off the boat taking him from Britain to Jamaica and within days established the UNIA, the vehicle through which he intended to make blackmen everywhere into an integrated nation. Before a decade was out he had in incipient nation of about six million souls in this organisation. By this act Garvey establishes himself as original. But if we are to learn from history and learn from Garvey's life we have to look beyond the figures and ask whether this miracle was Garvey's doing or whether an odd conjuncture of events helped him along. We have to ask whether success belonged more to circumstances over which he had no control or to Garvey's mental and spiritual strength. Let us therefore look now at the interplay between Garvey, the man, and the social and political environment out of which he carved the UNIA.

Garvey had inherited a world in which the black people in the New World had been historically sidelined and had historically devised programmes and actions for dealing with this. These programmes had been dominated by the free black intelligentsia, some from the West Indies and Britain but the larger number living in the North of the USA. In the early 20th century when Garvey emerged, the balance of power between black and white had not changed nor had the determination of the black intelligentsia to devise philosophies and programmes to right this in the favour of their people. Garvey therefore inherited a ground, which was fertile in thought and deed. By the mid-20th century the nature of this ground had changed significantly however. White power was moving into African lands and creating, as it did in the New World, black-skinned people who felt the need to define themselves in terms of their colour. There were now Africans at home feeling as alienated from the bases of power in the lands in which they lived, as Africans abroad.

To the extent that these new people were, like their New World counterparts, the intelligentsia, this extension could strengthen whatever movement was already in place. Other coalitions were more potentially possible however. The end of slavery in the USA South had produced a collectivity of alienated people who were by no means among the intelligentsia. Their post slavery condition brought them a freedom which was harassed by poverty, lynchings and by a literary culture which humiliated them. They had no protection from a state, which allowed the passage of laws designed to further humiliate them. Under slavery they had had the protection of their masters. Not even that was now available to them. The diaspora from the West Indies, forced out into the USA and Latin and Central America by the lack of social space for a free black people, were little better off. These people, presented an organisational challenge to the black intellectuals. How were they to be incorporated into what movement? Here was the tussle between man and circumstance. Here was a test on which Garvey scored higher than his contemporaries. Herein lay his originality. His capacity for focussed thought and action, his definition of himself, as well as his field oriented-approach to the challenge, put him above his peers.

While still a teenager and one in a managerial position,[53] Garvey with his eyes on his programme of social change in the conditions of the people who looked like him, sides with the workers in a strike and is served the ultimate punishment. He is fired. With no great fortune and no great experience of life as a labourer, this youngman finds his way to the Latin and Central American farms with his plan to learn about the condition of his people. There he does both manual and intellectual work, learning therefore the conditions relating to both. He also sharpens his skills at using his intellectual and linguistic gifts in the service of his programme and his people. He publishes a newspaper, gives public lectures and represents his people before the ethnically different bosses. A similar motive takes him to Britain. He learns what there is to learn there about his people resident there, about the way the government of the largest empire operates, spends some time on the inside of her reputedly great academic institutions and catches what glimpses there are of the conditions of his people on the African continent. It is in England that Garvey meets the Afro-Egyptian Duse Mohammed from whom he learns about Africa and meets, through the medium of the print, contemporary African-American thinkers such as William Ferris.[54]

By the time he reached the United States in 1916 Garvey through participant observation in the very many institutions that he met in his travels, had the kind of information with which to construct a general theory of the way in which the world behaves towards the blackman. Nor was Garvey purely the objective scientist: he was very clear in his mind that he was part of the data. And he was not only an anthropologist. Garvey behaves like an applied anthropologist. He does not stop at a theory concerning the relationship between black people and the rest of the world. He formulates a theory of action and creates from the data the kind of vehicle, which would put this action in motion. His contemporaries operated in a different way: the socialists and communists studied the philosophy of someone else and sought ways to bend their data to suit these foreign theories. One was inductive, the other deductive. Garvey let the data inform his theory and action. The data in all cases was the black people. Garvey's way and his resulting programmes thus maintained a humanism and a transparency that the others could not match. This approach would attract the new people unaccustomed to graduate-style intellectual discourse.

Where the socialists and communists waited for orders from the Kremlin on matters so germane to black people as how they should relate to whites, and Du Bois and the integrationists waited in their search for civil rights for blacks for assistance from the liberal whites in the newly founded NAACP, and where even the creative artists, the Jamaican Claude McKay among them, waited for adulation from white patrons, Garvey waited for no foreign mind. Garvey and his programme were, in contrast, in constant touch with the field; he could gather data easily and he could fine-tune his programme as the data required whenever he thought it needed adjustment. Garvey's programme also operated, contrary to the others, on the assumption that no fundamental change in the personality of the black people was required. He did not, as we have already indicated, see Jamaicans as different from Alabamans; neither the Jamaicans nor the Alabamans needed to change their nationality. He did not see his people as illiterate or literate – there was no place here for Du Bois' notion of a talented tenth leading the people. Garvey did not see some as ugly and others not. The black man was a being of a particular phenotypical kind, with a culture and past of his own and needs of his own. There was nothing wrong with what he had been given by the maker; the negatives were tacked on by others. Garvey worked with this. Black was as beautiful as anything else and Africa, from where black people originally came, as glorious as anywhere else. Black people, with this philosophy before them, could be at long last comfortable with themselves. That Garvey himself was as unlike white as was possible helped; that this "fat little blackman, ugly, but with intelligent eyes and a big head" as Du Bois had called him,[55] could, despite his looks, interface easily with whites, as evidenced by his meeting with the Ku Klux Klan, was an additional attraction.

Your physical and economic self, whatever they were, were welcome in Garvey's movement. So was your social self. Spirituality and the church are very important to black people. Although there was in the movement a chaplain general, it was not required that people change their religion or their denomination. Thus newcomers could literally come as they were. The UNIA, therefore, attracted into its fold people who were already involved in an organisation but wanted more than that organisation could provide. One of the needed things that most organisations had not thought of was an economic programme in which black people all over the world could be shareholders. Within four years of his entry into the USA, Garvey had established there the UNIA's Negro Factories Corporation. It managed a number of UNIA businesses – laundries, restaurants, a doll factory, a tailoring and millinery establishment and a printing press. Black people could through these agencies service themselves and keep their money circulating within their group. These industries also employed people. Blacks were now managers, workers and owners within an integrated economic system.

It had been Garvey's intention to have black people realise that power to transform themselves was in their hands. The businesses in the corporation did this and since nothing succeeds like success, each economic success brought more people into the UNIA. *The Negro World* the UNIA's mouthpiece carried news of these successes all over the world and brought new converts. By 1923, when Garvey was convicted, the black people of the world owned several pieces of real estate on which they had their Liberty Halls, their meeting place; they had businesses and they had ships – the Black Star Line. We must not believe that the UNIA was the only agency taking care of black people's economic and material needs. There was in the USA, for one, Daddy Grace's outfit. Here though, there was a mysticism and a response to the leader based on his mystical powers, that inhibited the empowerment that Garvey knew the six million people wanted and needed.

Through the UNIA black people also got the government Garvey knew they felt they needed and which he as a blackman felt he needed. They had a potentate, a titular head who resided in Africa, a president general and four assistant presidents general. The second, third and fourth assistant presidents general were responsible for set geographic areas; the president general oversaw their work and was assisted in this by the first assistant president general. There was an auditor general who was responsible for the accounts concerning the nation's financial business; there was a secretary general who was in charge of the divisional secretaries and a high commissioner general who was in charge of the UNIA's relationship with foreign governments. There were field officers who worked in the several divisions throughout the nation. There were several non-commissioned posts, which any person could hold – they could become part of the motor corps, the black cross nurses, or the legion and the children could fit themselves into the juvenile division. There were schools, there were elocution contests, there were plays and there were concerts. Within the UNIA any talent could be nourished. It was an umbrella for all those who had been left out in the cold by virtue of being black.

The UNIA supported itself financially. It was very important to Garvey's programme that black people be empowered. To accept financial support from elsewhere would lead to dependency on outsiders and dilute the movement's power so in this organisation, whose only requirement for admission was that the potential member be of African descent, dues were collected and used to administer the organisation. With this, each member knew that it was his dues, which bought the real estate which belonged to the organisation; his purchase of shares that bought those ships which to everyone's amazement were manned by black men. White power had pushed him outside of its power structure but he was inside of one, which was no less admirable and which was as functional. Historical alienation had been turned into creative and respected action. It was there for all the world to see. And they did see. The UNIA was recognised in Cuba by the government there as the representative of the foreign workers. Here in my view lies Garvey's originality and his contribution to history, black and otherwise – that he inspired black people towards the creation and operation of the UNIA. Through it Garvey made the continent of black consciousness, whose outlines predated him, into a nation.

As I think I have shown, Pan-Africanism was not the creation of any one mind; it was not the preserve of Delaney or of any one person from the USA, the Caribbean or anywhere else. It was a fact of history played out by the behaviour of several persons. I have isolated cooperation and incorporation as two key elements in this behaviour. That so many persons at so many different times and in so many different areas felt spontaneously moved towards this behaviour is what gives Pan-Africanism its essence. This feeling, common to so many, described a continent of black consciousness which included Africa and the geographic area to which Africans were dispersed from the earliest days of New World slavery to Garvey's time. Cruse seems either to have been unaware of or to have underestimated the historical dimensions of this continent. Garvey's researches revealed to himself this continent of which he was also a part. He sought to construct a state out of this continent. One of the questions we need to ask ourselves in this post-Garvey age is, has this continent, like Atlantis, vanished. If it has not, then we need to further ask ourselves whether we are part of this continent of sentiment. If the answer is yes, then we need to continue by asking ourselves whether it ought to be elevated to the status of state.

January 1997

AFRO-CARIBBEAN VOICES IN THE INTERNATIONAL ARENA

5

The Word of God, Christian version, was first made state under the Romans. It spread with their empire into the rest of Europe there to become also affiliated with the state. This word of God, this Christianity, was a system of truths as well as a way of life and according to one part of its mythology, the Pope was the reincarnation of St Peter, upon which rock, Jesus Christ is said to have said, he would build his church. The ensuing philosophy and behaviour made the Holy Roman Empire one big church over which the Pope presided assisted by the several temporal masters, who did the actual administering of the territories. That the Holy Roman Empire disintegrated by the 15th century into relatively small nation states, made no difference to the position of the Papacy. Small units or conglomerates, European powers at this time saw themselves and were seen as children of the Pope, and though they fought against each other, plotted against each other, poisoned each other, they remained Christian princes bound together by their allegiance to the Pope and to the word of God as he understood it.

This race of people and their brethren with whom we here, extracted from Africa, were forced for the last four centuries to relate, were very often fired by their religion to create converts. They had been into Turkey and as far as China. The 1453 fall of Constantinople, now Istanbul, to Mohammedan influences turned back this advance and trapped Papal Christianity in Europe. Its hegemony was assaulted from within in 1517, when Martin Luther's annoyance with Tetzel's indulgence-selling campaign drove him to nail his 95 theses on a church door in Germany[1] and to begin his country's withdrawal from the Pope's control. Less than 20 years later Henry VIII's wish to divorce his wife, and make a legitimate heir to the English throne of the child his mistress was carrying, led to another assault. Thus did Britain begin the process of breaking herself away from the Pope's jurisdiction. But neither in Germany nor in England was the Christian philosophy demoted with these secessions: it remained the system of truths and the way of life for Europeans until our present century. True, there were distinctions: in Greece and in Russia, the orthodox church, and in Western Europe the several brands of Protestantism, stood out distinctly from the rump, the Roman Catholic church. Nevertheless they all adhered to the same understanding of temporal and metaphysical truths which is called Christianity.

The change that came with these secessions and stayed in the 16th century and after, lay at a theological level in that Protestants no longer depended on the Pope and his priests to intercede with God and his Son for them. They carried their own pleas. It was the Protestants' responsibility to live their lives in accordance with the system of truth arising out of their reading of their God's word as it is written in the Bible. Some historians link this setting of one's own goals and dependence on self for their fruition, with the development of capitalism. Whatever the real connection between these two, the fact is that they occurred together and together pulled North America and Africa into their sphere. Great Britain was one of the major territories in which Protestantism and capitalism appeared together. Conjoined, they spread British influence throughout the world happily making for her the empire upon which 'the sun never sets'.

It is into this world, in which the combine of Christianity cum capitalism was the dominating ideology, that Festus Claude McKay was born in 1890. His particular part of this world was Clarendon in Jamaica, West Indies. A dozen years later came C.L.R. James and Malcolm Nurse, later to be called George Padmore, the former in 1901 and the latter after one or two years. Their birth place was Trinidad. All three were black-skinned men with obvious genetic links to Africa and social links to the history of capture, transportation and enslavement. They were also heirs to the anti-black prejudice of the post-slavery days of their respective islands and of the Western civilisation of which these islands were a part. Heirs they were, too, of the tension within a colonial system whose difficult question was, how can we help these ex-slaves and their children to develop their potential while seeing to it that they continue to serve us. All three faced these sociological circumstances.

McKay describes his father as a "real black Scotchman".[2] This description points to a particular tension in British colonialism. We have seen in the second lecture the problem which J.R. Williams, the new superintendent of education in Jamaica, felt faced him in 1906: he was to design a programme which made "active", "efficient" and "available" the "labour of a population ... of mostly very poor people".[3] By the time Williams came to do his reorganising, Claude McKay had completed his free years at school and his father, ofcourse, would have completed whatever formal schooling he had. Pre 1906 or post 1906 the intention of the schooling given by the colonial authorities was the same. The Sterling Report by whose recommendation state support had been given to schools for ex-slaves, the African-Jamaican population, had said in 1835:

> For although the negroes are now under a system of limited control which secures to a certain extent their orderly and industrious conduct, in the short space of five years from the first of August next, their performance of the functions of a labouring class in a civilised community will depend entirely on the power over their minds[4]

A grant had consequently been given for education, for controlling the minds of the great African-Jamaican majority so that they would remain labourers. The Protestant churches were given these funds and so took on the responsibility of turning Claude McKay and his parents into part of the labouring class so needed to continue Britain's capitalist enterprise. The Colonial Office's gift of education did not make Claude McKay or his parents into labourers, however: it helped to make his father a peasant who functioned in his village, like an English squire, "a real black Scotchman".

The family handed down to Claude, and therefore must have kept, an emotional relationship with a history of their past, of Africa, of the auction block and of their enslavement in Christendom. Family tradition on Festus Claude's mother's side held that their first Jamaican ancestor had been from Madagascar; that on the auction block he had asked for death rather than separation of his family. Some planter – obviously kind-hearted – bought the family as a group and settled them into his Clarendon plantation. There is less romance on his father's side. Nevertheless the ancestral link with Africa was there in the tales the family told. Here then is a McKay family that was aware of its black roots. Knowledge of roots, yes; practice of rites, no. This was not a family that practiced Afro-Jamaican rites. The post-1865 depression in the economy of the black section of the country which, as we saw in the third lecture, had inspired the development of Afro-Jamaican religious forms, had not invited the McKays to look to myal or any other Afro-Christian religion, nor were they seduced into family forms unsanctioned by the church.

This family had followed closely the system of truths and practices introduced to them by the Protestants, supposedly to turn them into pliable labour, to become a self-contained monogamous nuclear family. Marriage, part of the complex of Protestant thought and practice, contracted with another small but landed Christian nuclear family, for the bride came with some of that family's land, extended Festus Claude's father's small holding, which he had made himself after slavery, into the kind of agro-business which made him eligible to vote. "One hundred fertile acres" was indeed quite a holding for one whom capitalism had asked Protestantism to prepare for the status of labourer, for one belonging to a group which after the Morant Bay riot and the surrender of the Jamaica constitution had tremendous difficulties in accessing land as we learnt in the third lecture.[5]

In their escape from labouring for others, the McKays, these black people with a history of slavery, were exceptional; so too in their ability to read and write. The Crossman Report of 1883 to the Royal Commissioners had said of Jamaica:

> In 1881 the expenditure was six times as great as in 1861, but the number of children attending school and the number of these able to read and write was only twice as great. This is the more serious when we remember that, after deducting the adult whites (8,000) and 80% of the adult coloured population (60,000) it would appear that out of 250,000 adult negroes only 22,000 are yet able to write.[6]

Claude McKay's father, born about 1840 and literate, was clearly one of those few "adult negroes" who in 1881 could read and write.7 The size of his holding, his ability to vote and his literacy gave him squire status in his village. To him came people needing to interpret officialdom with its red tape and written papers. Within the larger Jamaican society and within Christendom, the McKays were seen principally as black people and therefore intellectually inferior and were unlikely to get jobs in the civil service or even in the officer rank of the police force in Jamaica or anywhere else in the world. Festus Claude, the eleventh child of this family was, despite this assignation, able to distinguish himself internationally not in work which involved brawn but in the literary arts, garnering respect in this enterprise not only among those of his colour and class but, as well and more so, among whites who were considered to be civilised. It was his poem that Winston Churchill Prime Minister of Great Britain used, unaware of its author's identity, to exhort his people to battle in the Second World War in the 1940s.

> If we should die, let it not be like hogs
> Hunted and penned in an inglorious spot ...8

The poem had been written to his own black people facing white mob violence in the United States of 1919. Apparently McKay's mastery of the language, received through the combine of capitalism and Protestantism veiled his origins, but after all he was the son of an anomaly, a blackman steeped in the ways of Presbyterianism, a "black Scotchman".

The governor of Jamaica might have shared the Colonial Office's purpose in giving education to African-Jamaicans with his privy council but certainly not with the public at large. There was therefore no way that the African-Jamaican public would know how they were seen by the Protestant/capitalist combine, and no reason for them to be angry at Britain and her people for offering them education as a means of keeping/making them a compliant labouring class. So few were able to access this education anyhow that the black educated became a tiny literati, reading journals and the latest opinions, servicing the teaching profession and observing the values of Christendom. Under these circumstances education could not appear in the mass mind as associated with the creation of the "labouring class" of any kind. Education became for them a status definer: those who had it were proud to have it and those who hadn't were respectful of those who had it. The Colonial Office's intentions towards the African-Jamaican were thus doubly masked – by the secrecy of officialdom and by the real function which it served in the black community. What could have been received in anger, were the intentions of the giver known, was instead accepted with joy and gratitude.

If his father was a "black Scotchman", Festus Claude's oldest brother was the native version of the Oxbridge don. For most of the years of his elementary school Festus Claude lived with his oldest brother U'Theo, who was a Mico trained teacher and a member of the literati indeed. The books and magazines found in his house covered the spectrum from sentimental novels to treatise on evolution. Festus Claude read these avidly, adding these imagined experiences and arguments to those he personally experienced in his village community. U'Theo, headmaster, farmer and choir master, exposed his church to the sounds and names of musicians popular in England, bringing an external dimension to Festus Claude's appreciation of music. The only child in his brother's household, there was no social place to which to banish him when the white missionary paid his weekly social call for lunch in the school master's house. News of social and political ideas prevailing in foreign, of the arts in foreign came into conversations. Young McKay learnt the facts and an orientation to knowledge, he also learnt how to converse and how to converse with a white foreigner.

At no time in Jamaica's Protestant/capitalist history was the ultimate seat of government in the island so that, though white people controlled political power, they were hardly seen in their delivery of it. Harsh laws were made by the Colonial Office but the maker was not seen, could not be identified and the anger it engendered could not be directed at it in true measure. In any case there was on spot the governor, the Crown's representative, who could tailor a message in such a way as to reduce its sting. Deflected anger towards white people was part of the colonial heritage. As it was in the formal political structure, so it was in social life.

Resident powerful white individuals, even under slavery, had been cushioned from the animus of their black workers by overseers and bushas. With emancipation, the personal contact

between white capital and black labour was even less. At no
time in the country's history did whites out-number blacks and
though there were a few white settlements, these were few and
far between. There was thus no close permanent white
neighbours to show the seamy side of white life and to direct
animosity straight into their black faces. The Jamaican child at
the turn of the century saw white-skinned people as the
bringers of goodies, the gift of education among other things; as
people who deliver and do not stay around to make demands.
Black anger against their social system tended to find its outlet
in resentment towards the resident coloureds. So it was with
Festus Claude and his coloured neighbour.

The natural ally of the black Jamaican, in his eyes, was the
foreign white, not the coloured native. Festus Claude had felt
and seen the kindness of the visiting white missionaries; he had
read their books and knew and respected their advances in
science and philosophy; he knew their language and was
writing poetry in it and he knew their music: he was
emotionally and intellectually ready for a connection with
Walter Jekyll.[9] Social confidence is a characteristic of the British
coloniser. He could travel to any point in his empire on which
'the sun never sets' and feel at home, for in every port was a
replica of his own society needing his help to make it more
authentic. Much more so for Walter Jekyll who being of the
upper class was the embodiment of British civilisation. Jekyll's
father was a Grenadier guard. He was a public school boy
ofcourse and was a bright one. He graduated with honours
from Cambridge, excelling in music, language, literature and
philosophy. He had taught and had published his thoughts. He
was in fellowship with others of his kind. It is his name that his
friend Robert Louis Stevenson gave to his famous character in
his *Dr Jekyll and Mr Hyde*. In search of a place in which to spend
his asthmatic days, Jekyll looked around the empire and chose
Jamaica. Jekyll had just the kind of exposure that would take
Festus Claude McKay beyond his brother's library, social
environment and political contacts.

Jekyll's class tended to romanticise the poor and
downtrodden. From his own mouth comes this admission.
Asked by the white governor of Jamaica to be allowed to
overnight with him in his cottage, Jekyll replies in the negative,

yet he is willing to accommodate McKay, the black peasant boy. McKay, observing this situation asks for an explanation and gets the response:

> English gentlemen have always liked their peasants; it is the ambitious middle class that we cannot tolerate.[10]

There were a lot of peasants in the Jamaica in which he settled and Jekyll set about collecting their stories and songs. It was in Brown's Town, St Ann, where McKay was apprenticed to a wheelwright, that Jekyll met the peasant boy who was to sit at his feet. Only someone with the social and intellectual authority of Jekyll could have turned around a person, socialised in the Anglo-Jamaican tradition as Festus Claude McKay was, to an appreciation of the Afro-Jamaican part of his cultural milieu – to the point where he could publish verse in the vernacular. Jekyll lived above Kingston and had the governor and his ilk in his social group. With the love of his life – his mother – dead, McKay moved to Kingston, joined the constabulary and was now nearer to Jekyll. A pen relationship was converted into a face to face one: he was very often in Jekyll's house. With Jekyll's encouragement McKay perfected his dialect verse and published in 1912 his first two collections, *Songs of Jamaica* and *Constab Ballads*. Jekyll made his library available to him, gave him subscriptions to journals which he thought worthwhile, taught him French and introduced him to his friends. Life with Jekyll was tantamount to a university course. It is this published poet, the first in Jamaican dialect, this youngman of peasant stock exposed to the ideas and writings of the foremost European minds, one who was comfortable with and succoured by white men, that set off for the USA in 1912 to enter university, 14 years before C.L.R. James left his Trinidad for the wider world.

In the British-held territories, including Jamaica and Trinidad, there was a dual system of education. There was a free stream, which took a child up to 15 years old. The best graduates from this went into elementary school teaching and the ministry, very often with further education through training colleges located in the islands. The fee-paying stream was secondary education. This began at about age 12 and fed into the university system in Britain. University training was not

available in the British West Indies except through mail. A
handful of scholarships in each territory allowed poor but
bright children to enter secondary school and to put themselves
in line for university education in Britain, either as fee-paying
or as scholarship students. This tertiary education prepared the
colonised for the higher professions – medicine and law,
allowing them to return home and move into the upper reaches
of the society. In the Trinidad of the youth of C.L.R. James and
Malcolm Nurse (Padmore) the colonial government went
further than the few scholarships: it offered free secondary
education to children of civil servants who passed the entrance
examinations. The schools to which these (male) children were
sent were Queen's Royal College and St Mary's.

The examinations sat at the secondary school level were those
sat by their age peers in Britain and the rest of the empire. The
young bright blackman from deep rural parts who had got a
scholarship knew from the outset that he was part of an
international net of students, he was part of an international
world. Since his tutors were usually foreign his sense of being
part of a world, larger than his island, was reinforced.
Trinidadian students did well. An ex-Prime Minister of
Trinidad, Eric Williams, is quoted as saying:

> one of the island scholars of 1911 was placed first among 57
> candidates in the British Empire in Agricultural Science ... of 83
> candidates who gained distinctions in History, four were from
> Trinidad. At the 1910 examinations one island scholar from QRC
> was placed first in the Senior Cambridge Examinations throughout
> the Empire[11]

It was only in 1815 that Trinidad officially became a British
colony. Until then it had been Spanish but in the later part of
the Spanish occupation, it had been settled by French-speaking
creoles, many of whom were coloured. Trinidad was not
Protestant; it was Roman Catholic and it came into the capitalist
system late. What came into this system, was a French-speaking
upper class of whites and French-speaking middle class of
coloureds who had to be made part of the Protestant/capitalist
system. The generosity of the British government in giving free
secondary school places to the children of civil servants, and the
financial support it gave to secondary education in general,

were intended to encourage the development of an English-speaking elite socialised in the ways of the British brand of Protestantism/capitalism. What this attention to scholarship did, was to increase Trinidad's literati and its tendency towards letters. Educated black people from the well-socialised Barbados came over to help with Trinidad's acculturation. Both C.L.R. James and George Padmore belonged to Trinidadian families that were touched by Barbadian norms and values. They both grew up in that double band, the family and the wider society, which stressed educational achievements.[12]

James' father was a school teacher and his house was like that of McKay's brother, well-stocked with books. James' mother was an avid reader. By the time the boy was ten he had read Thackeray and had been granted a scholarship to the premier high school in the land, Queen's Royal College, and thus was well on his way to testing his mettle with his peers in the empire, to another scholarship to university in England, to a profession in medicine or law and a place in the upper reaches of Trinidadian society. James shunned this path. The little boy, who in his reach to take Thackeray's *Vanity Fair* from its place on the bookshelf, had a good view of the village cricket pitch, chose as a youngman to focus his attention on his native society, and to do it in a decidedly Trinidadian way.

Trinidad came into the British Empire as a Crown Colony. It therefore did not have the history of playing the game of political parrying with Britain that Jamaica for instance had. Its European population was more French than British, yet it had no legal ties to France, thus it was not as drawn to watching and aping its European cousins as Jamaica was. The culture was instead oriented towards social analysis with a local flavour. This was there in the calypso; was there at the literary soirees; it was there in the novels, which were emerging. James the high school graduate became a part of this peculiarly analytical culture with its eyes turned on itself. He became a journalist covering cricket and approaching play from a detailed sociological perspective. He became a novelist and short story writer, using his analyses of the lives of the common people – the African-Trinidadians who had not got scholarships and were unlikely to become lawyers and doctors. He was part of a clique of literary men – Alfred Mendes, Ralph de Boissiere and

Albert Gomes, among them. With Mendes he edited the shortlived magazine called *Trinidad*. Gomes edited *The Beacon*. James' articles appeared in both.

James left Trinidad, at the age of 31, as a reputable cricket reporter, a fiction writer, one having some experience in the production of a magazine. He was moving into political analysis. He took with him a completed manuscript, *The Life of Captain Cipriani*, a Trinidadian, which he hoped to get published. He took with him his analytical mind, which had focussed itself on the life of struggling black people. Race and colour prejudice were not unknown in the Trinidad of James' youth. It functioned differently than it did in Jamaica. Here in Trinidad, race and colour were joined by other definers. Ethnicity for one, because there was a large Indian population, which was itself split along religious lines. Dissecting the race and colour line which was here, as in the other British Caribbean territories, were denomination – Protestant or Catholic, length of residence in the island and occupational orientation among others. This was a society of several sections, each highly tolerant of each other. There was strong adherence, for instance, to sectarian cricket clubs but these came together from time to time to compete against each other and to admire each other's form. The African-Trinidadian Learie Constantine had been nurtured by his club into an excellence that was regarded by all sectors of the society and, despite personal prejudices against his colour, he eventually became part of the national team.

Oxaal's *Black Intellectuals Come to Power* (1968) sensibly applies the phrases "plural acculteration" and "plural dissociation" to the norms supporting social interaction in Trinidad.[13] By the former is meant knowing the ways of the out-group and occasionally participating in them, and by the latter, the belief that each should attend to his own affairs. James, brought up in culturally diverse Trinidad, would have by the time he was 31 and ready to migrate, firmly internalised these characteristics. He is likely to have been, as a result, very concerned about his particular group but able to accept and work along with the differences in other groups. These characteristics allow easy accommodation into a foreign society. James in his particularly Trinidadian ways, was as ready for life in the international arena as Claude McKay was. He had spent a lot of his time in Trinidad in the colloquies of his literary clique, he could sail smoothly into the activities in Britain's literary circles.

Malcolm Nurse like C.L.R. James had roots outside of Trinidad: his mother was an Antiguan.14 His father's father had been born a slave in Barbados and came to Trinidad as a master mason. Padmore's father became an agricultural instructor with the Department of Education and a disgruntled man because, though the high quality of his work had been acknowledged with a promotion to senior agricultural instructor, he would have to stay at this level, for unspoken and unwritten laws decreed this to be the African-Trinidadians' boundary. Father Nurse resigned from the public service and, not just that, from Protestant/capitalism: he became a Moslem. His son does not appear to have been as academically gifted as C.L.R. James, but he did pass his academic exams at high school, did particularly well at pharmacy and took a job as a reporter of shipping news. Even if Nurse/Padmore had not been born and socialised in cosmopolitan, culturally diverse Trinidad, a job as a reporter of shipping news would have given him an international perspective. Along with this was a strong group sense, perhaps made stronger by his father's anger at the limitations imposed upon his colour and by immersion in his father's library of books written by Blyden, Du Bois and other black writers. There were many Garvey units in Trinidad in Nurse's youth, as we saw in the last lecture, and the *Negro World*, Garvey's newspaper, though proscribed, was smuggled in and widely read. A race conscious boy could in this environment find outlets of expression. One which this youth took was to offer a tribute to the 19th century Pan-Africanist Edward Blyden. Newly married and leaving a pregnant wife for the USA where he intended to train in medicine, Padmore left word that his child of whatever sex, be called Blyden. This young race conscious man from the culturally plural Trinidad society leaves his family in 1924, in his early twenties for Fisk University in Nashville, Tennessee, USA.

McKay was only two years out of his country when the Protestant/capitalist world ignited. War broke out between Germany and Russia involving all the great powers of the world. If we are to believe A.J.P. Taylor's account15 this war's beginning was the tragic-comic outcome of European culture. The archduke Franz Ferdinand, heir to the Hapsburg Austro-Hungarian Empire, had married for love, a mere countess – how could he! Given her lowly origins her children could not succeed their father to the throne nor could she sit with him on imperial occasions. Franz Ferdinand was however the field marshall and inspector-general of his country's army. His wife could share this military rank and so on their wedding anniversary, he decided to take her with him to review the army at Sarajevo, Bosnia's capital city. Bosnia and Herzegovina had been part of the Turkish Empire but had been annexed by Austria-Hungary in 1908. The inhabitants resented the separation from their ethnic roots and wished to ally themselves with Serbia. A schoolboy plot and a wrong turning pumped deadly shots into the bodies of the archduke and his wife. Though there was no evidence that the Serbian government was involved in these assassinations, the Austria-Hungarian government took steps to humiliate Serbia and eventually to declare war on her.

This according to Taylor was part of the normal diplomatic game. Serbia was part of the Balkans and the Balkans close to Constantinople, which was Russia's major route south. Everyone knew that the threat of another power's control of areas so near Constantinople would require a response from Russia. Russia's reaction was to mobilise her forces against Austria-Hungary. This pulled Germany into the game for she was an ally of the latter. She would now have to respond. Still a game of diplomacy, according to Taylor. Germany ordered Russia to demobilise. She refused. Germany declared war on her and thinking of ancient squabbles with France and the fear of being attacked by her while at battle with Russia, declared war on France too. Still a game according to Taylor, until technology, the darling of the early 20th century Protestant/capitalist world took over. Before diplomacy could kick in, the railway, unstoppable, was taking German troops into Belgium. Britain, in defence of Belgium, declared war on Germany bringing the people of her far flung empire into the war. By 1917, the USA was in the war, for German submarines had attacked her ships and Germany had offered Mexico help to recapture New Mexico from the USA. She took the side of the allies – Russia, France, Britain, Japan; Turkey came in on the German side. What was expected to be a short engagement lasted four years, bringing the east into the troubles of the west, for Japan and China entered the war too.

The allies won the war but the world from which they set off to fight was not that from which they now had to attempt to make peace. Three empires disintegrated – the Hapsburg Empire, the Ottoman Empire of the Turks and the Russian Empire. The first two crumpled into tiny states calling for independence and self-determination. In Russia the Protestant/capitalist system got its mightiest blow: it lost its philosophical hegemony. A.J.P. Taylor ends his discussion of the war with the words:

> The allies were not strong enough to make a new world. The world was left to make itself [16]

The black people of the world took this creative opportunity to attempt to carve out a new place for themselves in the world. Marcus Garvey's agents were in Paris for deliberation concerning the restructuring of the world, hoping to get a better deal for Africans at home and abroad; Du Bois was there too pulling Pan-Africanists into intellectual discussion concerning the new place which blacks ought to take; and here in Jamaica, Dr A.J. Thorne, writing from Beeston Street in Kingston, asked that His Majesty's government give further support to the plan to grant a concession of land in the British Central African Protectorate to people of the African diaspora willing to settle it. He had the support, he said, of Barbadians and of African-Americans and in particular the Tuskegee educational complex. In this document Thorne compared the European response to the German aggression against Belgium with the European approach to the Africans of the diaspora, and asked why moral suasion was so one sided. Why not help the West Indians who "did not migrate to these shores of our own volition". He was thankful for the gift of Christianity, for instance, but pointed out:

> We have not been restored to the lands from which we came; nor have we had any compensation whatever, to which we are undoubtedly entitled, after three hundred years of bondage ... yet

it cannot without truth be denied that the majority are virtually still
where slavery left them.[17]

James and Nurse/Padmore made no statements as far as we
know, about this peace; perhaps they were too young to react to
this creative opportunity. The changes brought by the First
World War were so thorough that opportunities stayed around
for their maturity. McKay, now in the United States of America,
reacted.

> But we, the blacks, less than trampled dust,
> Who walk the new ways with the old dim eyes, –
> We to the ancient gods of greed and lust
> Must still be offered up as sacrifice!
> Oh, we who deign to live but will not dare
> The white man's burden must forever bear![18]

he wrote in the "Little people". His words are the poetic
representation of the hurt which Dr Thorne feels at the way in
which the allies rushed to secure Belgium but did not turn their
eyes to see the suffering of the people of the African diaspora
"who did not migrate of their own volition".

The Treaty of Versailles ended the First World War. The anger
of Slavs at being forced into a political state with ethnically
different people was the sentiment which had fired the first shot
and had made the 1914 war into an idea and, shortly after, an
act. Germany's attack on little Belgium had been part of what
had inflamed the allies into military action. The end of the war
saw these contentions translated into the commitment of the
great powers to protect the independence of small states and to
recognise national sentiment. The word was 'self determination
of nation states'. It answered the vexations of the small states of
Europe. The poet McKay, like Thorne and the Pan-African
intellectuals, looked at the postwar meditations of the great
powers and their solution – the Treaty of Versailles – and were
hurt that only white nations had been decreed as weak and
worthy of the help of international backers to maintain their
nationalism and their freedom. McKay's poem, like Thorne's
proposal, like the Du Bois-organised Pan-African Congress, saw
the light of day in 1919, a time when Europe was responding to
European demands for self determination. Theirs is a reaction

to their invisibility in the eyes of the great powers.

It had taken several years for this level of black consciousness to make its way into McKay's poetry. True he did write and publish in the Jamaican dialect before he entered the USA and true his work was about the black Jamaican, but these were paintings of the Jamaican scenery, not the gut feeling of the involved:

> Black nigger wukin'laka cow
> An' wipin' sweat drops from him brow,
> Dough him is dying sake o' need,
> P'lice an' dem headman boun' fe feed.[19]

Not only was his consciousness as seen in his verse seated exclusively in one part of the African diaspora, African-Jamaica, but he denied Africa then:

> Jamaica is de nigger's place
> No mind whe' some declare;
> Aldough dem call we "no land race",
> I know we home is here[20]

Identifying with a wider race of black people and feeling their pain was not, in his Jamaican days, in McKay's heart.

There must have been some connection with black America somewhere though, for McKay left Jamaica to sit at the feet of Booker T. Washington, at the time the last word on the education of the blackman. He was also ofcourse moved by the desire to make something of himself in the traditional sense – to have, in accordance with his black middle class upbringing, a profession, to raise a family. Understandably, he did not see writing as a profession. But Booker T. Washington's Tuskegee was too basic, too full of unexposed young people, too trade oriented for one who had been under the tutelage of Walter Jekyll. He was shortly out of there and into a college in Kansas making himself into an agriculturalist. This didn't hold him either for, although McKay did not yet know it, he was not the normal black middle class African-Jamaican person. A gift of money made him choose to hasten respectability, to marry and to become a restaurateur. For this move McKay invited his girlfriend from Jamaica into marriage and moved to New York.

Within six months this plan had failed and McKay was left by himself to make what he could with it. He now recognised himself as more than the ordinary, recognised his need to define his own life style and started by forsaking the pursuit of university training. He settled down to take what jobs he could get. For a blackman in the USA these were service jobs. As waiter, busboy, railcar attendant, he got to learn and feel with the African-American, most of whom were consigned to these jobs. He took a room in Harlem, fast becoming the place where blacks of all nationalities met and his empathy with black people moved from Jamaican to a catholic position. As a black man in the United States of 1919, when northern whites returning from the war were angry at being displaced from the job market by blacks, when lynchings of blacks multiplied as the South tried to frighten blacks into staying home in their assigned place, McKay could not help but feel as black as his skin was and as frightened of the white mob as any native black. His sojourn in the USA, and his determination to take life where his true self led, had turned McKay at this point in 1919 – when the peace of Versailles was being arranged – into a member of the universal black race.

This new universally black self allied with McKay's Jamaican socialisation to make him a trend setter in the Harlem Renaissance. The First World War had shaken blacks out of their places. African-Americans had been to the war and had fought well. They knew now that they were worthy of the full rights of citizenship. They were in a militant mood. They had seen the white world crumble and had learnt from this that whites had no monopoly on God's love. Several riots, the largest being the Chicago riots of 1919 in which 58 people were killed, were their way of saying that the world had changed, our perception of the white world and of ourselves had changed, this country had to change. The black Caribbean followed suit: we here too made our statement through riots. The allies according to A.J.P. Taylor had left the world to sort itself out. Blacks were giving notice that they intended to take up this challenge.

Another group, which set itself to doing this sorting, was the non-establishment whites. These too were saying that change had to be and that they would help to make it. Some white

American writers, caught up with the nationalism of the time, looked within themselves for a style which reflected the realities of the country. They heeded Walt Whitman's earlier call for the regeneration of American civilisaton through literature.

> We have no tradition to continue; we have no school of style to build up. What we ask of the writer is simply self-expression without regard to current magazine standards. We would prefer that portion of his work which is done through a joyous necessity of the writer himself.[21]

said the *Seven Arts* edited by white Joel Oppenheimer and white Waldo Frank. Some of McKay's pieces were accepted, beginning a long relationship between a black man working in the pantry of the trains plying between New York and Pennsylvania and the white literati. Frank Harris, editor of *Pearson's Magazine*, came into his life. This man had earlier published such names as Oscar Wilde, George Bernard Shaw and H.G. Wells and like Walter Jekyll he saw a great talent in McKay. Harris invited him to put his intensity of feelings as a black man on paper. Out came the classic that had made his fellow workers on the train cry; whose emotional truth and poetic excellence forced the white press to accept it; and which Winston Churchill was to quote:[22]

> If we must die, let it not be like hogs
> Hunted and penned in an inglorious spot,
> While round us bark the mad and hungry dogs,
> Making their mock at our accursed lot.
> If we must die, O let us nobly die,
> So that our precious blood may not be shed
> In vain; then even the monsters we defy
> Shall be constrained to honour us though dead!
> O kinsman! we must meet the common foe!
> Though far outnumbered let us show us brave,
> And for their thousand blows deal one deathblow!
> What though before us lies the open grave?
> Like men we'll face the murderous, cowardly pack,
> Pressed to the wall, dying, but fighting back[23].

There had been black conscious poems before but these had been in the romantic Ethiopianist mode, hoping for the time

when Ethiopia would stretch forth her hands unto God or the
time past when Ethiopia was the place where the Gods loved to
be. McKay's poem was seated in the present conditions of black
people, the voice was that of the black man of the present. It
spoke to the blackman wanting to be the 'new negro', the one
who fights back rather than slinks away. The poem brought
black people and their present condition into the ambit of art.
This was what the new black writers wanted to do, this is what
they were to do in creating the Harlem Renaissance. McKay's
writing was to become a beacon. White friends and publishers
had encouraged him towards faith in this style and they had,
through their journals, publicised his feelings and his art and
with sales made it possible for him to see writing as a part
career, if not a whole career. After him the writers of the
Harlem Renaissance and their work, though framed by black
conditions and black issues, cooperated with and used the
agencies of whites.

The meeting of black and white had philosophical
underpinnings. It was during the 1914 war that Marxism with
its anti-capitalist, anti-Christian rhetoric was made state. By
1917 Russia had a socialist government which was bent on
giving power to the ordinary citizens, whose labour had
maintained a Christian monarch and disproportional wealth to
those who owned the means of production. It was the Russian
soldiers who, as fed up of being the class that lost its life in a
war they didn't create as soldiers in France and Germany, voted
with their feet to end the war. The socialist government signed a
treaty with the Germans, and the Russian people settled down
to evolve an alternative ethic and practice, which they intended
to export to the rest of the world. This ethic celebrated the unity
of workers everywhere and saw a moral distribution of the
world's goods as a possibility. Here was a new morality for
those who felt that the combine of Protestantism and capitalism
had failed to keep the world at peace and had caused
immeasurable suffering and loss of life. The black race knew
itself to be the most exclusively working class race; if the
Russian Marxist practice didn't have them in mind, they knew
that they should. Socialism became popular throughout the
black world. In the USA it constrained whites to define
themselves firstly as workers and to consider as peers all other

workers. Theoretically at least, whites and blacks were now equal.

The new ethic mandated close working relationships between blacks and whites and on an equal footing. Since black was synonymous with worker and worker with socialism, it was difficult for blacks to avoid seeing themselves as socialists. McKay was one of the blackmen for which the one meant the other. His "Capitalist at Dinner", published as his "If we must die" by the white socialist Eastmans, showed him to be as sanguine about the death of capitalism, a concern of socialism, as about the conditions of black people:

> The entire service tries its best to please
> This overpampered piece of broken health,
> Who sits there thoughtless, querulous, obese,
> Wrapped in his sordid visions of vast wealth.
> Great God! If creatures like this money-fool,
> Who holds the services of mankind so cheap,
> Over people must forever rule,
> Driving them at their will like helpless sheep –
> Then let proud mothers cease from giving birth;
> Let human beings perish from the earth.24

The union between definition of self as blackman and the acceptance and work within the alternative, universal socialism, was much clearer and much more lasting with Malcolm Nurse/George Padmore than it was with McKay. McKay in the middle and late years of his life dallied around the world physically and to some extent, philosophically.25 He had been part of Sylvia Pankhurst's communist journal *Dreadnought* in England; had there met and talked with the likes of Bernard Shaw; had been to Russia; and, supported by the leading Japanese communist Katayama when the American branch disowned him, had not only been invited to the platform to sit behind Zinoviev at the 4th Congress of the Communist International, but had stayed behind and had appeared on the reviewing stand at the 1923 May Day parade, with this Zinoviev, the head of the branch of Soviet communism, which controlled the world spread of this alternative ethic. Taking seriously the need for the world to understand the condition of blacks, McKay had proceeded, writing novels from Europe and

North Africa, which depicted life mainly in black America. The African-American reading public was not pleased with these exposures and McKay felt and was alienated from the people about whom, and for whom, he wrote.

Stalin's ascendancy in Russia brought changes in several quarters, McKay's political vision among them. It helped to turn McKay from communism but it did not push him into any other branch of socialism as it did C.L.R. James. In his middle years, McKay was voicing loudly an almost Garvey-like conviction that the hope of black people lay in their unity and self-reliance, not in a colour-blind universal organisation. McKay's life ended in 1948 after another World War had massacred the world. This one left him with the conviction that the hope for blacks of the USA, in a world torn by these wars, lay with the Roman Catholic church and its good deeds. Hope lay, he seems to have been saying, in personal humanitarian efforts. McKay had gone far past the socialist ethic, past even the Protestant/capitalist ethic; he had gone back past Henry VIIIth and Martin Luther, back to the ethic of the Holy Roman Empire revised to link faith and good works into a personal sword.

Nurse/Padmore's life reads like a sharp arrow undeflected from its target. So focussed was he that he had no place in his scheme of things to share his musings with posterity: he appears to have left us no autobiographical essays. Even his birth date is not clear to us today. It is through his reported actions that one finds his purpose and in his friend C.L.R. James' recollections of his life. Nurse/Padmore left Trinidad at about 22 years of age for Fisk University in Tennessee, USA. Like most progressive youths of his Trinidad he thought of training to be a doctor. His first year in the USA found him instead studying the new science of society at Columbia University in New York. Medicine was out, he thought of the other choice that socially mobile males in Trinidad made – law – and proceeded to Fisk to do his pre-law courses. There he studied botany and zoology, a natural science option was natural for him: he had done well at home in pharmacy. But the bulk of his programme reflected an interest in the social sciences, for Nurse/Padmore chose to do with his natural science option, international relations, political science and negro sociology.

Fisk was quite politically exciting. The students there had mounted a three weeks strike, which had earned them the positive notice of the major black intellectual figure – W.E.B. Du Bois. At Fisk Nurse/Padmore was involved in public speaking. It seems he was thinking not only of analysing society but of exhorting the whole or parts of it. He got good practice at Fisk and made a name for himself in this regard but, like McKay before him, he yearned for something more than the South. There are suggestions that the Klan was displeased with his activities and he became frightened. It seems more likely, given his actions, that Nurse/Padmore, a child of the British Empire, was seeking out youths with like experience with whom to cooperate on some plan for change, using his knowledge of social science. From Fisk he had established communications with Benjamin Azikiwe, later to be the first president of Nigeria. He sought help from him in establishing an African student organisation to foster racial consciousness and a spirit of nationalism. The notion of nationalism was the popular vision in the post World War One era. Nurse/Padmore sought to establish a student organisation, which would focus its attention on the protection of the sovereignty of Liberia. This state as we know was the most outstanding attempt by Africans of the diaspora to reclaim a space in Africa. The Europeans at the Treaty of Versailles had guaranteed the sovereignty of several new states. Obviously Nurse/Padmore saw the need for the Liberian experiment also to be protected and saw that it would have to be done by Africans and Africans of the diaspora. His position at this point was clearly Pan-Africanist.

Nurse/Padmore left Fisk and the South for New York's Law School but took no courses and dropped out. His mind was elsewhere. Here in New York he joined the Communist Party. Medicine, law and the ambitions of the colonial child for a place in the social system of the empire, were now dropped for the scientific reorganisation of the international society, for this was communism's aim. This ideology had come to see the race, consigned to the position everywhere of hewers of wood and drawers of water for the rest of the society, as crucial to the realisation of this new white materialist dream of a world governed by the proletariat, the workers. Black intellectuals were targeted internationally. Naturally, Howard University in

Washington, which had in its student body the highest
concentration of would-be black intellectuals from foreign
lands, was a target. This is where Nurse was planted. Between
1927 and 1928, Nurse became Padmore when on the party's
business. Out would go the empire with which he was familiar;
in would come another more to his liking.

Padmore's work as a communist at this stage required little
adjustment. It was rather like work towards black nationalism.
He was in league with another West Indian at Howard, Cyril
Oliviere who was president of the Garvey club and together
they planned a demonstration against the British High
Commissioner who was due to open a new building at Howard.
Mimeographed documents were circulated referring to this
officer as the representative of a 'bloated' empire and accusing
him of having master-minded the deportation of Garvey, an
event which had taken place very recently. College
investigations discovered that the protest was the work of
George Padmore of the Anti-Imperialist Youth League, but
there was no such student on the register ... Padmore's double
identity was paying dividends.

This college student and husband moved between
Washington and New York as if it were Port of Spain and
Tunapuna or Kingston and Spanish Town, between one identity
and the other. In New York as George Padmore he helped
another West Indian, Richard Moore, with the black-oriented
communist weekly the *Negro Champion* later to be called *The
Liberator*. He helped with the Harlem Workers' Centre, attended
the Bertram Wolfe school for workers at the party headquarters
and.earned a living as a janitor. Clearly Padmore believed that
communism would do the levelling that would bring black
people their just deserts and he worked with all his heart within
it. Other West Indian blacks, senior to him such as Moore with
whom he worked on the party's newspaper, had a theory that
in trade unionism lay the instrument of change, thus Padmore
along with them supported the American Negro Labour
Congress, an arm of the communist movement in the USA. The
theory and praxis of change, which these black intellectuals
followed, was that African-American negroes would be the
vanguard of the international labour movement until Africans
were ready. Meanwhile Padmore worked for the readiness of

Africans and for the preparedness of African-Americans until both could merge to assume power in the ranks of the international proletariat.

Padmore's hard work was noticed by the executive of the Communist Party in the USA and he was rewarded with a ticket to Moscow. It is doubtful whether he and his wife knew that this was a one-way ticket. The fact is nevertheless that she refused to accompany him and Padmore was now a mind unfettered by family. In 1930 this African-Trinidadian was made head of the Negro Department of the Profintern with headquarters in the Kremlin. He was often on the stand with Stalin and Molotov as they reviewed the army on the May Day parades, and intimate enough with Molotov to be buying razor blades for him on his excursions out of Russia. He was sent to Vienna by the party to take over the editorship of the *Negro Worker*, from the African-American communist, J.W. Ford. This literary device was the instrument designed to bring the African and the African of the diaspora into international communism. From this vantage point, Padmore tried to woo African-Americans away from the influence of such leaders as Du Bois with his notion of the development of the negro races in stages, the first being the talented tenth; from Randolph with his mild socialism; and from Garvey with his racial separatism. In his *Negro Worker and the Imperialist War – intervention in the Soviet Union*, he ridiculed Garvey and called Du Bois a petty bourgeois negro intellectual. Padmore's programme spread far and wide, even into the hands of Elma Francois,26 that Vincentian washerwoman who was leading a working class movement in Trinidad;27 Uriah Butler of the Trinidad Oilfield Workers was nourished on it. From his base in Europe, Padmore, through his writings, gave black malcontents everywhere a conceptual framework within which to meditate on the issue of change in their position within the global system. It is within this space that he researches and writes *Life and Struggles of the Negro Toiler*. By 1933 Padmore had resigned from the Communist Party.

This was not an about-face. Liberia and the future of black people on the international scene was as dear to Padmore as ever. It is in fact this age-old preoccupation that forced him to sever his links with the party. There were rumblings foretelling

the Second World War and Russia needed allies against
Germany. The French and the English were the most likely but
they were colonial powers. Comintern, the section of the
Communist machinery, which had been specifically assigned to
disturb relationships between the classes in the empires of the
Western powers, was put on the back burner. Stalin the new
leader of Russia was in any case moving towards a theory of
socialism in one state, which meant the development of the
Russian soviet system prior to the export of change
internationally. Padmore considered this a betrayal of the hopes
of black people. Padmore explained to his friend James.

> I stayed there because there was a means of doing work for the
> black emancipation and there was no other place that I could think
> of.[28]

With this betrayal there was now clearly no need for him to
stay in what he considered an organisation which did not have
the interest of black people at the fore. In 1934, a year after he
had severed his connections with the party, he was formally
dismissed for arguing negro unity on race rather than class lines
and that he had attempted with Du Bois to raise five million
dollars to bail out the Liberian leaders on the mistaken
assumption that reform could come from the capitalist class.
Padmore had indeed been looking around, in view of his
disappointment with the direction of communism, for more
congenial fellow travellers and had told Du Bois that though
Liberia had her faults, white politicians were no better than
black ones and it was their duty to save the "black baby from
the white wolves".[29]

Padmore's new associates were now black, and unity among
such black skinned, black minded thinkers part of his goal. To
this end he tried to link the young Afro-French intellectuals
with older ones such as Du Bois and helped them to convene a
Negro World Unity Congress, designed to look at the negro
problem in the light of the current worldwide and economic
crisis and the rise of Nazism, that acute form of nationalism
which would be happy with the extermination of the negro.
Without his *Negro Worker* and the Red International Labour
Union (RILU), which had supported it, Padmore now needed
an organ. For this reason too, it was necessary to court Du Bois

who was the editor of *Crisis*, the mouthpiece of the NAACP, the National Association for the Advancement of Coloured People. A vibrant correspondence began between the two, Du Bois in the USA and Padmore now living in England. In England he met a boyhood acquaintance, C.L.R. James. They worked together and have become known as the architects of modern Pan-Africanism. Encouraging and developing the minds of potential black leaders was now part of the job Padmore assigned himself. Nkrumah of Ghana is one of his successes. So the boy brought up in Britain's white capitalist, Protestant/capitalist orientation, whose father had made a tiny chink in that system, was now intent on making a wider hole; he was now undertaking the development of a black socialist empire.

C.L.R. James accepted nobody's isms. If he arrived at a position similar to that of any one else it was because it lay in the trajectory of his own. This is a quality he had revealed from the time he opted out of the pursuit of university education, medical or legal degree and a place in the higher reaches of Trinidadian society. C.L.R. James was a mind more cerebral than most. Racial snobs he managed to see as data rather than as affronts to his person. By the time James reached England at the age of 31 his approach to life was more than mapped out: he was on a clear path – journalist and novelist and short-storywriter – good enough to be reviewed in the English press and to catch the eye of the literary giant, Edith Sitwell. His more distinctly political work was in embryo, in manuscript form, but James' mind was obviously ready to expand in this direction. His socialisation into Trinidad's cosmopolitanism would stand him in good stead, but, in any case, Trinidad was part of the British Empire with its particular brand of Protestant/capitalist ethic; it was the extension of home that America wasn't. Purposeful as ever, he had gone to England with a set programme: he was to help Learie Constantine, the African-Trinidadian cricketer, with his autobiography. Working from such a milieu and with cricket reporting already one of his gifts, James found work with the *Manchester Guardian*. His analyses drew comment in this birthplace of cricket and joined his fiction to give him and his name visibility; but more, the experience of covering matches, led him to the sociology of Britain. With this sociology and that of Trinidad revealed to him, James was moved to hypotheses concerning social class and naturally to a reading of Marx, Engels, Lenin and Trotsky. From this reading he emerged a Trotskyite.

As a native of a colonial territory, James had ofcourse meditated on the colonial condition and on the meaning of empire. The manuscript in his bag, *The Life of Captain Cipriani*, touched on this matter, and his *pamphlet The Case for West Indian Self-Government* was not far behind. James' reading of socialist thought moved him to see the colonies on the same plane as the working class within the framework of international affairs With this notion the colonial question now finds a theoretical place in socialist thought. Continuing in this vein, James examines the revolution in the French-held Haiti of the late 18th and early 19th centuries and gives the world, in his *Black Jacobins*, an understanding of its first successful working class revolution. Emphasising the fact that these successful revolutionaries were black and underlining the military and organisational skills of these black people, James' *Black Jacobins* gave the world not only socialist analysis but a positive view of blacks, well needed in the mid-1930s, when a racial nationalism that would make of the negro a non-entity was rife. *Black Jacobins* first appeared as a play, *Toussaint L'Ouverture*. It was staged in London where James had by now resettled. He was obviously involved not merely with the English writing circle, but also with the international set of intellectual blacks, for the leading actor in this play was Paul Robeson, African-American athlete, bass and communist. *Toussaint L'Ouverture* was staged in 1936 and *Black Jacobins* appeared in 1938. In this year James' international perspective was manifested in his *World Revolution*. It was the first comprehensive study of the Comintern, the arm of communism which had been devised for proselytising the world. Stalin's adoption of the notion of socialism in one country had, as we have seen, meant the death knell for the Comintern. James, at this time at any rate, believed in the concept of international action towards change. This work was anti-Stalin, pro-Trotsky. A year later, James translates Boris Souvarine's *Stalin*, from French, to make it available to English readers and to become the authority on Stalin. Those who were thus informed could now take the move, which

James studies had forced on him, towards Stalin's rival, Trotsky.

Italy had incensed the black world in the mid-1930s with her aggression towards Ethiopia. Blacks from the USA to the smallest English-speaking part of the British Empire were sounding their protest in strikes and rebellions. More than Howard University in Washington DC, USA, the universities in Britain were home to the young intellectual minds of the international black world who expected, and were expected, to assume leadership roles in their countries on their return homes. James with Padmore nurtured the anti-imperialist, pro-black nationalism sentiment of this cream through the International Africa Service Bureau. James chaired the African Friends of Abbyssinia, an organisation whose name speaks its purpose, and he edited the *International African Opinion*. The mission statement of the International Africa Service Bureau, the parent of the other two was:

> [to] assist by all means in (our) power the un-coordinated struggle of Africans and people of African descent against oppression which they suffer in every country.30

With this statement, Pan-Africanism went past the sentimentalism of Blyden and even the creativity of Garvey to explicit confrontation with the existing social order, still the capitalist/Protestant order. It didn't matter to James and to Padmore – brought up in a culture in which different coalitions minded their own business and cooperated with each other where and when their interests met – that they did not support the same brand of socialism. They shared a feeling towards the black world and this was enough. There was room for cooperation.

Among the members of the International Friends of Abbyssinia, formed by James and eventually taken over by Padmore, were Kenyatta of Kenya and the first Mrs Garvey. They lectured on political issues and when the issue of the Ethiopian war subsided, they put their efforts into the International African Service Bureau. Padmore chaired this and James edited their journal. They wrote letters to Members of Parliament, so that the Colonial Office could know that intelligent opinion was watching their behaviour towards their

colonies; they courted the left wing of the British Labour Party;
they wrote books. Padmore contributed *How Britain Rules Africa*
and *Africa and World Peace*, Kenya's Kenyatta wrote *Facing Mt
Kenya* and Ghana's Dr Danquah, *African People and God*. Quite a
library of analyses of the black condition was being made for
the international world to note. With the organisation and the
theoretical work which they did through their lectures and
writings, James and Padmore created a social and intellectual
framework within which aspiring black leaders could formulate
and refine their ideas towards social change in their countries –
this within the notion of a black international somehow linked
to an international workers' movement.

In 1938 James had moved to the USA and had caught the
attention of the *New York Times* and the *Times Magazine* as the
man who had debated with Bertrand Russell, who had written
in 1917 in the same edition of *Seven Arts* in which McKay was
published:

> Mankind cannot afford to risk another great war. Every advance in
> technical civilization must make war more deadly, and a great war
> a hundred years hence might well leave the world in the exclusive
> possession of negroes. If we wish to avert this calamity we must be
> bold, constructive, and not afraid to be revolutionary.[31]

By the response of the audience, the "negro" had won. The
American press knew James to be a speaker who could talk
without notes, spouting the relevant statistics. His section of the
socialist movement noted James' theses and at its 1939
convention declared that "blacks were destined by the whole
historical past to be, under adequate leadership, the very
vanguard of the proletarian movement".[32] As Padmore had
been sent to Howard, James was now placed in the USA by an
international socialist organisation intent on making the world
into one state. James was the principal member of the Socialist
Worker's Party that visited Trotsky in Mexico in 1939 where he
had been given asylum. At this meeting with Trotsky where he
presented his pre-analysis of the African-American situation,
Trotsky gave him his blessing:

> I believe the party should utilise the sojourn of Comrade James in
> the States (the tour was necessary to acquaint him with conditions)

but now for the next six months, for a behind-the-scenes organisational and political work in order to avoid attracting too much attention from the authorities. A six month programme can be elaborated for the Negro question, so that if James should be obliged to return to Great Britain, for personal or through the pressure of the police, after a half a year's work we have a base for the Negro movement and we have a serious nucleus of Negroes and whites working together on this plan. It is a question of the vitality of the party. It is a question of whether the party is to be transformed into a sect or if it is capable of finding its way to the most oppressed part of the working class.[33]

Blacks, and the African-American in particular, were thus the key to the party's sense of itself as an instrument for the transformation of socialism from the ideas of a sect to an instrument for change in the place of and the condition of the working class. James, now J.R. Johnson, went underground to collect data towards designing a programme to give the blacks their place in the world order. After 15 years worth of data, seduced by his love for a young white American woman and by America's call to a freedom from old ways of thinking, James found that he had moved past Trotsky into an appreciation of how ordinary men and women interact with the social world around them; had moved to a social psychological approach to phenomena, a position, which is clear in his 1963 work *Beyond a Boundary*. For this new James the individual human being's spirit and not the party or the system was now the basic active unit. James' sojourn in the USA had opened his eyes to the tremendous creativity within the ordinary man and accordingly his centrality to political action. The problem for political philosophy, as he now saw it, was how to make socialism reach its greatest height – democracy – by allowing the individual's creative powers to develop and express themselves. He now saw the 'party' as a hindrance and that the hegemony of the proletariat had to mean the overthrow of the party itself. Such a position obviously meant his break with Trotsky and he did so.

James was now on his own, a philosopher with faith in the creativity of people as the solution to the world's problems, a philosopher with the feeling that when this energy is unleashed in African-America and linked with that of the rest of the black world, the new civilisation created by the existence of the new world, would have a transformative effect on the whole world. Important to this analysis was the fact that the world with its technological advance in communications, was already a unit. The bases of mental activity had to change with it: the old European distinctions of art versus culture, intellectuals versus the people, politics versus everyday life, had to go. A fusion of these was what was now necessary. James followed this position towards a clearer Pan-Africanism, sure that black colonial people were going to play a decisive role in the shaping of the new world society. He and Padmore worked together once more, Padmore more concretely, jockeying Nkrumah and Ghana into fulfilling their West Indian dreams. James was now a kind of guru looking at and looking for the other bright young people, who would realise the dream of the new world, guiding their work by his comments. The development of women's potential was close to his heart: a relatively new thing in his time.

Unlike McKay, Padmore and James pressed on to envisage a new world order. Protestant/capitalism, which they had inherited from Europe and the materialist intellectualism of Soviet Russia, arising in their lifetime, was to be replaced by creativity of the personality. James seemed to see that which was formed by the New World and the colonial experience of the people brought there from Africa, as the vanguard of change. Padmore's focus on the development of an African leadership elite suggest that this vanguard was the continental African. At the activist level James was more broad-minded lending his intellectual skills through talks and his writing to the development of a wide range of personalities.

What lesson is here for us in the lives and works of the three internationally regarded black men? The question is: are we the present crop of black thinkers, the change agents James expected to emerge? More generally, does our sense of the world require us to conceive of it in terms of race as Padmore and James saw it or do we see the world as the circumstances of the dying McKay suggested – a bright future ushered in by the good works of christianised individuals?

February 1997

FROM JUBA'S HEAD

6

In the previous lectures we have looked at the condition of the Africans of the diaspora. We have looked at the circumstances, which brought them to the New World. We have looked at the conditions in which they lived. We have looked at how they changed these conditions, the world they made during enslavement, the theories they devised and their consequent actions towards their emancipation. We have looked at several men and the part they played in liberation and in designing strategies for survival in and out of enslavement. All of the men at whom we have looked are dead. Now we want to look at the contemporary scene: what are intellectual Africans of the diaspora saying about the societies in which they have been reared and which they could influence by their behaviour. We want to look at the female mind and at female actions. We have chosen to look at one African-Trinidadian born in 1944 and one African-Barbadian-American born some years earlier, both are novelists. So we have the task now of looking at the female commentary on the society and looking at it through the lens of fiction. In these lectures we have tried to look at our societies and the behaviour of our forefathers within our societies with the intention of learning about ourselves and our societies, the better to equip us to diagnose and prescribe programmes for the health of our nation. Can fiction help us in this task? Let us see whether fiction has any informative value. First a definition.

"Fiction" according to the Oxford Classical Dictionary is "the action or product of fashioning or imitating", "a supposition known to be at variance with the facts but conventionally accepted". Its shorter version adds "thing feigned or imagined, invented statement or narrative; literature consisting of such narrative esp. novels". The Webster's Dictionary says much the same thing: "something invented by the imagination or feigned ... an assumption of a possibility as fact irrespective of the question of its truth". Critical to the general definition of fiction according to these sources, is that which is fashioned, invented by a mind and is communicated to an audience willing to suspend its sense of fact to enter into the created truth. This definition of fiction calls into being a person feeding her invention to others. It calls into being a social psychological set, which includes one skilled in techniques of persuasion, for the willingness of others to suspend their sense of reality hinges ofcourse on the power of the novelist to invent.

Fiction can be about saints in heaven, gods be-sporting themselves on Mount Olympus, a horse – Black Beauty, a spider – Anancy, things which do not speak of the life of the audience; it may be about human beings, so like the audience, that they identify with the subject matter and begin to perceive themselves or other human beings in the light of this fictive matter. Abraham Lincoln is said to have credited Harriet Beecher Stowe and her literary invention *Uncle Tom's Cabin*, with inspiring the civil war, which eventually took African-Americans out of legal enslavement.[1] Harriet Beecher Stowe perhaps did do this for, like Charles Dickens, she was talking to her group about issues which concerned them. Stowe and Dickens used their imagination to create social situations very much like the real ones to which they wished to draw their readers' attention. A great deal of Caribbean novelistic fiction is of this kind – the creation of models of social situations for the direction of the group-mind to the real situation. A great deal of it is intentionally so: is intended to be a commentary on the society and is intended to influence our behaviour towards our societies. We focus on Merle Hodge from Trinidad and Paule Marshall from Barbados/America as novelists whose inventions are so close to reality that they could have a social function intentionally or otherwise.

Merle Hodge's comments on the functions of fiction indicate that she is not only likely to use fiction in this way but feels that fiction ought to have a social and cathartic function:

> The proper role of fiction in human societies included allowing a people to "read" itself – to decipher its own reality. The storyteller offers a vision of the world, which is more coherent, more "readable", than the mass of unconnected detail of everyday experience. Fiction also brings to our attention and puts in place parts of our reality that are not visible to us or are normally

overlooked, allowing us to form a more complete picture of our
environment than our own observation allows.2

I have seen no like comment from Paule Marshall. Our
examination of these two women and their works will
nevertheless question the ability of their work to sensibly
inform us about the goings on in our societies. This we will do
in order to judge the credence of what they say and decide to
what extent we should therefore allow what they say to
influence our behaviour. We look at Hodge's first novel *Crick
Crack Monkey* and Marshall's third, *Praisesong for the Widow*.
Techniques normally used to simulate reality are language,
choice of character and the combine of time and place. We will
look at these factors towards assigning credence to these works.

This lecture has another set of interests. Hodge and Marshall
are women from two different parts of the African diaspora.
What light do they and their work throw on the condition of
women in their particular societies? This question takes us into
a comparative examination of the works and of the social
settings they may depict. The areas of comparison could be
legion. In my study of theory and methods of sociology in my
student days, there was a term, which was often used. It was
'heuristic device', a mental and verbal construct devised to
make more visible, ideas and the connections between them. To
help me identify the areas for comparison, I have called on the
heuristic device, 'Juba's head', the title of this lecture. Juba is a
female name popular throughout the African diaspora. It has
also been popular as such among the Bambara, the Wolof, the
Vi and the Mende of West Africa.3 It is clearly a name brought
over from Africa to us in the New World. Juba will be for me in
this lecture, a female New World intellectual's sense of feeling
connected to Africa.

We shall see the Trindadian Hodge and the Barbadian-
American Marshall as great-granddaughters of Juba who made
the crossing to the New World. We shall see whether these
women's works indicate an intimacy with the existence of
Africa and its diaspora; whether they write out of this
consciousness; whether their works indicate that they are not
only born Juba, but feel Juba. The notion, Juba's head also
allows us to posit characteristics of femaleness in Africa of the
diaspora. In Bambara the word Juba is more than a person's

name. It refers to a hen, who has young children. Among the Wolof too, it is more than a female name – it refers to tough-tough hair on the head. We have chosen to assign the quality of mental toughness and nurturing of her young to Juba and ask ourselves now, whether the black women in these inventions of Hodge and Marshall are portrayed as mentally tough-tough, as creatures who take care of their young. Among the Yoruba, where the word might also be a female name, it is the verb. Juba in this case means "to pay homage" and "to acknowledge as superior". We translate this to represent deserved reverential behaviour to or from a female. Are females so presented to us, in the two novels that we will examine closely? Do these female writers see anything in the societies, we have established here in Africa of the diaspora, which deserve reverence?

Lynne Fauley Emery says, talking of the Africa from which the New World Africans were taken:

> specific tribes did seem to prefer certain types of dances. Yet even among the wide variety of tribes brought together in the Caribbean, some dances were enjoyed by nearly all the slaves: the Calenda, Chic, Bamboula, and Juba.[4]

She adds that Juba was brought from the islands of the Caribbean to southern USA where it is a well-known dance. Juba's dispersion indicates a spread of concepts of femaleness, among other aspects of culture. What commonalities in the lives of the Jubas of the southern USA and the Caribbean do the works of Merle Hodge, the Trinidadian and Paule Marshall, the African-Barbadian-American see and present to us the reader?

Juba has been called a challenge dance. Emery quotes an 1844 description of the dance as done by Africans in Cuba:

> Presently a woman advances and commencing a slow dance, made up of shuffling the feet and various contortions of the body, thus challenges a rival from among the men. One of these, bolder than the rest, after awhile steps out, and the two often strive which shall first tire the other; the woman performing many feats which the man attempts to rival, often excelling them, amid shouts of the rest. A woman will sometimes drive two or three beaux from the ring yielding her place at length to some impatient belle[5]

Are our women of such in male-female relations, that one could out-perform and drive two or three men from the ring?

Juba, the dance, has obviously percolated in time, changed but is still around. It was once a dance done at wakes but has moved out of this enclosure; it survived the outlawing of the drum in the USA to become the act of replacing the drum sound. This is done by the patting of parts of the body, thus the term 'patting juba'.[6] Is there a concern in Hodge or Marshall with the expression of African sensibilities and the way in which, like the concept 'Juba', they have defied external pressure and resurrected elsewhere in the cultural expressions of the people of the African diaspora? And do their works suggest that they have a reverential attitude to that which was brought from Africa and which survived here?

In this study of the works of Merle Hodge and Paule Marshall, we want to see

• to what extent do their works have a social function
• whether language, choice of character, and the time-place combine have been specially ordered to serve as conduits of a message

Guided by our heuristic device – 'Juba's head' – we look too at

• whether the models of the societies which they have created present women as tough yet nurturing
• how they evaluate the societies in which Africans of the diaspora live and which they – the novelists – must have, by their very presence in them, helped to create
• the extent to which their works indicate a connection between the African-Caribbean and African-America
• whether, if they approach gender relations, the woman is a challenge to the man and likely to be more hardy "driving two or three beaux from the ring"
• whether they are concerned with the re-interpretation of African culture in the New World occasioned by the establishment's onslaught against it

We deal with them in chronological order, Hodge's *Crick Crack Monkey* (1970), and Marshall's *Praisesong for the Widow* (1983). We can assume from Hodge's own words that her work is intended to have a social function. In the article quoted above she says:

I began writing in my adult life, in protest against my education

and the arrogant assumptions on which it rested; that I and my
world were nothing and that to rescue ourselves from nothingness,
we had best seek admission to the world of *their storybook*[7]

What social function does Hodge intend?

Caribbean fiction can help to strengthen our self-image, our
resistance to foreign domination, our sense of oneness of the
Caribbean and our willingness to put energies into the building of
the Caribbean union[8]

And why is this strengthening and resistance necessary?
Because she continues,

Caribbean people suffer great ambivalence regarding their culture
... .We recognise our culture only in a negative, rejecting way: we
see in our people tendencies and characteristics which we regard
as aberrations to be stamped out[9]

How does *Crick Crack Monkey* answer Hodge's charge?

Crick Crack Monkey is set in Hodge's birthplace, Trinidad, in
what seems from the presence of the Americans at the 'base'
and from the absence of any mention of independence
celebrations at school, to be in the pre-independence post war
era, which would be in the late 1940s to late 1950s. The model of
society that Hodge uses is not the yard of C.L.R James' *Minty
Alley* (1936), the village of Claude McKay's *Banana Bottom*,
(1932/33), the upper class of John Hearne's *Voices Under the
Window* (1955), an ethnic group of Naipaul's *Mystic Masseur*
(1957), and later works such as *House for Mr Biswas*, or an area
in the Caribbean mind as in Wilson Harris' *Palace of the Peacock*
(1960). And though the chief spokesperson is a child, Hodge's
Crick Crack Monkey does not, like Michael Anthony's *Year in San
Fernando* (1965), build its model around childhood in Trinidad
and it certainly is not the 'growing up' novel of George
Lamming's *In the Castle of my Skin* (1953). Hodge's first novel,
unlike the first Caribbean novels of the artists above, views the
whole society. Her model is of Trinidad. Clearly she intends to
talk about the total society and some of its institutions.

    Hodge's model of Trinidad is built around two primary units,
Tantie's household in Santa Clara, a non Port of Spain part of
the island and that of Aunt Beatrice in the capital, Port of Spain.

According to Lloyd Braithwaite in his ground-breaking work on Trinidad's social structure, *Social Stratification in Trinidad*,[10] place of residence is an important criterion of social status in that island. Highest value is placed on residence in the capital, Port of Spain, all other areas fall behind, the more rural coming last. Santa Clara is one of the more rural conglomerations. Hodge has in this way made her Trinidad sociologically authentic, close, intimate and real for those whose "self image is to be strengthened". Any native can find himself in this model, though *Crick Crack Monkey* without explicitly saying so is predominantly interested in the African-Trinidadian part of the society. Any native can be informed and therapeut-icised if Hodge has the skills to now fill in the details, isolate the problem and convince him/her of the necessity of action.

Caribbean households rarely appear without children in them. In these two households there are children who, naturally, are to be socialised therein. The openness of the household, at the economically poorer and usually more Afro-oriented part of the society, is a feature of Caribbean life. That the community, and in particular blood kin, should see to the welfare of children and, particularly the distressed, is also part of the culture. This article of faith contributes to the openness of the household. Emigration from one's troubles is also a part of Caribbean life, which adds too to the openness of the household, for children, left behind by parents' flight, have to be nurtured. In accordance with this understanding of Caribbean life, two children are left in Tantie's household when their mother dies and their father chooses to emigrate. There are no customary laws to determine where such abandoned children should be placed. An informal and acrimonious battle could ensue between relatives. It does so in *Crick Crack Monkey* between Tantie, father's sister, and Aunt Beatrice, mother's sister. In the process the two sub-cultures battle and the native whom Hodge wants to inform, gets a dynamic and comparative view of the nature of each. Hodge is filling in the details.

Child shifting is central to this culture of open households. The child is a part of different affective sets and likely to be named by each as the emotions flow. Thus Tee in Tantie's household, is sometimes called Cyntie, but her right name is Cynthia and her younger brother, Toddan, has a right name –

Codrington. In the novel, as in real life, the use of these 'right'
names makes the situation, in which they are used, less familiar.
Tee and Toddan are shifted between the two households – Tee
more than Toddan for she, at the time of the action, is about to
be fitted for life, for high school. In Aunt Beatrice's Port of Spain
household, the children's right names are used and those who
live there, Bernadette, Carol and Jessica, never have their names
changed with the mood or the personality of those addressing
them. Their household is not open: not even the child next door
can speak to – much less play with – these children and those
who enter the household. With the exception of the domestic
helper who has to conform anyway, all share the same culture.

The Santa Clara household does not operate in this way, in it
there is a another resident nephew of Tantie's – Mickey. He has
a whole network of young men hanging about at the bridge
down the road and though they do not actually come into the
home, the children do go out to them with Mickey and are
exposed to their subculture. Here, in the personalities of these
young men, Hodge makes us see very starkly the result of the
socialisation into negation and rejection of Caribbean
experiences to which she alludes in her comments above. These
young men have given themselves names of white movie stars –
Audie Murphy, Rock Hudson, Gary Cooper – and their
conversation is about the content of cowboy movies originating
in the USA. They subject these imports to so little Caribbean
analysis that Krishna, whom by his name we assume to be
Indian, can say:

'An' then the other guys reach, an' then, ol'-man, then yu jus' see
Red-Indian fallin-dong all over the place – ba-da-da-da-da – pretty,
boy, pretty![11]

Several 'uncles', short term paramours of Tantie, pass through
her open household. They too are in an intimate relationship
with the children. They bring presents, chauffeur them and
Tantie here and there, and make enquiries about their
behaviour. Mr Henry's voice is heard as the children shout their
excitement to him; Mr Christopher, the drunk dragged home by
his wife, Miss Terry, passes with his song. Like Mickey's gang
Tantie's household has ethnic Indian connections. Doolarie, a
little Indian girl, sees herself as so much part of household and

is so seen by the children that it takes Aunt Beatrice and her
Port of Spain ways to eject her from a family gathering.
Motherers are a critical part of African-Caribbean life. Whether
they have actually borne children or not, whether the children
in the household are theirs or not, it is a culturally prescribed
duty of women to 'raise' children. Abiding by the truth of the
culture, Hodge puts in her model of the Santa Clara life in
Trinidad, several motherers to whom the children might turn in
times of trouble. Trouble is in this case their kidnapping by their
Aunt Beatrice, who Tantie calls "The Bitch":

> We had clear instructions what to do if The Bitch turned up while
> neither Tantie nor Mickey was there – we were to run over to
> Neighb' Ramlaal-Wife and stay there; and if Neighb' Ramlaal-Wife
> wasn't there we were to go Neighb' Doris or to Tan' Mavis, or
> down to Marva-Mother. Half the street was involved in the
> barricade against The Bitch; (p. 10)

Hodge is describing just about any yard or lower income
residential setting in the English-speaking Caribbean.

The children's social and affective network on Tantie's side
does not stop here. It goes into Pointe d'Espoir, physically and
socially further from Port of Spain. Here was where Ma,
Tantie's mother, lived in her household of several apparently
parentless grandchildren. Here was a network of other Ma's –
Ma-Henrietta, Ma-Josephine, old farming women. Here the
African history and sensibility was clearest:

> Ma said that I was her grandmother come back again. She said her
> grandmother was a tall straight proud woman who lived to an old
> old age and her eyes were still bright like water and her back
> straight like bamboo, for all the heavy-load she had carried on her
> head all her life. The People gave her the name Euphemia or Euph-
> something, but when they called her that she used to toss her head
> like a horse and refuse to answer so they'd had to give up in the
> end and call her by her true-true name ... She couldn't remember
> her grandmother's true-true name. But Tee was growing into her
> grandmother again, her spirit was in me. They'd never bent down
> her spirit and she would come back and come back and come back;
> if only she could live to see Tee grow into her tall proud straight
> grandmother. (p. 19)

Ma passed on with this knowledge of the past, gems, nonsense
verse, stories – the 'nancy stories, we now know have been
carried from West Africa.

No live old people were in the Port of Spain network; there
was no link with an African and slave culture of the past. Here
children slept one to a bed, there was a husband/father and a
mother so insecure about the sub-culture in which she moved
that she was unable to give guides to her daughters concerning
right behaviour. Here was clear the rejection and tendency
towards negatives that Hodge wished to purge from her
society. Though Aunt Beatrice could give no guides to her
daughters concerning how to behave, she was fulsome on what
should be rejected. Among them "niggery-looking dresses"(p.
77), "coolie affairs" (p. 78). Here there was no representation of
the Eastern mix in the Trinidad potpouri – no Ling, the Chinese
grocer of Santa Clara, and no permission for Tee to go back
home to the wedding of the Indian neighbour, Moonie. Here
Tee is seduced into a rejection mode, while herself being
rejected by Port of Spain's middle class culture: her cousins
laugh at her clothes, present her to their friends as "'some lil
relative Mommer found up in the country'" (p. 81), the teachers
at the high school ignore her; she is lost in the maze of kneeling,
genuflecting, standing, reading from a missal, the behaviour of
the Roman Catholic church which now replaces the pentecostal
Sunday school of her Santa Clara life. She begins to reject.

Instead of going to Santa Clara for the school holidays, she
goes with her Port of Spain family to a beach house, complying
with a breach of promise to Tantie. The child who had loved
and defended Santa Clara and its way of life could now be
embarrassed by Tantie's behaviour. Aunt Beatrice did not seem
about to send her home, a situation which could bring Tantie to
"Aunt Beatrice's front door to tell her what was what, the
thought of which gave me [her] an unpleasant shiver" (p. 86),
she therefore took it upon herself to inform her that she would
not be coming home (p. 86). This child for whom the trip from
Santa Clara in the company of the villagers with their pelau and
roti, dalpouri and chicken had been more prized than
Christmas, now sat in the stands beside whom? – an American
tourist; like him watching Carnival as a staged event, and
feeling embarrassed at the memory of "Ramlaal's inelegant

truck into which we used to pile with a herd of neighbours and neighbours' children for the trip to Coriaca to see Carnival there"(p. 86). Tee has not rejected Tantie and Santa Clara for anything tangible: in fact, she finds herself in an unconscious act openly rejecting Aunt Beatrice as well. She "savagely" (p. 93) slaps Aunt Beatrice's hand which she had put out to help her out of the way of a group of night-time merrymakers catching crabs on the beach. Tee has become Cynthia, the middle class African-Trinidadian young woman, who knows only how to reject. Hodge has drawn us to the problem.

The family in Port of Spain, given what we know of the sociology of Trinidad, represents for Hodge the new upwardly mobile African-Trinidadian. They are so new that, unlike with Tantie, there is no live mother/grandmother. All this household had to link them to the past is an old photograph "as faded as a photograph could manage to be" (p. 81) of Elizabeth Helen Carter, an ancestor said to be white. According to R.T. Smith, the sociologist, there is embedded in Jamaican culture a myth of the white father.[12] Zora Neale Hurston had much earlier in her *Tell My Horse* (1938), commented on the fact that upwardly mobile Jamaicans all spoke of their white father. Hurston comments:

> Black skin is so utterly condemned that the black mother is not going to be mentioned or exhibited. You get the impression that these virile Englishmen do not require women to reproduce. They just come out to Jamaica, scratch out a nest and lay eggs to hatch out "pink" Jamaicans.[13]

Trinidad has a plantation history and a history of colonisation by the English. It also had a resident upper class that could trace its genetically pure roots to France. As in Jamaica, the white ancestor would be prized. Hodge gives her Trindadian an ancestress.

Aunt Beatrice has struggled to keep the photograph of the white ancestress alive. She claims that one of her daughters resembles her though, according to Tee, her features are so eroded that any such comparison would be impossible. As defiant of form, as the photograph, is the culture, which Aunt Beatrice wants to hand down to her daughters. What she has helped them to develop instead, and which is very recognisable and which she admits and herself abhors, is a style of relating to her which is ill-mannered, with little consideration, love or respect. They treat each other in like manner. Aunt Beatrice is disappointed in her handiwork and feels rejected by her daughters. There is very little affect coming from her resident husband, Uncle Norman, who in *Crack Crack Monkey* has less apparent involvement with the family than Tantie's short term mates. It is into this island of rejection that Tee has graduated. Out of touch with Tantie, she does not know that Ma, her grandmother, has died; that she has been calling for her; that she had finally remembered her grandmother's name which she had wanted Tee to add to her names so that she could "come back and come back and come back".[14] Tantie, assuming that Ma was now part of what Tee rejected, had not bothered to remember this 'true-true' name.

Whether of his own accord or on advice from Tantie, Tee's father sends for his children. The attitude towards her changes in Port of Spain, "my standing was that of a pariah who had suddenly inherited a title". She was going away; she had someone significant abroad. Her cousins now spoke of her to their friends as a first cousin who was so bright and had come first in her form. Her teacher was eager to talk to her "with the same besotted expression she had on her face when she probed some girls in the class with questions about their mummies and daddies". To be able to get away from home, from Trinidad, from Jamaica, from the Caribbean is a truth of the upwardly mobile African-Caribbean person that Hodge has presented in her work. Emigration, this ultimate form of rejection, is viewed differently by the two aunts.

Tantie was a weeping drunk at Tee's farewell party and when Mickey had planned to go to the USA on a short course to better himself she had raved and questioned the need for Mickey to migrate:

> 'Wha you put up-there, yu put some-ting up-there? Me ain' know what you understan it have up-there – it ain' have no blasted Heaven here but it ain' have that no-whe'-is allabout have ketch-arse – any damn place yu is you does have to haul yu arse out the bed when the mornin' come; yu vest does ha' to wash, yu ears does get wax an' if yu ain' shit yu belly does hurt yu. Me ain' know if you think yu does come different like if yu cross-over the blasted Jordan or what.' (p. 64)

Nevertheless, Tantie had signed the papers that allowed him to go for he was underage, and though she had then claimed that only God and His Mother could get her to send Tee and Toddan to their father in the "Golden Gates", she seemed to have instigated their departure in much the same way as she had acquiesced in sending Tee to live with her Aunt Beatrice, when she won the government exhibition. There was something which Tantie, the old way incarnate, knew she could not fight. Tee with no fight at all was eager to leave Trinidad and the confusion, the rejection and consequent nothingness into which the tug-of-war between the two orientations in the culture had pulled her. Hodge fingers the nub of the problem and situation, which defeat Tantie. It is the education system, which for Hodge produces this negative state in Tee and brings into being a force before which Tantie is forced to surrender. This education system encourages its products into an unreality, a fairy tale world.

Women are everywhere felt to be the earliest and the crucial socialisers of the nation's young. Hodge must feel this way too or at least be aware that this is felt to be so, for in her critique of the socialising institutions in Trinidad, it is the women, Tantie and Aunt Beatrice, on whom she has chosen to focus. She takes us too to the basic school – Miss Hinds' school – where Tee learns nonsense words totally unrelated to her experience or that of anybody else:

> Gen Terjesus me kan mile
> Loo kupon thy little chile
> Pi teemy impliss City
> Suh fumee to come to thee (p. 27)

where the child's attempt to make sense of these sounds renders "impliss", a qualifier of the word City. Here too we see the potential of the unveiled and malicious gossip and the prejudice of those supervising the young in the school system to sully the reputation of their households, and to alienate them from their primary carers. Tantie knows of the evils of the system but she also knows that education is the route to social mobility for her precious children. What can she do about it? This is the challenge that *Crick Crack Monkey* puts to the readers in the social psychological set of which its inventor is a part.

The question is posed in such a way that all can be convinced of the need for action. So much of *Crick Crack Monkey* is sociological analysis, with serious applied possibilities, perhaps intended, yet its content is as available to the man in the street as it is to the education specialist, for Hodge has produced a facsimile of Trinidad/Caribbean in the native style. *Crick Crack Monkey* is not only written in the vernacular but employs the popular Trinidadian style of orature, the calypso. The long established art form of the lower income Trinidadian, the calypso takes sensitive societal issues into the public arena and makes them accessible to general discussion by presenting them in the language of the people and from their most comical perspective. Can a woman steal a man from another woman as is often claimed? The acceptance of this possibility brings disquiet into the community and into the people's parliament.

> Good morning, is Miss Santa living here
> Yes, Yes is me.
> Well a woman make a complaint to me
> That you tief she man from she
> An as a police is mi bounden duty
> To charge you with larceny.
> You see, Santa take this big man from St James
> And tie him like her cow in Mouvant
> Sun and rain wetting the man and he can't get away poor fella
> Sun and rain wetting the man and he can't get away poor fella.[15]

In the midst of the laughter, each person quietly absorbs the tragedy. In like manner Hodge through Tantie brings the quintessential problem of the Trinidad society into discussion. Tantie disapproves of Mrs Hinds' school and through her we disapprove of the educational system in Trinidad, yet in the absence of better,

> We marched down to Mrs Hinds, Tantie muttering all the way her disapproval and disgust blasted government would'n build school for the chirren what the blasted government there for but to build school for the chirren now look my cross I have to put the chile by these shitters all they know is to run behind Revern' arse an' he wife smell every fart they blow when it was black-arse Reverend Joseph God res' he soul they used to find their arse to Hell up in Coriaca Church on a Sunday morning me I would shit on all o'

them jus' you remember you going there to learn book do' let them
put no blasted shit in yu head. (p. 22)

We collapse with laughter but we feel Tantie's question, how
can our children get their education without having the system
put "blasted shit" in their heads. This is the question which
Merle Hodge's calypso puts to her audience.

Hodge does focus on Juba. They are tough, nurturing, it is
they rather than their men whom we see on the battlefront.
Clearly the female characters which spring out of the head of
Hodge, this African-Trinidadian born in 1944, as seen in her
first novel *Crick Crack Monkey*, project the image of Juba carried
over from Africa. But this inherited native toughness is severely
challenged according to Hodge's work, by New World
conditions. We see tough-tough Tantie collapsing under it, into
drunkenness as she caves in and allows her children to go off to
the "Golden Gate" (p. 64); we see the warrior Tee bent by it. It
was a common practice in the West Indies and elsewhere, as we
saw in the first lecture, for the enslaved to be stripped of their
name and assigned any name that suited the fancy of the
master. Ma's grandmother, the oldest of Hodge's Jubas, was
tough enough to force "The People" to call her by her "true-
true" (p. 19) name. Ma was reverential towards this behaviour
and wanted to perpetuate it into the current generation. It was
her hope that Tee would be that tough-tough Juba whose
"spirit" they could never "bend down": Tee's initial promise
did not mellow into that woman; the socialisation system which
came with progress did not allow her to be.

The real 'Bitch' that railroaded the juba-ness of Tee and Tantie
was not Aunt Beatrice, whom Tantie had thus named: it was the
system of values, which was encouraged by the way the
education system functioned. This Hodge shows us clearly, she
not only analyses her society but shows us what has to be
changed. In this analysis we are left wondering, where does the
sense of being part of Africa of the diaspora leave us, for Tee
fails to be a Juba and the link with the African past is
irrevocably broken when Ma dies without passing on the 'true-
true' name and the essence of her personality to Tee. That
Hodge makes this breach so poignant indicates that she sees
this break with Juba as psychically significant and tempts us to
think that it is so at the personal as well as the fictional level.

The fact remains, despite the fictional and possibly the author's personal sadness at this thwarted transmission of Juba-ness, that Hodge has presented us with a broken link. In her calypso style of having us weep or laugh our own way to the cerebral conclusion, Hodge seems to want us Caribbean people to understand that a new self is needed for our time, and that we had better begin to create it.

In a similarly calypso way Hodge makes powerful statements about the role of men in the Caribbean by making them marginal to her narrative. Uncle Norman, the one husband in the work adds little more than a cheops to any discussion and but for his driving Aunt Beatrice here and there we would think him part of the grave. Mrs Hinds' husband is little more than a ghost. He had gone up to England, fought in the war, nearly became a lawyer and is so removed from the reality of those he calls "little black nincompoops" (p. 29) that circumstances force him to teach for a living, that the picture of Winston Churchill, to which they refer as "Crapud-Face", is virtually God's image for him. Hodge makes these men uncomfortable misfits in the lives of their women. The most active and comfortable mates are Tantie's temporary consorts: we at least see them giving a watch to Toddan, giving Tantie gold teeth and giving pep talks to the children. Are these women challenges to their men? Do two or three tire before this Juba leaves the ring? It would seem so. We leave *Crick Crack Monkey* with the feeling that the male role and particularly men's relationships with women and children within the household in Hodge's part of the African diaspora is underdeveloped and this whether he be a resident and legitimate husband/father or not. Is there a message here that the instrument of change will have to be the women, that we will have to revolutionise ourselves to deal with our present and the need for change?

Marshall's *Praisesong for the Widow* is not, like Hodge's *Crick Crack Monkey*, located within a national boundary: it is located in the Africa of the diaspora, and this, in its spiritual manifestation as well as its physical.[16] Without her words it is not possible to know whether Marshall intended her work to have a socially therapeutic function. The end product however, fits nicely into an argument for the celebration of black consciousness. On the last two pages (pp. 255-256) Marshall has her heroine, Avey, committed to spreading the word concerning the need for blacks to (re)connect with their racial past. She is now eager to cooperate with the missionising zeal of her last daughter Marion, whose populist black power stance had hitherto annoyed her. This middle class African-American widow went to Carriacou, an island in the Caribbean, and there made a spiritual connection and reconciliation with her racial past. On her return home she intended to spread the word concerning the necessity for re-connection:

> on the street corners and front lawns in (her) small section of North White Plains. And the shopping mall and train station. As well as the canyon streets and office buildings of Manhattan. She would haunt the entrance ways of the skyscrapers (p. 250)

She would establish a summer camp for passing on knowledge to black children about their ancestors.

This middle class black woman is going to be a 'witness' passing the message at street corners. That her middle class readership can identify with this eccentric behaviour is due to Marshall's skilful suggestion that re-connection is vitally necessary to the mental health of all black people no matter how far up the social and economic ladder they may be. Her skill in convincing us of this, leaves us with the impression that she, like her heroine, is herself a committed Juba, a female intellectual knowing and feeling a sense of connection with Africa and inspired into guiding others towards this path. Marshall captures our empathy for her heroine and her family and her heroine's subsequent political position, by making them a typical and very believable unit, like us her black readers, having middle class strivings. Thus we see ourselves in these people, fighting our way through the system and thus we enter easily into therapy and healing with the heroine.

We meet the heroine on a ship in the Caribbean Sea, on a pleasure cruise which has gone sour for her, and she has decided to return home to New York. We see her packing, having decided to disembark when the ship docks in Grenada and from there to find her way home. In Grenada she accepts the invitation of an old Carriacouan man to go home with him to a celebration in honour of the ancestral spirits. There she is re-born into a sense of her African-ness, which she had long been resisting. Through this woman's musings we see black life in lower income New York, rural black life among the Gullah of South Carolina and we see life in the black Caribbean. Marshall makes us see a cultural entity, Africa of the diaspora, an area which defies physical boundaries.

The characters Marshall puts into this world are Avey Johnson whom we follow as a young childless wife through to her life as a widow. We see her husband J - Jerome Johnson - and the family they made. We see Avey's travelling companions - Thomasina Moore, a light skinned aggressive middle class African-American woman and Clarissa, the bullied. We see Lebert Joseph, a 90 year old Carriacouan who helps Avey to find her way to her ancestors and we see several warm Carriacouans led by Lebert Joseph's daughter, Rosalie Parvay. Very important to this collection is the picture of a black couple en route to the middle class. We meet its joylessness and we meet the African-oriented culture of the island of Carriacou. *Praisesong for the Widow* like *Crick Crack Monkey* pits two cultures against each other. Here, however, there is a clear winner - the socially inclusive Afro-oriented culture, which transcends national boundaries and links New World blacks with Africa. In shifts between states of mind and between places and times, Marshall takes the reader through the joyless middle class North White Plains living room back to the winning pleasures of honeymoon in black lower-income jazz-filled Brooklyn, USA, into Tatem, South Carolina, and the arms of the African culture of rural South Carolina, and forward to Carriacou and the embrace of the Caribbean people, who live this culture.

The psychic journey is the device Marshall uses to show us the black continent which New World slavery had established and which she seems to be inviting contemporary blacks to recognise and to claim. The journey begins in Tatem, South Carolina, USA. About this region, John Henrik Clarke says:

The sea islands of Georgia and the Carolinas, like most islands, are cultural incubators and containers ... The lack of contact with the mainland helped to preserve some of the important features of the African culture. Because the Africans were not sold and resold as often as those on the mainland, some of their ancestral family patterns remain to this day.[17]

In this part of the African diaspora in the USA, lies the myth referred to as Ibo Landing. In Paule Marshall's *Praisesong for the Widow*, the acceptance of this myth is an act of faith and empathy with the racial past of Africans of the diaspora. According to this myth, a shipload of Ibos was brought to this area, which John Henrik Clarke describes. As pure Africans they could "see in more ways than one" (p. 37), according to Marshall's fiction. Brought on to the shores of the USA, with one look they knew that it was a socially unhealthy place. They turned around, chains and all, and not bothering to take the small boats that had shuttled them to the shore from the ship, they pressed on through the water.

> When they got to the ship, they didn't so much as give it a look ... They feet was gonna take 'em wherever they was going that day ... When they realised there wasn't nothing between them and home but some water and that wasn't giving them no trouble, they got so tickled they started in to singing (p. 39)

The father of Avey, Marshall's heroine, had roots in this area. Not everyone even in this area had the faith to accept this myth. It was so accepted by the grandmother of Avey's father's great aunt, Aunt Cuny who intends to pass it on. Avey is to be the vehicle of transmission and was so selected even before she was born. Aunt Cuny had sent to tell her pregnant parents that she would be a girl and that she should be named Avatara after Aunt Cuny's faith-keeping grandmother. She had insisted that at age seven the child be sent to her in Tatem every summer for a month. Avey at age ten showed lack of faith in the myth, she asks of these Africans walking home on the sea: "But how come they didn't drown, Aunt Cuny?" (p. 39). Aunt Cuny's response to this expression of doubt, was one which disturbed this heiress-apparent to the faith throughout her life.

> Slowly standing on the consecrated ground, her height almost matching her shadow which the afternoon sun had drawn out over the water at their feet, her greataunt had turned and regarded her in silence for a long time ..."Did it say Jesus drowned when he went walking on the water in that Sunday School book your Momma always sends you with?"(pp. 39-40)

For Aunt Cuny the revering of and the faith that there was

righteousness in the ancestors and their behaviour, is a religion second to none. Avey's distress at her inability to share Aunt Cuny's faith, to accept the myths of her own racial group and by extension, to accept her group, manifests itself in a nightmare, which she has on her pleasure cruise. In this nightmare, she is in a nasty fist fight with her Aunt Cuny. It is in Carriacou that the resolution of her problem with Aunt Cuny and her faith come to her.

This is an island 13 square miles in area. It is the largest of a string of tiny islands called the Grenadines and is politically part of Grenada. Like the sea islands of the coast of Georgia and South Carolina, Carriacou was a producer of sea-island cotton through the medium of enslaved Africans. Shortage of labour after Emancipation had caused several estates in the Caribbean to import free labour from Africa and the Orient. In Carriacou this need did not exist. Thus the Carriacou culture remained virtually unchanged. In this regard, as we have heard from John Henrik Clarke, it resembles the sea islands of Georgia and the Carolinas. A part of Carriacou's long standing culture is the ancestor cult called the Big Drum. This is a ceremony in which live members of the clan pay respect to the 'Old Family'. It is at this ceremony that Avey makes her peace with Aunt Cuny.

The social anthropologist M.G. Smith tells us that in Carriacou:

> the important kinship units are individual families and larger groups of kinsfolk who trace their relationship to one another through the male commonly to a depth of three or four generations.[18]

He further tells us that this kinship system remains in the face of the British rules concerning naming and illegitimacy, for it is the 'blood' of the male in the veins of a person, not the status of the relationship between the cohabiting couple, that establishes status in the clan. This is, he says, a patrilineal group, rarely so well-defined anywhere else in the English-speaking Caribbean. Whether she had prior knowledge of this or not, Marshall does write this anthropology into her fiction: that Carriacouans are going home to celebrations in their respective families is clear; that he, a male, is the head of the clan, with which he has invited Avey to celebrate, is clear to us in the actions and the words of Lebert Joseph. Smith further states that Carriacou had no large estates, thus an absence of cleavages between folk and elite. Carriacou, this island, obviously approaches the classless society of small farmers and fisherfolk each revering its own ancestor, each in agreement with the other that this should be. This part of the anthropologist's view of Carriacou society appears too in Marshall's *Praisesong for the Widow*, and heightens the pathos of the struggle of the African-American couple to move through the pluralities of class and race to middle class status within their society. The people of Carriacou, like the people everywhere in the Caribbean, journey out to more economically attractive labour but these return for the ceremonial big drum. It is these people returning home to beg pardon of their ancestors that set Avey on the path to reconciliation with Aunt Cuny and an appreciation of the myth of the landing of the Ibos.

Marshall in her creation of Avey and of Avey's association with Lebert Joseph helps us, the reader, to take a fairly smooth step from Tatem, South Carolina, to Carriacou in the West Indies, for Avey, like the Carriacouans, feels a patrilineage. It is her father, who even after transportation from Tatem in the plantation South to the industrial North of the USA, remains the rice-eating Gullah; it is through him that the faith-keeping females make the link between Avey and the old ancestors. So, in this patrilinearity and this respect for the ancestors, Carriacou could be Tatem. Marshall pushes other identicals through the behaviour of the old women. The old mothers at Tatem's church nurture and support the church rituals with their 'amens'; with their looks they guide the acolyte in the crossover from sin to saving. Here in her own transition to saving, Marshall's Avey relives in dream-state her near vomiting during a church sermon and finds the actuality on the boat on which she is crossing over to Carriacou; finds the old women with whom she sits, aware, like the mothers of the Tatem church, of their nurturing function, silently taking charge of her, and with their wordless sounds encouraging her to expel the sinful contents of her inside, binding her body when diarrhoea takes over and guiding her, now weak, to a place of rest, to the psycho-physical space where a new life will begin. The women of Tatem and of Carriacou are one and the same.

There are parallels too in the act of excursion. As with the Carriacouans, the excursions by boat on the Hudson river which Avey's father used to take her on as a child, are family affairs. As here on the boat in the Caribbean, there are groups of families celebrating the same intention – "to lay claim" (p. 112) *"We gonna put on our robes and shout all over God's heaven"* (p. 192). Carriacouans, Marshall tells us, take this excursion, not only to beg pardon of their ancestors ceremonially, but to tend to their farms, family land, to lay claim. Marshall puts these connections between Carriacouans and the people of Tatem, South Carolina, in a wider African scenario. The reader is urged towards translating the commonalities between the two places and peoples into African sensibilities, by the descriptive vocabulary which the author uses. The lines on Lebert Joseph's face, for instance, are etched "like scarification marks of a thousand tribes" (p. 161).

Her characters too, express deep emotions through this medium:

> He would lie within her like a man who has suddenly found himself in a temple of some kind, and hangs back, overcome by the magnificence of the place, and sensing around him the invisible forms of the deities who reside there: Erzuli with her jewels and gossamer veils, Yemoja to whom the rivers and the seas are sacred; Oja, first wife of the thunder god and herself in charge of winds and rains (p. 127)

This particular one was Avey's husband's experience of making love to her.

The central action in *Praisesong for the Widow* is Avey's re-connection with her past, and we can't help but wonder here whether Hodge's Tee, when her teenager turns into widowed 50-plus, will not be on the same journey. There are parallels in the world invented by the two novelists which tease us into such a thought – the power of the aunt in the socialisation of the child, for one. Tee grew with aunts both of whom felt that the shaping of her life was their business and we do feel that they would have felt this way, even if her parents were around. We don't know what circumstance made Aunt Cuny so powerful in the life of Avey's father that she could be allowed to name his daughter and to claim her for a month every summer. Marshall leaves us with the fact that she was a powerful great aunt. The powerful aunt is an African-Caribbean truth and obviously an African-American one as well. The linkage of the situation invented by Marshall and that invented by Hodge out of their understanding of their particular culture, to West Africa where the aunt is the kingmaker, the Queen Mother, is inescapable. Whether consciously or not, the female Barbadian-African-American and the African-Trinidadian are operating within the same article of African sensibility transported to the diaspora, and it is possible to see rejecting Tee as a younger version of the faith-finding Avey.

The importance of name is another parallel between them. Hodge's Ma refuses to answer to the name the "people" gave her and insists on being called by her 'true-true' name, which name apparently carries one's essence; for in Hodge's invention, Ma's capacity to resist being bent by others is to be passed on to Tee, the modern day Juba-to-be along with the name. Similarly, Aunt Cuny wants to and manages to get Avey to be named after her myth-preserving grandmother. Marshall also lets Avey's husband, after he has changed his character, change the name he is called and used to call himself. That names carry one's character and attach one to a group past and to a social burden, occurs in several cultures and is very much a part of West and East African understandings. Here is another article of African consciousness which, deliberately used or otherwise, links the minds of Hodge and Marshall and makes them both to some extent or the other, Jubas. Both women also treat this racial past with reverence, though they seem to differ in the part it must play in the present and the future. Hodge seems to say 'forget it' while Marshall says 'hang on to it'.

Further parallels exist. They are there in these novelists' treatment of old women, for instance. Both Ma, Tee's grandmother and Tantie, but more particularly the older of these two, is a tough-tough Juba, recognising and in the more extreme case, refusing to give up her African identity. Avey's father's female ancestors, Aunt Cuny and her grandmother, play the same part, refusing to give up their connection with Africa. These old women are determined persons: they are determined, and more explicitly those in Hodge's case, to re-create African selves in a new generation of women. The two works also share their sense of women and particularly old women as nurturers. It is with respect to men's role in the lives of women that we find the greatest divergence. Hodge's middle aged women are Jubas – they tire out and out-perform men, and men's contribution to the life of the group is inconsequential. Marshall turns all of this around. Avey is powerful enough to get her husband to change his lifestyle but Marshall puts a negative on this power. She makes it clear to us that this woman has, by this action, played Eve: she has sinned. For this among other acts, she needs expiation and the re-creation, which is the major burden of *Praisesong for the Widow*. In fact the title of this book is misleading, for Marshall's work is as much about the widow's husband as it is about the widow, and though the praise might be sung by the widow, it certainly is sung to men among others. To this extent Marshall's heroine fails to be a Juba as per the heuristic device we have created, for Marshall this is no failure, for her notion of Juba invokes a pair. "I needs a partner. The Juba calls for a pair" are words Marshall puts into Lebert Joseph's mouth (p. 180) and we are left to believe that the "pair" could be a man and a woman as Lebert Joseph and herself, though he does explain that the Juba is a woman's dance.

Understandably, an important entity in Marshall's *Praisesong for the Widow*, not seen at all in Hodge's *Crick Crack Monkey*, is the dyad – the male and female in interaction in a family setting. We see each in Marshall's invention, trying to cope with life but the concerns of one is never paramount to the concerns of the dyad. We see the transformation of Jay, Avey's husband, through the dressing and undressing metaphors which Marshall uses and we also note that it is Jay rather than Avey who first gives credence to the story handed down in Avey's family about Ibo landing. She told him the story expecting him to treat it as a joke but his response was:

I'm with your Aunt Cuny ... I believe it Avey. Every word. (p. 145)

It is Jay whom we see involved with black culture. It is he whom we see listening to jazz, dancing, being funny. It is he whose life is sacrificed, whose death releases Avey from a course towards which she had badgered him into taking their lives; it is his decease that releases her into a "tabla rasa", into "walking on a flawless apron of sand, not a footstep to be seen" (p. 153), walking towards a new and more palatable history which another man helps her to write. *Praisesong for the Widow* bigs up Lebert Joseph, the 90 year old man with the "door slightly ajar"(p. 157) and through which "opening there came a cool dark current of air like a hand extended in welcome" (p. 157). Avey took this hand, which eventually led her to a reconciliation with the spirits of her ancestors and the understanding, which she now wishes to broadcast – that an acceptance of your African forefathers is necessary to your social-psychological peace; that your ancestors of the African diaspora ought to be revered and that there is a continent of black consciousness that we all can plug into and be healed. It was a position for which her own father, who had left Tatem, South Carolina, but not its blackways, had prepared her to take. Marshall's blackmen are central to the lives of their women.

In her treatment of black society, Marshall invites us to a conclusion that is different from that of Hodge. Is there a place for both in the thinking of us who are the new generation and will make the next generation? Can we forget the past and press on with new creations as Hodge seems to be saying? Seems to me we can do both. The Tee in us can go back, as Avey did, to find our true-true name and after this journey, thus armed, do what we feel has to be done to make our world a better place. One of the tasks, that seem to await us, is the transforming of Juba from the competitive being who tires out and discards her men, into the image presented by Marshall – a part of a pair, a woman dancing in tune with her mate, waiting and being waited for by her partner. Can we mark out a path for Tantie by which she may get education for her precious children without them having to absorb mess? Can Aunt Beatrice stop badgering Uncle Norman into nothingness? Can Miss Santa and that unnamed woman stop feeling that they can haul and pull that man from St James to Mouvant and instead have dialogue with him concerning the development of appropriate forms of expressing and maintaining loving relationships between men and women?

April 1997

WRITING YOUR VILLAGE HISTORY – THE CASE OF WOODSIDE

7

Mon say Christopher Columbus discover on yah
But I say Christopher Columbus find dreadlocks on ya.
Him go again, him come again,
Bring Babylon on ya.

The Rastafarian brethren of the Twelve Tribes of Israel airing this song in the 1975 could hardly have read Van Sertima's *They Came Before Columbus* (1976), yet they knew that the African presence in the New World predated that of the European. And I have often heard my African-American colleagues saying of Bob Marley's 'Buffalo Soldiers', "Where did he get that piece of information? So few people know about these buffalo soldiers". Imagination and meditation can do a lot. Jamaican wisdom holds that, "Anything black people say, if it nuh go so, it nearly go so". What black people say, as a result of applying imagination and meditation to an issue, given the paucity of records for a conventional history of us, we should perhaps accordingly see as hypotheses to be tested, as leads to be followed in writing our family and local history, for it might "nearly go so". It is with this taking-what-my-black people said seriously that I started the research into my own village history. It is a path that I am recommending to you. I began with the myths circulating in my village and I want to show you how using them as an entry into the past can unearth data towards the reconstruction of the history of our myth-makers and myth-keepers and how it has provided me with a case history of the relationship between the enslaved and their master, between the plot and the plantation, between the big and the little traditions.

I believe that our emotional relationship to the space about which we want to write, colours our approach to the work. It was so in my case. Let me therefore share with you the highlights of my sentimental relationship with my village for I know that the research process which I recount here is intimately tied up with my motives for undertaking the project and that this desire, to write my village's history through the myths it holds, had its beginnings very early in my existence. My village is called Woodside. It is in St Mary, one of the north-easterly parishes of Jamaica.

My parents, moving to this village only months before my birth, naturally did not inherit a large support group. My father had come at the invitation of his big sister who was also a stranger in this village. She had come to teach and after a very short time had settled into marriage and house-keeping with a man whose father had been a late arrivant into the village. My father's brother had taught here too but he was leaving and it is his holding that was to form the base of my father's agricultural concern. This concern was not much, for having found the money to buy the house and the land, there was nothing left to do anything else.

Three months after she 'dropped me' in the house on the spot on which I now live, my mother, seeing the writing on the wall, returned to the profession she had left to be a housewife, and took a job teaching outside of the village. She took my sister, three years older than I, with her. It was the happy coincidence of the mailvan or the breadvan, heading for these parts when she was on her break, that took her back to home and to me. My father meantime was trying his hand at several little businesses in order to get some cash. All of these took him away from his new home and from me, for objectively shorter times than my mother, yes, but for me, too long. Today he was a lumber salesman; tomorrow a salesman of patent medicines and the day after a little court-reporting. I was left with servants, new to the family, and occasionally with my aunt.

"Mr and Mrs Sippi made me feel at home", says the singer. The village, my one constant presence didn't come in to hug me. Miss Rachel for instance, the nana who had brought me into the world, didn't seem to feel the need to take a caring relationship further and swept her silent self past me as if I was nothing more than a tree. She knew that the navel string she had severed had been planted in the yard under the blue bell tree, a tree which strangely enough gave forth white bell flowers; she must have said, "Now you are planted here, be no more stranger, fend for yourself". It was I, I saw, not my mother and father, new to the place, nor the people of the place, who would have to make the effort to get to know and make a companion of this place, this presence into which I was thrust. I had to get to know the village on my own. My research into the history of my birthplace began. I had to listen, for young and terribly ill, I couldn't walk, nor talk, much less read or ask questions. I heard Mass Richard Walker's son, Mass Cecil blowing a mournful horn upon the hill; Mass John Hermitt's song as he accompanied himself on his guitar:

Oh what a shame/she has lost her name/don't know who to blame/making a fame with shango bachelor.

I used my nose to acquaint me with the place: the smell of the cedar trees. The hurricane of 1944 brought me a new life. My mother got a job at the local school and my father's journeys out lessened too. I was now part of my family and very happy, but I never forgot my old companion Woodside, now my friend. I continued to get to know her. Why were there so many ferns at this section of my place? Some people must have lived here long ago. And this rock-house, large enough to hold a bed, did some-body long ago, on the run like Rhygin, rub his lode-stone for luck here as he hid from his pursuers?[1] There were a million such questions in my head concerning my village and her past. I listened.

Some answers lay in the oral traditions – in the songs, in the foundation myths, in the language, in the style of walking and talking and generally what of themselves the people about me chose to retain. I stored the questions Woodside forced me to ask and what answers she could give me until the resources came for my historical treatment. The resources came as I grew, in little bits but did come, allowing me to attempt some 50 years after my birth, a passable history built from what my village had told me about herself, a history which I hoped would go into the elementary school; for I had come to believe by then in the therapeutic value of knowing one's history. The history motivated by love, has been written. It is called *Woodside, Pear Tree Grove P.O.* If your experience with your place has been like mine, an emotional one, you have no choice but to pay attention to what your "black people sey" and go on and write that village or family history. A good place to start, as I did, is with the myths.

There are four clearly articulated traditions in Woodside. In historical order they are: the myth of the Spanish occupation; the myth of the haughty slave mistress; the myth of the body-less tomb; and the myth of the founding mother. It is with the second and third that, given my leaning after formal tertiary education towards oral history and archival history, I have been able to work. I present them, interwoven and my interaction with them below, an interaction which subsequently developed into a history.

The Myth of the Haughty Slave Mistress and of the Body-Less Tomb

The story is told that Woodside was an estate owned by a slave mistress who was very haughty – the word 'haughty' or the word 'proud' is usually used to describe her. When she got married, goes the story, a red carpet was spread from a gate called "pillar gate" for about two chains to the present site of the Anglican church which was where the house she was to live in was situated. She was so haughty that she had to put on gloves to take money from her slaves. However, she came down so low that she had to walk about the district with a calabash bowl begging salt from her ex-slaves. Her husband, 'young' Neilson went to England and died (at sea), there is a monument in the churchyard to him. No body is in it. Mrs Neilson's son was a 'drunkareddy' who sold off hunks of the Woodside property and drank off the money that he got for the estate's lands. He predeceased his mother.

I grew up hearing this story into which the two myths are collapsed, and was very familiar with the monument which was in the church/school that I attended for the first 11 years of my life. In the past two years I have heard much the same tale from people older and younger than I with the occasional embellishment, such as that Mrs Neilson used to eat lizards and that she was reduced to surviving on bananas roasted by a man with the largest possible leg ulcer, one who apparently in her heyday would not have dared to get near to her. My focussed thinking began with my bother about these two intertwined myths.

What bothered me about these myths, was why a group of people would keep on handing them down and in the kind of detail that made you see a lonely deranged woman asking for pity, yet tell the tale with so little pity. There is no word that

Mrs Neilson was responsible for the whipping of any slave or any other kind of physical distress normally associated with bad treatment of people during slavery. Instead, she is accused of the eye-pass: being proud and disdainful towards her enslaved workers. What was the norm attending the relationship between mistress and slave? Did Mrs Neilson flout this? The answer to this, required that I see the people around me as myth-makers and myth-preservers and that I look closely at them in this role and look at their relationship with the site of the tale and the characters in the tale. I would have to look at the social action on the Woodside estate during slavery. The scribal and the oral had to meet to interrogate these related myths.

My concentrated research into the history of Woodside began with a recorded interview of Mr Vernal Kelly, born 1912, by then one of the oldest residents of Woodside and certainly one of the most knowledgeable concerning this area, having been brought up here and having been a civil servant in and about the area. I needed to define the physical structure of the site of the myths. From Mr Kelly I had got a descriptive outline of the area he saw to be Woodside. His description was based on the Woodside church and the school which was kept in it. This building, it was common knowledge in the village, had been part of the great house to which the red carpet taking the young bride led. Residences of the students who attended this school and of the people who attended this church are what, for Mr Kelly, formed the boundaries of Woodside. Using his definition I approached the school records for the years 1928-1948, the period immediately following the mandatory end of his elementary schooling, where I found that at this time Woodside's boundaries were further afield.

To establish and to date the existence of Woodside, the physical site of the myths, I approached the government archives. The oldest map of the area found there, that of 1804, had nothing to say about Woodside nor any of the place names mentioned in the two parochial sources, except Palmetto Grove and Hopewell, but it had personal names on it, and one that was on the monument – Neilson. There were two such names, but with the help of the map's placement of Palmetto Grove and Hopewell, I was able to identify which Neilson was related to the monument in the Woodside churchyard. No Neilson remains in Woodside today but there were surnames carried by today's residents of Woodside. People in the district who shared the surnames of those on the 1804 map and those mentioned by Mr Kelly, my informant, were now selected as the local 'archives'. It is these people plus the Map Collection at the National Library of Jamaica, the wills, deeds, estate accounts, slave registers and baptismal records at the Island Archives and Public Records Office that help to describe the 'social action', it is the site of the myth. Thanks too to the students and faculty of Gettysburg College, the students of Randolph Macon College who helped the families to describe their family trees.

My return to my village stories, not now as eager listener but as investigator, a return particularly to that about the body-less tomb which had 'no body in it, for the master had died at sea', showed me the following inscription:

> Here lies the body of John Neilson Esq who departed this life XXVth June MDCCC aged LXI years. His widow Frances Maidstone Neilson has erected this marble [undecipherable] mournful testimony of her affection and regret.

And this was the tomb that the tradition claimed had no body in it! Hundreds of us had been visiting the church and its splendid tomb since its construction. Some of us could read. Granted the dates were in roman figures and perhaps difficult to decipher but the definitive phrase "here lies the body" was in plain English. Why had the hundreds of us who had played jacks on that tomb not seen it? Why did the myth-makers and myth-preservers make this mistake? One reason must be that the tale was told with such passion and assurance that a new generation never felt the need to double check. That I think was my position, but the investigator in me now needed a fuller reason for my compliance and for the distortion of history. Analysis of the oral and archival sources eventually made it clear that there were people during slavery who were in a very strong position to feel that they knew the truth about the tomb, people who had the passion and the opportunity to broadcast their version into a tradition.

These records tell us that Frances Maidstone Neilson, on the death of her husband John, names we see on the tombstone, left Jamaica for England in 1801 apparently taking with her the son and heir to the Woodside property, William John Neilson, then only ten years old.[2] The property was left to the care of William Neilson, quite likely the surveyor and resident owner of a property close to today's Carron Hall. William John Neilson returned to Jamaica as a doctor of physic and medicine around 1811 at the age of 21 and, as it was stated in the arrangement with William Neilson that he should, took over responsibility for his inheritance.[3]

John Neilson, William John's father, had been a pretty important man in the area. He was a major in the regiment. The cost of the uniform for this post, met by the occupier, was, according to Brathwaite's *Creole Society*, exorbitant and to get this honourable position, one had to have friends in high places.[4] Quite apart from this, John Neilson is likely to have, with William, the surveyor – who might have been his brother – controlled a run of about a thousand acres stretching in all directions from the property on which the monument to John Neilson lay.[5] At his death John Neilson left buildings and pastures, he had been a big and active man in the area. Young William John would inherit his father's property and social status. That he was a doctor (British-trained, I assume), a captain in the militia since 1817 and an assistant judge from 1811-1827 would add to his importance.[6]

Thanks to Haiti's problems with its revolution, Jamaicans could now profit from coffee production. By 1806, as one of the maps consulted shows, the Neilson lands were into coffee and before long William John had made his Woodside plantation into the largest coffee estate around.[7] What happened to this young master, this medical doctor, this magistrate would be news. His marriage choice would have been news. William John had died by 1829.[8] He was no more than 40 years old. The death of a young man of his status would be news; it would leave a hole in the social class of which he was a part.

William John died at the time when emancipation was in the air. The notion was exercising both blacks and whites, both masters and slaves. Enslaved labour was what the planters built their business on; it was not a light thing to them that enslaved people as well as important British thinkers, who could make their case before a British government which ruled them all, were thinking like the enslaved, that they should be emancipated. The position their master William John took on the issue was crucial to the enslaved people of Woodside, whether he lived or died was crucial to their future. If he was against their freedom, would a more sympathetic master come with his death? If he was on their side, would his successor be like him? William John's death would be carried in the heart and the memories of the enslaved; it would be part of what marked time for them. The circumstances surrounding his decease would live on in their memories.

William John made his will in December of 1828 and he was dead by June of 1829.[9] He was a doctor; he probably knew that he was very ill, could die from his illness and should organise life for his dependents by disposing of his property through the medium of a will. He may also have thought that he could safeguard their future by saving his life. He had studied abroad, had contacts with England where his mother had gone after her husband's death and where he sold his coffee, and he could afford to go for treatment there. It is quite possible that he went off to find a cure and died on the way, died at sea according to the village legend. His wife Jane Eliza was pregnant in December of 1828 with her seventh child, all under 21 years old. In 1833 when her under-aged daughter, the eldest child, is about to be married, only 6 children are mentioned.[10] This pregnancy must have been aborted or died in infancy. It is hardly likely that Jane Eliza, pregnant, miscarrying or with a newly born babe would leave her many children to attend her husband in England or wherever he might have gone by sea to seek treatment.

William John had been close to his mother. They had quite likely been in England together in his school years and on his return, she was definitely in Woodside, going with him and his wife to weddings in the area and keeping her own set of slaves and no doubt household.[11] It is my suspicion that it was Mrs Frances Neilson, Senior who accompanied William John to seek medical attention and came back with 'no body'. This is what Woodside's enslaved people knew and had to know – that the master had died away from home and that his body was not returned to Woodside. But why did they believe that the monument was raised to his memory?

It is inconceivable that the slaves milling around his house during William John Neilson's lifetime had not, in the normal business of the day, noticed the splendid polished marble tomb with its removable top. If the 'monument' was around at this time, it would have been known to house someone other than Dr Neilson. Clearly the monument was not there then but was built close to the time when he died. Frances, who was around until at least 1832, must have at this time given her husband's grave its splendid tomb,[12] put ofcourse in the yard where he had lived, had been buried nearly 30 years before, and where her deceased son had recently lived. For those who didn't know where the old master, husband of Frances and father of William John, probably called John by the family, was buried, the tomb would have been built for their recently deceased master of Woodside.

William John, when he returned to Jamaica to enter into his inheritance, had reorganised his estate physically and it seems given its name to his reorganised and expanded patrimony. I say this because whereas an 1806 map, the earliest pictorial reference we can find to the Neilsons as land owners, does name the area by which their land is bounded by its estate name, the Neilson property is referred to as "In coffee by Mr Neilson".[13] This "Mr Neilson" would ofcourse not be William John who was at this time, 1806, a child, possibly in England with his mother. Ten years later, in 1817 William John acquires Alexander Wright's property.[14] He might also at this time have built his marvellous pillar gate surviving into the 1960s, the like of which is seen nowhere else in the immediate area. Now too, William John Neilson's property, referred to as Woodside, and its gate, have become markers: the deed to the 100 acres bought from Wright is described by reference to the 'Woodside Gate'. This property bounded by the road passing Petersfield to Palmetto Grove on one side and a "rivulet running into the Rio Sambre on the other"[15] came to William John with its enslaved workers and we recognise it today as the John Crow Hill-Jumper area. These workers, as I shall later show, might not have known of father John Neilson's death and burial in 1800.

William John, also in 1819, swopped with James Deans 25 acres in the area between Carron Hall and Palmetto Grove for an area between Hopewell and Palmetto Grove.[16] The same could be said for this group of enslaved workers, living even further away from the spot where his father John had been buried, if any slaves did come with this small run of land.

Beginning in 1817 masters had to register their enslaved workers by name. Several were registered in one name only. William John Neilson was one of those masters, the majority of whose slaves had two and in some cases three names.[17] The new names were called their "alias", their real names being what they were called before making the multiple-name transition. The forefathers of several of us now began to have two names, duly registered in pen and ink at Spanish Town! With their relationship to their owners being more significant to the governing authorities than their relationship with their kin, the enslaved usually had the surnames of those who were their masters at the time of their birth.

Of the 150 persons in his possession in 1817, only 11 carried William John's surname and were therefore likely to have been with his father at his death.[18] One, who was 24 years old when the old man died and could have known where John Neilson's grave was and that it was he not his son who was being tombed, died by 1820, eight years before William John.[19] Two others were a year old and one four years old when father John Neilson died and unlikely to have first hand knowledge of his death and burial. This leaves eight possible eye witnesses. But could they create a tradition? One of this group, the Africa-born Margaret Neilson who has descendants consistently living in Woodside over the years 1817 to present day.[20] There are many others, not of this group of possible eyewitnesses, whose descendants have stayed here to tell their version of who was buried how.

William John had on his estate in 1817, in addition to this eleven, 139 other enslaved workers. Orlando Patterson, an authority on the matter of slavery in Jamaica, tells us that it was unusual for estate owners to sell slaves individually unless they were skilled workers.[21] William John was building a business which required manual labour: he was likely to have bought new slaves for manual work after 1811 and bought them in groups. The slave returns for the triannual years 1820-1829 note no additions to William John's human possessions by direct

purchase.22 The 139 enslaved persons who are not called
Neilson are therefore those who came with his 1817 purchase of
the John Crow Hill-Jumper area and the swopped Hopewell-
Palmetto Grove area.

The bulk of William John's slaves, then, were likely to be new
to the family: they would not know the family's history and
would know nothing of father John Neilson and his death and
burial, 17 years before their transfer. Woodside's history begins
in the minds of the village, with William John's spectacular
marriage. Clearly the myth-makers began collating information
concerning Woodside at this point, a possible indication that the
place did not exist for them before that. Several people in
Woodside today, apart from the descendants of the African
Margaret Neilson mentioned above, can trace their history back
to ancestors enslaved here.23 William John's 1817 and post 1817
slave possessions have had ample opportunity to pass their
misperceptions on into tradition.

A group, positioned to know things and/or to seem to know
things and whose comments would be regarded as fact, is the
set of personal slaves of the widow. Mrs Jane Eliza claimed in
1829 that 14 of her deceased husband's slaves had been hers.24
These 14 include a 35 year old woman and three of her children
whose ages range from one to 15. A fourth is listed as Jane
Eliza's property but not mentioned in the transfer: he is ten
years old. Another woman, 33 years old, is in the group. Her
three children who have been claimed along with her, are
seven, five and two. There are three men – 46 years old, 37
years old and 33 years old. By 1832 the 37 year old is sold away.
There is one 18 year old girl who is a first cousin to the ten year
old and there is a 46 year old woman who up to this point has
no children. The last is a 38 year old mother whose children are
not listed among Mrs Neilson's personal property. What these
report of the Great House and its runnings could become a
tradition.

Death and sale rob Mrs Neilson of some of her human
property in 1832.25 In this year she admits to having 13 slaves.
She has bought none. She has had two births. Clearly the slaves
she claimed in 1832 are still with her and still well positioned to
hear and know the business of the big house. None of these
people carry the Neilson name and, relatively young, they are

likely to have come to Woodside after the death of father John
Neilson and know nothing about him. What they say however
about the deceased master and the mistress would be taken as
gospel, and with so many young and impressionable children
among them, what they are quite likely to have witnessed – the
building of a tomb about the time their master died, but not
containing his body – is likely to have been passed over into the
story of the body-less tomb. The offspring of most of these
reside in the village to this day and talk about the 'monument',
the marble top of which, incidentally, was stolen in 1996 during
the study period.

Within the incident of the transfer of slaves from the
Woodside estate to the personal property of Jane Eliza, seems to
hang a tale which could influence her slaves' perception of Mrs
Neilson. William John Neilson had asked three persons to be
executors along with his wife. The document noting and
rationalising the transfer of slaves is signed by only two.[26] It is
signed in June of 1829, sometime after the death of William
John. By September of the same year, the third, William
Andrews has renounced his executorship having – "never acted
or interfered with affairs of the estate or concerns of the said
testators", he was "desirous of relinquishing, disclaiming,
releasing and renouncing said Executorship and the Trust".[27]

A James Neilson nearby had also died and his wife had taken
over some of her husband's human possessions but she had
purchased them from her deceased husband's estate.[28] Should
Jane Eliza have bought the slaves she claimed to have been
always hers? Were the other two executors, William McKay and
Barnaby Maddam, aiding and abetting her in fraud? Is this
what Andrews wished to distance himself from? Whatever the
case, there was some misunderstanding surrounding Mrs
Neilson and her deceased husband's estate. Household slaves
have ears and do want to know. There are 14 people who
would have known that something not so right had been done
and that the widow was implicated. There were seven adults,
some with grown children, to whisper to those in the field that
something wasn't quite right about the master's will, and the
mistress was involved with it. Moreover, that wrong-thing, had
something to do with them.

Again, William John Neilson's will required the manumission

of William Beckford and Selina Montague.[29] This would have been effected and noted in the 1829 return of slaves. The only manumission noted is that of a woman, Jeanette Neilson aged 42. None is recorded for the next filing, 1832.[30] Did Mrs Neilson by-pass her husband's death wish? Word does leak out. More than likely, the master's intention was known to the enslaved population: Beckford as an age-mate and Selina, the child of one who bore the Neilson name. "But see here. What a thing! What a disgrace! The mistress tief the people dem freedom", would be whispered all around the Woodside estate.

There seem to have been other incidents, which would not warm the workers' hearts to their mistress: William John Neilson, between 1817 and 1828, is recorded as selling just one slave, a 63 year old man.[31] Between 1829 and 1832, his widow had sold three, one a female child less than two years old, one a 37 year old man, and one a 48 year old African man who had been with the estate since 1817 if not before.[32] Then Mrs Neilson began to put her hand, if not her face into public estate business: she signed the crop accounts in 1837. Was she taking over reigns of the estate? The coffee estate was moving towards the abandonment registered in 1848.[33] Mrs Neilson would now be seen as the interfering woman who had helped to move the estate towards abandonment.

Did Mrs Neilson put herself on the front line in 1836-1837, to squeeze the last drop of labour out of her former slaves, now apprentices, before the end of slavery? Such a position would be understandable from the owner's point of view but that squeeze would be felt by the workers who would be further alienated from her. Diana Wilson and Jestina Sewell, young women under 30 years old were not willing to stick out the apprenticeship period and wait for free emancipation, supposed to have been in four years time, in 1840. They bought out the rest of their time for £35 each in 1836.[34]

Mrs Neilson also seems to have tried to interfere with her workers' religious freedom. Many of William John's enslaved labour force, in 1817, had multiple names, indicating that they had been christianised. In 1831 there was an English Baptist church a mile away, which was so well attended that a bigger structure was needed. There are several enslaved persons on nearby Palmetto Grove estate, listed as 'American' and one on the Woodside estate. American slaves in Jamaica were very often Christians of the Native Baptist tradition. George Gibb, an American ex-slave was proselytising in the St Thomas-in-the-Vale area, into which Woodside falls at this time. The chances are that William John's enslaved people were English and Native Baptists. William John himself was in 1820, if not before or after, a Quaker. Between 1817 and 1831, only 48 of Dr Neilson's 162 slaves are listed as Anglican, many of this 48 being children. Very likely the bulk of Woodside's enslaved Christians were of the non-Anglican brand. The word is that Mrs Neilson tried to force these workers to go to the Anglican church services and they instead would gather at a cave called Daddy Rock, to discuss their own affairs.[35]

If this is so, then the woman was interfering now with God's business, trying to get people to change their religious persuasion. Early Woodside people experience Mrs Neilson now, not just as someone who does something odd with her husband's will, who stifles the will of a deadman to free some of them, under whose hand the estate's coffee business is in ruins, but one who tries to impose her will upon the free flow of the spirit. Did Mrs Neilson really interfere in this way?

Mrs Neilson does sign herself in the 1829 slave returns as if she is a Quaker.[36] Where then is the substance to the above charge, for the Quakers had a record of toleration of the version of Christianity practiced by their enslaved workers? Could Mrs Neilson have moved from the Quakers to join the Anglicans who by 1831 were charged by the establishment to brainwash the soon-to-be-free into philosophic conformity with it? The records show that in 1881 she gave 15 acres of land and her house to the Anglicans.[37] She may indeed have gone into the pre-Emancipation days as an Anglican and as one working with them to control the behaviour of the soon-to-be-free workers. These oral and the archival records do indeed suggest that the interaction between Jane Eliza Neilson and her slaves/apprentices was a troubled one. "Another white witch of Rose Hall" is how Mr Raniki (Remekie), whose ancestors did not even get to Woodside until after Emancipation, describes her.[38]

The legend concerning the Neilsons accuses William John Neilson's wife Jane Eliza and her son of impoverishing the estate by selling off the lands bit by bit, and the heir of spending the money on drink. William John had been the premier coffee planter in the area, owning at his peak 162 slaves to neighbouring Rock Spring's 44, neighbouring Smailfield's 34, neighbouring Richmond Hill's 39 and neighbouring Waterton's 36, all of which were in coffee too. Louisiana, another neighbouring coffee estate, was the nearest to Woodside in economic terms. It had about 131 slaves. William John Neilson's Woodside was at least 734 acres. Only Louisiana of the others had as many as 350 acres.³⁹

By 1832 the number of slaves and the returns from the farm had gone down and the estate registered itself between 1832 and 1848 as a failed coffee estate.⁴⁰ It is true that William John had left his wife Jane Eliza and his eldest son George in possession of the estate but George was the second to last of six children, the eldest in 1833, Helen Ismail, being less than 21 years.⁴¹ Any decisions could hardly have been his. Jane Eliza did not seem prepared to be a titular head only: she signs the estate returns in 1837.⁴² Being so publicly involved with the running of the estate, she put herself in the position to be seen as the poor manager and to survive in village history as the murderer of Woodside estate.

Land appears to have been sold around the time of William John's death. By 1832, John Ewart, quite likely the eventual stipendiary magistrate and assemblyman of St Thomas-in-the-Vale, today's Bog Walk to Louisiana area, is listed on the official returns as having a small estate called Woodside.⁴³ This seems very much like the part of the Neilson property left by John and which abutted Patience Hermit's land in what seemed to be the Richmond Hill/Pear Tree Grove area.⁴⁴ The Woodside estate is listed in 1840 as being 734 acres.⁴⁵ The only official record of sale that I have seen is for a piece of land a little over six acres, sold to William Cousins in 1842.⁴⁶ The document carries the name of Jane Eliza and George. The map of 1880 gives Woodside 680 acres. This means that between 1840 and a little before 1880, when the map was prepared, the Neilsons had only divested themselves of 54 acres. Whence then the charge that Jane Eliza and her son mismanaged and sold off the land bit by bit?

While neighbouring estates such as Petersfield, Palmetto Grove and Smailfield systematically and legally sub-divided their lands and made them available to ex-slaves, and Windsor Castle close by went further by 1843 making itself into a village of registered small settlers, Mrs Neilson apparently held on doggedly to Woodside, allowing leases and rents, sale and possibly squatting of miniscule acreages.[47] There are on the map no neat divisions in Woodside as in other places; there are just the words 'small lots', 'small settlements'. I grew up in Woodside hearing the terms 'lease and sale' and 'heir and sale'. The one is an arrangement by which the person leasing has the first offer to buy the land he is leasing and the other is an arrangement that the leasee or the tenant's heir be given the first choice to buy the land his parent is renting or leasing. The popular existence of these terms indicate that Mrs Neilson was slow to sell Woodside's lands and that the ex-slaves felt forced to find ways of assuring some permanent relationship between themselves and their children on the one hand and the lands they cultivated in Woodside on the other.

This would be an annoying route for one who had the money and could make an outright purchase. Then there must have been those who missed the stability of a social organisation in which there was an economically strong resident master (preferably male) who would serve as a wage-payer and a moral authority. This could only come about if Mrs Neilson would sell out to someone who could return Woodside to social and economic prominence. Mrs Neilson's approach to disposing of her land meant that no large landlord could come in and offer labouring jobs as had happened all around. It was this resistance to selling and this 'bit by bit' approach to disposing of what land she did sell, rather than the 'selling out' of her lands, that must have really angered Woodside's newly freed people. It must have been with vexation that the ex-slave population saw this white woman, an ineffective landowner, standing between them and what they could use.

By 1880, whether by her agencies or that of another – a lawyer perhaps or the Anglican church – more than half of Mrs Neilson's Woodside was in the hands of people whose names are very familiar to us today. Bogle, Sheriffe, Conridge, Rennickie (Remekie/Raniki), Walker, Hermit, Williams, Thomas, Hamilton, Richard, Stanbury, Johnson, Conie, Meade, Evans, Payne, Willis, Walsh, Lord, Morrison and more, were by

1880 all tax-paying users and some definitely owners of land in Woodside.[48] Most of these people had lands of less than 20 acres. Some were as small as an acre.

According to the map of 1880, naturally prepared before that date, Mrs Neilson's Woodside was 680 acres large. Oddly enough the name on this map is written without the 'i'. What are we to make of this? An error? Or did the Neilsons change their name to Nelson? There certainly has been no sign of the Woodside Neilsons in the official records since 1842 when Jane Eliza and her son George, then over 21 and official heir, sold six acres of land surrounded by their own land to a William Cousins.[49] There has been no death certificate for either of these people, nor is there one for William John, George's younger brother. There is no landowning Nelson in these official records either. Once again it is the word from the village and other informal sources that present some notion of what happened to the Neilsons.

William John Neilson and Jane Eliza had six children. The eldest was Helen Ismail. She was followed in order of birth by Isabella Francis, Frances Eliza and Mary Ann and then the boys – George William and William John Jr. According to William John's will of 1828, his mother Frances was to get a yearly income of £500.[50] Jane Eliza was to get a clear £1000 per year and each child £2000 per year at the age of 21. The estate went to Jane Eliza and their eldest son George and to William John Jr should George predecease him. In 1833 Jane Eliza with Hugh Donald McKay, at one time and perhaps still her overseer, sought to get Helen Ismail's money released to her betrothed, James Marshall.[51] I presume that this marriage did take place and that Helen Ismail changed her name to Marshall, took her money with her to that family and moved out of my historiographical gaze.

My own mother, newly married, pregnant and no longer in her teaching job, accustomed to the busy-ness of her mother's farm and bakery and now living on a tiny strip of land in a one-bedroomed house, must have been very bored. While she waited in 1937 for my sister's birth and while she nursed her, she pasted clippings from the newspapers in her scrap book. She didn't know much about putting dates on clippings and it is by chance that some pieces survive with the date of the newspaper. One such is the report of the farewell function given for Inspector Neilson of Manchester on his retirement. Somebody in more recent times thought this inspector important, for they sent several bits of information concerning him, in a file, to the National Library. From my mother's clipping I noted that Inspector Neilson was light-skinned and straight-haired; from the clippings in the archives, that he was the son of Frances Neilson of St Andrew; that he was definitely quadroon, that the inspector's parents were not married and that he took the name of his mother. Could she be Jane Eliza's daughter and Frances Neilson's granddaughter in St Andrew with a mulatto lover, could this Frances Neilson be Frances Eliza of Woodside?

Several voices have pointed out the spot in Woodside, where 'Miss Neilson daughter' lived. She died and was buried there too, if we are to believe a recently collected tale of one passing himself off as an obeah man, arranging to teach another the art and taking him to the place described as Miss Neilson's daughter's home, to raise the duppy of Mary Ann Neilson.[52] There even is a report that this daughter of 'Miss Neilson' had a baby for William Ferguson a black ex-slave.[53] Quite possible, there was a slave by this name in Mrs Neilson's household. This baby grew up, her name is known and handed down to me. Mary Ann, the last daughter of Dr and Mrs William John Neilson apparently then stayed on in Woodside in an area of the property that was called Neilson and certainly, as far as her sex life was concerned, was integrated into the ex-slave society. There has been no word on Isabella Francis and apart from his propensity to drink, none on George, the heir. Two daughters with illegitimate children, one got by an ex-slave, is not the picture her ex-slaves, themselves struggling to be upright Christians, see as a successful mother, add to that a drunken son. Mrs Neilson had failed on another measure.

So there is documentary evidence to suggest that early Woodside people had experienced Mrs Neilson as someone who had pitted her will against theirs, even meddling with their spiritual life; who had been dishonest and in a way that affected them negatively; who was a stumbling block in the way of their economic development; who had failed in her own business as an estate manager; and failed as a parent. In her failure is the notion of fall, capable of being glossed, as in the myth, as 'from red carpet to roast banana'!

Mrs Neilson stayed physically in Woodside until the 1860s if not later, begging salt, it is said, from her ex-slaves. Other white and ex-slave holders like herself had either died or left the vicinity. Mrs Neilson like any other human needed company and if she couldn't have it from those parallel to her in status, she would take it from any other human being. To beg is to link socially with others. Mrs Neilson was seeking social intercourse. Where were the rituals to convert a master-servant relationship into a neighbour-neighbour relationship? They had yet to be written for this post-emancipation situation was a new one. The literature on apprenticeship talks about getting the slaves to adjust to freedom and a social adjustment is implied. Little is said about helping the master class to adjust socially. Without role reforming rituals, Mrs Neilson's reaching out would seem the insensitive insult of one who has failed to acknowledge the pain which the system she had operated had caused, and the consequent right to anger of those so pained.

Finally, had Mrs Jane Eliza Neilson been proud and principled; been able to make a success of the farm her husband left her; been able to bring up her sons as successful professionals, medical doctors like their father; if she had been able to find the right suitors for her daughters; if she had been poor and sick but kept her distance, the oral history of black people would have left her alone. As it is, she was an unfortunate combination – proud 'with nothing back a it'. She became an object lesson, her life epitomising the saying: "pride goeth before a fall". "How are the mighty fallen". The village knew the scriptures. "The Lord shall laugh them to scorn, the Lord shall have them in derision", they knew the psalms. Woodside was happy to have evidence of these biblical truths and revelations. The myth-makers and preservers could always be warned and warn their children accordingly, for the scriptures were revealed in Mrs Neilson's life right before their eyes; her story had a function to perform. "Vengeance is mine", saith the Lord, "I will repay", and he had kept his word for here was the mistress begging salt from us in a calabash bowl, not even a crockery one. The moral order was secure.

Interrogating the myth of the body-less tomb and of the

haughty mistress took us into the history of social action in the village of Woodside and provided information which can now be made public, doing what Kamau Brathwaite once called for – letting us see the face of ordinary black folks, so-called slaves, freedmen and their free-born descendants. This exercise has brought ordinary Jamaicans, who have given the stories handed down to them, into the research experience, helping them and us to see ourselves and our ancestors in the historical process. 'Anything nega sey, if a nuh so it go, it nearly go so.' Try using the myths handed down to you about your family or village to right/write your history. Black people need your view of our face. And the archival material is there to help you to interrogate your myth.[54]

May 1997

NOTES

Chapter 1

1. Orlando Patterson, *Slavery and Social Death – a comparative study* (Cambridge, Mass: Harvard University Press, 1982).
2. Erna Brodber, 'Mammy Edith', in *Life in Jamaica in the Early Twentieth Century – a presentation of ninety oral accounts*, Unpublished. ISER Doc Centre, StTFa p. 31, 1980
3. 'With Forebearers from Guinea', ISER Doc Centre, 48 StcFa, p. 6.
4. Patterson, *Slavery and Social Death*, p. 112.
5. Patterson, *Slavery and Social Death*, pp. 310-313.
6. Patterson, *Slavery and Social Death*, p. 119. Says Patterson "Of the estimated 7.4 million [Africans] transported [to the New World] between 1701 and 1810 .... over 70% were kidnapped".
7. Igor Kopytoff and Suzanne Miers, eds, *Slavery in Africa – historical and anthropological perspectives* (Wisconsin: University of Wisconsin Press, 1977).
8. Kopytoff and Miers *Slavery in Africa*, p. 40.
9. Kopytoff and Miers *Slavery in Africa*, p. 338.
10. Patterson, *Slavery and Social Death*, p. 128.
11. Patterson, *Slavery and Social Death*, p. 55.
12. Patterson, *Slavery and Social Death*, p. 55.
13. Patterson, *Slavery and Social Death*, p. 55.
14. Philip Wright, *Lady Nugent's Journal of her Residence in Jamaica from 1801-1805* (Kingston, Jamaica: Institute of Jamaica, 1966).
15. Wright, *Lady Nugent's Journal*, p. 69.
16. Wright, *Lady Nugent's Journal*, p. 76.
17. Wright, *Lady Nugent's Journal*, p. 81.
18. Wright, *Lady Nugent's Journal*, p. 29.

Chapter 2

1. See Ira Berlin, *Slaves Without Masters* (Oxford: Oxford University Press, 1974), and Orlando Patterson, *Slavery and Social Death* (Cambridge, Mass: Harvard University Press, 1982).
2. Philip Wright, *Lady Nugent's Journal of her residence in Jamaica from 1801-1805*, (Kingston, Jamaica: Institute of Jamaica, 1966), p. 98.
3. Wright, *Lady Nugent's Journal*, p. 12.
4. Wright, *Lady Nugent's Journal*, p. 182.
5. Wright, *Lady Nugent's Journal*, p. 143.
6. For further information see Gad J. Heumen, *Between Black and White – Race, Politics and Free Coloureds in Jamaica 1792-1865* (Westport: Greenwood, 1981).
7. Heumen, *Between Black and White*, p. 11.

8. Much of the information on the Haitian revolution comes from Chapter 11 of Parry and Sherlock, *A Short History of the West Indies* (London: Macmillan, 1960).

9. C.L.R. James, *Black Jacobins: Toussaint L'Ouverture and the Saint Domingo Revolution* (London: Secker & Warburg, 1938).

10. Parry and Sherlock, *A Short History of the West Indies*, p. 163.

11. Parry and Sherlock, *A Short History of the West Indies*, p. 161.

12. The data in this and the three succeeding paragraphs are from Orlando Patterson, *Sociology of Slavery* (Jamaica: Sangster's Bookstore, 1967). See especially Chapter IX.

13. Parry and Sherlock, *A Short History of the West Indies*, p. 164.

14. See Orlando Patterson, *Sociology of Slavery*, Chapter 1, sub-heading 'The white society during slavery'.

15. Published by API 1977, p. 25.

16. George Eaton, 'Trade Union Development in Jamaica', in *Caribbean Quarterly*. Vol 8 1962-63, p. 44.

17. For instance his work, 'The Meaning of Freedom: blacks in politics and labour struggle in Jamaica, 1838-1865' presented at the *Conference on Slavery, Emancipation and the Shaping of Caribbean Society*, 8-10 December 1988, at St Augustine, UWI, Trinidad.

18. Edith F. and Samuel J. Hurwitz, *Jamaica – A Historical Portrait* (London: Pall Mall Press,1971), p. 162.

19. This book was published by Harcourt and Brace, 1971. It has provided a great deal of information on the American situation presented here, the table on p. 39 being the source of the figures in this paragraph. Other valuable references on the American situation are Wilson Jeremiah Moses, *The Golden Age of Black Nationalism* (Oxford: OUP, 1978), and *Alexander Crummell* (Oxford: OUP, 1989); Edwin Redkey, *Black Exodus* (New Haven: Yale University, 1969); Herbert Aptheker, *Essays in the History of the American Negro* (New York: International, 1964); and C. Eric Lincoln, *The Negro Pilgrimage in America* (New York: Bantam, 1967), and *The Blackamericans* (New York: Bantam, 1969).

20. Lucille Mathurin-Mair, *A historical Study of Women in Jamaica from 1655 – 1844*, PhD thesis UWI Mona, Jamaica, 1974, p. 26.

21. David Walker's appeal ... with introduction by James Turner (Baltimore: Black Classic Press, 1963).

22. Psalms 68, verse 31.

23. Peter Hall, *Autobiography of Reverend Peter Hall* (Accra: Waterville, 1965), p. 5.

Chapter 3

1. Emancipation Songs collected in Woodside, St Mary, Jamaica 1996.

2. *Jamaica. Minutes of the Council. July, 1832 to September 1839*. Jamaica

Archives, 1b/5/3/24 March 1834.

3. For this and other data in this piece, I rely heavily on Thomas C. Holt's, *The Problem of Freedom -race, labour and politics in Jamaica and Britain 1832-1838* (Baltimore: John Hopkins University Press, 1992), p. 16.

4. Edward Long, *The History of Jamaica*, Vol II (London: Frank Cass, 1774), p. 352.

5. Holt, *The Problem of Freedom*, p. 105.

6. As at note 2. May 1938.

7. Holt, *The Problem of Freedom*, p. 53.

8. Holt, *The Problem of Freedom*, see chapter 5.

9. *Great Britain Parliament, House of Commons select committee on sugar and coffee planting* (DETAILS, 1848), p. 229.

10. STM 51, Map Collection, National Library of Jamaica.

11. STM 1397, Map Collection, National Library of Jamaica.

12. STM 586, Map Collection, National Library of Jamaica.

13. STM 614, Map Collection, National Library of Jamaica. Map undated. Reference says it is about 1857.

14. Orlando Patterson, *The Sociology of Slavery* (Kingston: Sangster's Bookstore, 1967), p. 84.

15. Patterson, *The Sociology of Slavery*, p. 80.

16. Wills: Liber 109.112 and 110.103. Island Record Office, Jamaica.

17. Holt, *The Problem of Freedom*, p. 145.

18. Erna Brodber, 'Oral Historian' 60StjFa in, *Life in Jamaica in the Early Twentieth Century: a presentation of ninety oral accounts*, ISER Documentation Centre, Mona, Jamaica, 1980.

19. Holt, *The Problem of Freedom*, pp. 151-152.

20. Erna Brodber, *The Second Generation of Freemen in Jamaica 1907-1944*, PhD Thesis, University of the West Indies, 1985.

21. George Eaton, 'Trade Union Development in Jamaica', in *Caribbean Quarterly*, Vol 8, 1962-1963, p. 44.

22. Holt, *The Problem of Freedom*, p. 174.

23. Ansell Hart, *The Life of George William Gordon* (Jamaica: Institute of Jamaica, [n.d.]), p. 122.

24. Hart, *The Life of George William Gordon*, p. 120.

25. Swithin Wilmot, 'Black Labourers and White Missionaries: Conflict on the estates in Hanover, Jamaica, 1838-1847', in *The Jamaica Historical Review*, Vol LXIV, 1984, pp. 18-27.

26. Swithin Wilmot, 'The Meaning of Freedom: blacks in politics and labour struggle in Jamaica, 1838-1865' presented at *Conference on Slavery, Emancipation and the Shaping of Caribbean Society*, December 8-10, 1988, St. Augustine, Trinidad. Unpublished. Cited with the kind permission of the author.

27. Swithin Wilmot, *Emancipation in Action: workers and wage conflicts in*

Jamaica, 1838-1848. Unpublished. p. 15. Quoted with the permission of the author.

28. Lorna Simmonds, 'Civil Disturbances in Western Jamaica 1838-1865', in *The Jamaica Historical Review*, Vol LXIV, 1984, pp. 1-17 and especially p. 7.

29. Robert Stewart, 'Conflict in the Jamaican Baptist Church: Thomas Dowson and J.M. Phillippo, 1842-1850', in *The Jamaica Historical Review*, pp. 28-41.

30. Simmonds, 'Civil Disturbances'.

31. Wilmot, *Emancipation in Action*, p. 18.

32. Wilmot, *Emancipation in Action*, p. 19.

33. Wilmot, *Emancipation in Action*, p. 19.

34. Hart, *The Life of George William Gordon*, p. 122.

35. Holt, *The Problem of Freedom*, p. 216.

36. Holt, *The Problem of Freedom*, p. 63.

37. Holt, *The Problem of Freedom*, p. 229.

38. *Wars of Respect* (Kingston, Jamaica: API, 1977).

39. *Jamaica Almanack 1811-1832.*

40. Patterson, *The Sociology of Slavery*, pp. 181-188.

41. Holt, *The Problem of Freedom*, p. 167.

42. Holt, *The Problem of Freedom*, p. 167.

43. F.R Augier et al *The Making of the West Indies* (London: Longman Caribbean, 1960), pp. 178-179.

44. Holt, *The Problem of Freedom*, p. 255.

45. *Baptist Missionary Herald*, June 1845, p. 93.

46. Holt, *The Problem of Freedom*, p. 205.

47. STM 586, Map Collection, National Library of Jamaica.

48. STM 51, Map Collection, National Library of Jamaica.

49. *Register of Property Tax 1/8/1869-31/7/1870.*

50. *Statement of Land Tax and Arrears paid in St Mary, 1881-1882,* Jamaica Archives.

51. Holt, *The Problem of Freedom*, p. 16.

52. Veront M. Satchell, *From Plots to Plantations – land transactions in Jamaica 1866-1900* ISER, Mona, Jamaica, 1990.

53. Information in this paragraph is from Satchell, *From Plots to Plantations*, particularly chapters 5 & 6.

54. *Handbook of Jamaica*, Government of Jamaica, 1882.

55. Patrick Bryan, *The Jamaican People 1880-1902 – Race, Class and Social Control* (London: Macmillan Caribbean, 1991).

56. Brodber, 'Man Boy' 5CMb, in *Life in Jamaica in the Early Twentieth Century.*

57. Brodber, in *Life in Jamaica in the Early Twentieth Century.*

58. Olive Senior, 'The Colon People', in *Jamaica Journal*, Institute of

Jamaica, Vol II, nos 3 & 4, p. 62.

59. Olive Senior, see the above as well as her 'The Panama Railway', in *Jamaica Journal*, Institute of Jamaica, no 44.

Chapter 4

1. Harold Cruse, *The Crisis of the Negro Intellectual* (New York: William Morrow, 1967).
2. This and the succeeding quotes are from Cruse, *The Crisis of the Negro Intellectual*, pp. 120-131.
3. Winston James, 'Harold Cruse and the West Indians: Critical Remarks on the Crisis of the Negro Intellectual', in *Holding Aloft the Banner of Ethiopia* (London: Verso Press, 1998), indicates that Cruse severely edited Domingo's communication. He might not really have been "supercilious at all".
4. Cruse, *The Crisis of the Negro Intellectual*, p. 123.
5. Robert Hill, *Marcus Garvey and the UNIA Papers* (California: University of California Press, 1983).
6. See Tony Martin, *Race First* (Connecticut: Greenwood Press, 1976), p. 8.
7. Jeanetter Smith-Irvin's *Marcus Garvey's Footsoldiers of the Universal Negro Improvement Association* (New Jersey: Africa World Press, 1989).
8. *Class*, Island Record Office, Kingston, Jamaica, 12 January 1992.
9. Smith-Irvin, *Marcus Garvey's Footsoldiers*, p. 70.
10. Smith-Irvin, *Marcus Garvey's Footsoldiers*, pp. 15-16.
11. 'Garveyism in California', in *Garvey, Africa, Europe, the Americas*, eds Maureen Lewis and Rupert Lewis (Jamaica: ISER, 1986).
12. The data for this and the succeeding paragraph are from the 14th census of the USA, Vol.II Table 14. Figures concerning the UNIA are from Martin's *Race First*.
13. Martin, *Race First*, p. 287.
14. Martin, *Race First*, p. 15.
15. Smith-Irvin, *Marcus Garvey's Footsoldiers*, p. 57.
16. Tony Martin, 'Marcus Garvey and Trinidad, 1912-1947', in Lewis and Lewis, *Garvey, Africa, Europe, the Americas*, p. 73.
17. Smith-Irvin, *Marcus Garvey's Footsoldiers*, p. 70.
18. Martin, 'Marcus Garvey and Trinidad, 1912-1947', p. 63.
19. Cruse, *The Crisis of the Negro Intellectual*, p. 124.
20. Cruse, *The Crisis of the Negro Intellectual*, p. 129.
21. P. Olisanwuche Esedebe, *Pan-Africanism – the idea and movement, 1776-1963* (Washington D.C: Howard University Press, 1982), p. 3.
22. John Henrik Clarke, 'The American Antecedents of Marcus Garvey', in Lewis and Lewis, *Garvey, Africa, Europe, the Americas*.
23. Clarke, 'The American Antecedents of Marcus Garvey'.

24. Clarke, 'The American Antecedents of Marcus Garvey'.
25. Clarke, 'The American Antecedents of Marcus Garvey', p. 5.
26. Clarke, 'The American Antecedents of Marcus Garvey', p. 5.
27. Clarke, 'The American Antecedents of Marcus Garvey'.
28. Edward Blyden, *Christianity, Islam and the Negro Race* (Edinburgh: Edinburgh University Press, 1967), p. 155.
29. Mary Prince, *A Black Woman's Odyssey through Russia and Jamaica – the narrative of Nancy Prince* (New York: Marcus Weiner, 1990), p. 48.
30. Leroy Graham, *Baltimore, Nineteenth Century Black Capital* (University Press of America, 1982), p. 254. It is interesting to hear from Akasha (Gloria) Hull in the late 1980s that August 1st is still celebrated in Delaware.
31. Margaret Busby, *Daughters of Africa* (New York: Pantheon Books, 1992), pp. 75-76.
32. See editor's comment on the poem, Busby, *Daughters of Africa*, p. 75.
33. See Barry Chevannes,'Revival and Black Struggle', in *Savacou* no 5, June 1971. Shirley Gordon, *God Almight Make We Free* (Bloomington & Indianapolis: Indiana Press, 1996), is excellent for information on this and other African-Jamaican intinerant preachers in Jamaica.
34. Robert Hill, *Marcus Garvey and the Universal Negro Improvement Association Papers* (Berkeley: University of California Press, 1933).
35. Selwyn Cudjoe, 'The Audacity of it all: C.L.R. James' Trinidadian background', in *C.L.R James' Caribbean*, eds Paul Buhle and Pajet Henry (Durham: Duke University Press, 1992).
36. Psalm 68, verse 31.
37. Wilson Jeremiah Moses, *The Golden Age of Black Nationalism 1850-1925* (Oxford: Oxford University Press, 1978), p. 24.
38. Prince, *A Black Woman's Odyssey through Russia and Jamaica*, p. 53.
39. Gordon, *God Almight Make We Free*, p. 66.
40. Peter Hall, *Autobiography of Rev. Peter Hall* (Accra: Waterville, 1965), p. 5.
41. Tony Martin, *The Pan African Connection – from slavery and beyond* (Massachusetts: The Majority Press, 1983), p. 9.
42. Esedebe, *Pan-Africanism*, p. 15.
43. Robert Hill, 'Before Garvey: Chief Alfred Sam and the African Movement 1912-1916', in *Pan African Biography*, ed. Robert Hill (African Studies Center, UCLA and Crossroads Press, 1987).
44. For more information see Edwin Redkey, *Black Exodus – black nationalist and back to Africa movements 1890-1910* (New Haven & London: Yale University Press, 1969).
45. Redkey, *Black Exodus*.

46. Hill, 'Before Garvey', p. 69.
47. Martin, *Race First*, p. 82.
48. Martin, *Race First*, p. 111.
49. Martin, *Race First*, p. 6.
50. Martin, *Race First*, p. 30
51. Martin, *Race First*, p. 33.
52. Cruse, *The Crisis of the Negro Intellectual*, p. 125.
53. Information on Garvey's early life is available from the many texts on Garvey.
54. Martin, *Race First*, p. 6.
55. Martin, *Race First*, p. 297.

Chapter 5

1. For more information, see Myron Gilmore, *The World of Humanism 1433-1517* (New York: Harper and Brothers, 1952).
2. Wayne F. Cooper, *Rebel Sojourner in the Harlem Renaissance* (New York: Schocken, 1987), p. 9.
3. Quoted in Edith F and Samuel J. Hurwitz, *Jamaica – a historical portrait* (London: Pall Mall Press, 1971), p. 162.
4. 'Extract from Report of Sterling Committee to the British Government, 11 May 1835', in Shirley Gordon, *A Century of West Indian Education* (London: Longman, 1963), pp. 20-21.'
5. Cooper, *Rebel Sojourner in the Harlem Renaissance*, p. 4, quotes McKay as saying that his father had "at least hundred acres".
6. 'Crossman Commission 1883', in *Sources of West Indian History*, F.R. Augier and Shirley C. Gordon, compilers (London: Longman, 1962), p. 77.
7. Cooper, *Rebel Sojourner in the Harlem Renaissance*, p. 4. Missionaries had "instructed him in the fundamentals of reading and writing".
8. Cooper, *Rebel Sojourner in the Harlem Renaissance*, p. 100.
9. The information concerning McKay in this and the following paragraph are from Cooper, *Rebel Sojourner in the Harlem Renaissance*.
10. Cooper, *Rebel Sojourner in the Harlem Renaissance*, p. 29.
11. Oxaal, *Black Intellectuals Come to Power* (Massachusetts: Schenkman, 1968), p. 62.
12. Much of this data arises from reading Oxaal, *Black Intellectuals Come to Power*, and from C.L.R. James' autobiographical piece, *Beyond a Boundary* (Kingston, Jamaica: Sangster's Book Stores in association with Hutchinson, 1976).
13. Oxaal, *Black Intellectuals Come to Power*, pp. 23-24.
14. Information on Padmore unless expressly stated otherwise comes from James R. Hooker's *Black Revolutionary, George Padmore* (New York: Praegar, 1967) and C.LR. James, 'George Padmore: Black

Marxist Revolutionary', in *Rendezvous with Victory* (London: Allison & Busby, 1984).

15. A.J.P. Taylor, *The First World War* (Harmondsworth: Penguin, 1963).

16. Taylor, *The First World War*, p. 257.

17. C/O 137/731 dispatch 197 Probyn to Viscount Milner Secretary of State.

18. Cooper, *Rebel Sojourner in the Harlem Renaissance*, p. 102.

19. Cooper, *Rebel Sojourner in the Harlem Renaissance*, p. 42.

20. Cooper, *Rebel Sojourner in the Harlem Renaissance*, p. 38.

21. Cooper, *Rebel Sojourner in the Harlem Renaissance*, p. 81.

22. Churchill is generally understood to have used this poem in his exhortations to the British people on the eve of their entry into World War II.

23. Cooper, *Rebel Sojourner in the Harlem Renaissance*, p. 100.

24. Cooper, *Rebel Sojourner in the Harlem Renaissance*, p. 102

25. Cooper, *Rebel Sojourner in the Harlem Renaissance*; see also Winston James, *Holding Aloft the Banner of Ethiopia* (London: Verso, 1998), for details and analyses of McKay's later years.

26. Rhoda Reddock, *Elma Francois* (London: New Beacon Books, 1988), p. 13.

27. 'Writings from the Nation', in *The C.L.R. James Reader*, ed Anna Grimshaw (Oxford: Blackwell, 1992), p. 290.

28. James, *Holding Aloft the Banner of Ethiopia*, p. 255.

29. Hooker, *Black Revolutionary, George Padmore*, p. 33.

30. Olisanwuche P. Esedebe, *Pan-Africanism – the idea and movement, 1776-1963* (Washington D.C: Howard University Press, 1982), p. 124.

31. Cooper, *Rebel Sojourner in the Harlem Renaissance*, p. 84.

32. Paul Buhle, *The Artist as Revolutionary* (London: Verso, 1988), p. 72.

33. James, *Holding Aloft the Banner of Ethiopia*, p. 47.

Chapter 6

1. Harriet Beecher Stowe, *Uncle Tom's Cabin* (Boston: John P. Jewett, 1852).

2. Merle Hodge, 'Challenges to the Struggle for Sovereignty', in *Caribbean Women Writers*, ed. Selwyn Cudjoe (Massachusetts: Calaloux, 1990), p. 205.

3. Lorenzo Turner, *Africanisms in the Gullah Dialect* (Chicago: University of Chicago, 1941). Thanks to Dr Maureen Warner-Lewis for providing this reference. Several West Africans as well as Brazilians have told me of the popularity of the name in their part of the world and the similarity of meaning.

4. Lynne Fauley Emery, *Black Dance* (Pennington, N.J.: Princeton

Book Co., 1972), p. 21.

5. Emery, *Black Dance*, p. 27

6. Emery, *Black Dance*, p. 185. According to Emery Juba, the dance, came from Africa to the West Indies and from here to the USA "where it evolved into a rhythmic, stamping, clapping, patting type of dance". I have heard African-American friends talk of "patting juba" as a challenge dance game they participated in as children. We find the reference again in the past in a quote Emery takes from Hearn's post civil war description of a dance in a Cincinnati dance hall – the dancing became wild, men patted juba and shrieked" p 146.

7. Hodge, 'Challenges to the Struggle for Sovereignty', p. 202.

8. Hodge, 'Challenges to the Struggle for Sovereignty', p. 203.

9. Hodge, 'Challenges to the Struggle for Sovereignty', pp. 203-204

10. Lloyd Braithwaite, *Social Stratification in Trinidad*, SES Vol 2. 1953.

11. Merle Hodge, *Crick Crack Monkey* (London: Heinemann, 1970). All further references are to this edition and are included in the text.

12. Personal conversation, 1981 with R.T. Smith.

13. See Bob Callaghan, Introduction, in Zora Neale Hurston, *Tell my Horse* ([1938]; Berkeley: University of California Press, 1981).

14. Hurston, *Tell my Horse*, p. 19.

15. King Solomon, early to mid 1950s. Thanks to Gordon Rohlehr.

16. Paule Marshall, *Praisesong for the Widow* (Plume, 1983). All further references are to this edition and are included in the text.

17. John Henrik Clarke, in his foreward to *African Presence in the Carolinas and Georgia – Sea Island Roots*, eds Keith Baird and Mary A. Twinning (New Jersey: African World Press, 1991), pp. v-vi.

18. M.G. Smith, *Plural Society in the Briish West Indies* (Kingston: Sangster's Book Stores, 1974), p. 223.

Chapter 7

1. Rhygin was a Jamaican outlaw of the late 1940 popularised among the folk. His life is canonised in Perry Henzel's film *The Harder They Come* (10A West King's House Road, Kingston, c.1972).

2. Deeds LOS 487.169 1801, Island Record Office, Jamaica.

3. *Jamaica Almanack*, 1811.

4. See Edward (Kamau) Brathwaite, *The Development of Creole Society in Jamaica 1770-1820* (Oxford: Clarendon Press, 1971), pp. 26-31

5. Mentioned as such in B. W. Higman, *Jamaica Surveyed* (Jamaica: Institute of Jamaica Publications, 1988), p. 296.

6. *Jamaica Almanack*, 1811-1828.

7. STM 583, Map Collection, National Library of Jamaica.

8. Slave Returns for St Mary 1B/11/7/5, 1B/11/7/6, 1B/11/7/42, 1B/11/7/58, 1B/11/7/92, 1B/11/7/103, 1B/1/7/113, Jamaica

Archives, Spanish Town, Jamaica.
9. Wills: Liber 109.112 1828 and 110.103 1829, Island Record Office, Jamaica.
10. Deeds LOS 786.167 (1833), Island Record Office.
11. Slave Returns for St Mary 1B/11/7/5, 1B/11/7/6, 1B/11/7/42, 1B/11/7/58, 1B/11/7/92, 1B/11/7/103, 1B/1/7/113; also register of Marriages etc for St Mary 1817-1825 & 1828, Jamaica Archives.
12. Slave Returns for St Mary 1B/11/7/5, 1B/11/7/6, 1B/11/7/42, 1B/11/7/58, 1B/11/7/92, 1B/11/7/103, 1B/1/7/113, also 1B/11/7/126, Jamaica Archives.
13. STM 583, Map Collection, National Library of Jamaica.
14. Deeds LOS 687.164, Island Record Office Jamaica.
15. Deeds LOS 687.164, Island Record Office Jamaica.
16. STM 569, Map Collection, National Library of Jamaica.
17. Slave Returns for St Mary 1B/11/7/5, 1B/11/7/6, 1B/11/7/42, 1B/11/7/58, 1B/11/7/92, 1B/11/7/103, 1B/1/7/113, Jamaica Archives.
18. Slave Returns for St Mary 1B/11/7/6, Jamaica Archives.
19. Slave Returns for St Mary 1B/11/7/42, Jamaica Archives.
20. Margaret Neilson's daughters, Celestina Neilson and Pamela Cunningham produced children by Walker and Hermitt. These families still live in Woodside.
21. Orlando Patterson, *Sociology of Slavery* (PLACE: Sangster's Bookstore, 1967), p. 81.
22. Slave Returns for St Mary 1B/11/7/5, 1B/11/7/6, 1B/11/7/42, 1B/11/7/58, 1B/11/7/92, 1B/11/7/103, 1B/1/7/113, Jamaica Archives.
23. Erna Brodber, *The People of my Jamaican Village* (Jamaica: b l a c k s p a c e , 1999).
24. Slave Returns for St Mary 1B/11/7/103, Jamaica Archives.
25. Slave Returns for St Mary 1B/11/7/126, Jamaica Archives.
26. Slave Returns for St Mary 1B/11/7/103 and 113, Jamaica Archives.
27. Wills: Liber 110.103 1829-1830, Island Record Office.
28. Slave Returns for St Mary 1B/11/7/113 1829, Jamaica Archives.
29. Will: LOS 109.112 1828-1829, Island Record Office.
30. Slave Returns for St Mary 1B/11/7/126, Jamaica Archives.
31. Slave Returns for St Mary 1B/11/7/6 1817, Jamaica Archives.
32. Slave Returns for St Mary 1B/11/7/6 1817, Jamaica Archives.
33. Appendix to the seventh report from the select committee on sugar and coffee planting, Great Britain Parliament – House of Commons, 1848, pp. 229.
34. Estate crop accounts (Woodside, St Mary) 1B/11/4/81.24, Jamaica Archives.

35. Talks with Mrs Pearl Crossman who had learnt this from Mrs
    Gladys Walker who was very informed about the history of
    Woodside and had written the first published historical account of
    the village (1972). This account – three pages – appears in *The
    Banana Church*, a pamphlet to commemorate 150 years of service
    given by the Anglicans to the area.
36. As with her husband in 1820, she signs a document edited to read
    "if a quaker, affirm". See Slave Returns for St Mary 1B/11/7/103,
    Jamaica Archives.
37. Search facilitated by Mr Melbourne B. Wint of the Anglican
    Church Office. According to the information he prepared for me,
    "Neilson, J et al" gave 15 and 1 rood to the "Incorporated lay
    body". This land was conveyed and transferred in 1881 by
    certificate of title NS11/Folio 217.
38. Talks over several years with Mr Arnold Remikie/Ranniki/
    Ramiki who seems to have been of new African stock, coming into
    the island in the 1840s and into Woodside by the 1880s.
39. *Jamaica Almanack*, 1811, 1821, 1826, 1828, 1832, 1840.
40. Appendix to the seventh report from the select committee on sugar
    and coffee planting.
41. Wills: Liber 109.112 1828 and 110.103 1829. Also Deeds LOS 786
    folio no. 167, Island Record Office, Jamaica.
42. Estate crop accounts 1B/11/4/77/230, Jamaica Archives.
43. *Jamaica Almanack*, 1828, 1832.
44. StM1089, Map Collection, National Library of Jamaica.
45. *Jamaica Almanack*, 1840.
46. StM558, Map Collection, National Library of Jamaica.
47. StM51, Map Collection, National Library of Jamaica.
48. *Register of Property Tax from August 1st 1869 to July 1st 1870 and
    Parish Council of St Mary – statement of land tax and arrears paid in St
    Mary 1881-1882*, Jamaica Archives.
49. StM558, Map Collection, National Library of Jamaica.
50. Wills: Liber 109.112 1828 and 110.103 1829. Also Deeds LOS 786
    folio no. 167, Island Record Office, Jamaica.
51. Deeds LOS 786.167 (1833) Island Record Office.
52. Tale told to me in 1995 by Noel (Bishie) Walker, great-grandson of
    the enslaved Mary Ann Drew.
53. Information given in 1995 through personal communication, by
    Mrs Leonora Brisset great grand daughter of the enslaved, Mary
    Ann Drew.
54. Told to me in 1995 by Noel (Bishie) Walker; and talks with Busha
    Brown and his older and distant cousin, Eustace Brown, 1995.

INDEX

WHEN I WAS A CHILD

When I Was A Child
Copyright © A. B. McClintock
Illustrations copyright © E Bruce
Published by Kilmunart
ISBN 978-1-78280-209-9

Printed by E & R Inglis Ltd, 84 John Street, Dunoon PA23 7NS

This book is dedicated to Ann's
granddaughter Hannah who has
brought her grandparents so much joy.

CONTENTS

INTRODUCTION

Ann McClintock is a former university lecturer in psychology and communication. In the course of her career she has had to write a great deal of what she would call "academic stuff", including a couple of textbooks. This book, however, is anything but academic. It is simply a selection of the poems and stories she has jotted down over the years in spare moments on spare paper and generally handwritten.

The book has been illustrated by Elizabeth Bruce, a member of the Glasgow Society of Women Artists, who has exhibited throughout the UK. Liz is an enthusiastic supporter of the Open Studios phenomenon and was Chair of Cowal Open Studios for three years from 2010-2013.

Although most of the works are written in the first person, they are not autobiographical. Some of the settings, however, are based on real places or events.

For example, for those of you who have never visited Glasgow, the smell that emanates from some of the stations of the Glasgow underground metro system is so distinctive that no native of Glasgow could ever forget it. A smell compounded of damp earth, disinfectant, urine and what can only be described as "wet dog" wafts up from the nether regions and, in the days when smoking was allowed, mingled with the smell of cigarettes, fish and chips and the freshly inked newspapers the vendors sell at the station entrances.

The Waverley, too, is real – the last sea-going paddle steamer in the world. Every year it is in danger of disappearing due to lack of funds to maintain it. And every year people and funding organisations rally round to ensure that it keeps on going. The illustration on the front cover is reminiscent of the days when Glasgow children came "doon the water" on the Waverley for a day out at the seaside. And, though this is Scotland, it didn't always rain!

For those who don't remember his TV shows, Uri Geller is a real broadcaster and parapsychologist who claims, among other things, to be able to stop or start clocks at a distance simply by the power of his mind.

And there was once a chance encounter on a train with an exceptionally well dressed old gentleman. But the rest of the story, like all the others, is pure, unadulterated fiction.

THE LOTTERY

I won the lottery last week!
Well, no, I didn't actually win it.
But I had all the right numbers –
even the bonus one

And it I'd been my Aunty Jenny
instead of me I would have won.
But then again, maybe I wouldn't.
Aunty Jenny would never have bet
on the lottery in the first place

Och, I can see I'm confusing you.

So let me tell you the whole story
from the beginning.

To do that I have to go back a long
way; to the first world war, in fact.

You see, my Uncle Jim was stationed out in Ireland during the war and there he met and fell in love with a young Irish lass called Jenny McQueen. He didn't marry her at the time because, like all the young men, he didn't know if he'd survive the war and he didn't want to leave her a widow wumman, maybe with a bairn to support as well.

But Jenny was the seventh child of a seventh child, so, of course, she had the second sight. She predicted that Uncle Jim would survive the war, that he would come back for her and that she would be waiting for him. And so it turned out. After the war Uncle Jim went back to Ireland and there she was, waiting for him just as she'd said. So delighted was he to have found her again that he married her there and then and brought her back home to Scotland as his bride.

I wasn't born then, of course, but they tell me she caused a great sensation with her height (she was nearly six feet tall) and her flaming red hair. They'd never seen anyone like her hereabouts. They said she must have kissed the blarney stone before she left Ireland for she had the gift of the gab. She'd say things like "words are a silken cord that can weave a mantle so fine that only the angels can tell the tale of it." Och, she had the words alright!

Anyway, because she had the words and the second sight, another thing that Aunty Jenny could do was read the future in the tea cups. She'd get you to drink down to the last dregs, turn the cup upside down and birl it round three times in the saucer. Then she'd look inside and say things like, "Oh, I see a bit of sweetness here, and there's news of a wedding – or perhaps an engagement - within a three. Yes, definitely within a three. But whether it's three days or months or years, the cup doesn't say." And, sure enough, the person would hear of a wedding. Aunty Jenny's predictions always came true.

She taught me to read the cups because I am the third child of a third child, and, though the second sight isn't as powerful in a third child as it is in a seventh child, it's still there all the same. To tell you the truth, I'm not sure if I did predict the future or if I just used my imagination and made it all up. But people used to say I showed a lot of my Aunty in me, so maybe I did see something without realising it.

It wasn't only in the teacups that Aunty Jenny could see things. Oh dear me no! She could understand dreams and find things that had been lost. My cousin Nan went to her in a great state one day because she'd lost her wedding ring. Aunty Jenny said,

"I'll just have a bit of cheese for my supper. That should help me to dream and we will see what we will see….."

Aunty Jenny was a great believer in a bit of cheese to help the dreaming process. Of course, it didn't always work. Sometimes it just kept her awake or gave her the heartburn. But when it did work it was a powerful stimulus.

The night Cousin Nan asked her to find her ring Aunty Jenny dreamed that it lay in the bottom corner of the bed sheet, gripped tight in the jaws of a pair of false teeth. Cousin Nan rushed off right away to look at the bottom of the sheet, though she wasn't too keen on the false teeth bit. Sure enough, there was her ring, wedged right down in the corner of the bed and not a false tooth in sight. Aunty Jenny said that was to be expected. Dreams are dreams, after all and they take poetic licence. You can't just take them at face value. They have to be interpreted. That's where the gift comes in!

Aunty Jenny's gift even extended to dreaming the winner of races – though she could never tell if it was horses or dogs she saw and, of course, she couldn't give the whole name, just an impression of, say, a crown or a scarecrow, or the initials of a name. But she never put a bet on herself. She thought that was a sinful exploitation of her gift. She'd tell the butcher or the fish man, though, when they came round with their vans; and if they put a bet on and it came up a winner they'd slip her an extra bit of fish or meat. Which, they told me, was very welcome in those days!

Well, it's a far cry from these days today and Aunty Jenny is long dead and buried. But I dreamt about her the other night. I dreamt I was sitting at my dressing table brushing my hair. In the mirror I could see Aunty Jenny. She was standing on the stage and she was calling out the winning numbers for the lottery. As the balls came down I could see them in the mirror as plain as I could see myself. There they were:

12, 13, 32, 34, 41, 42,

and the bonus ball; 11.

So I bought a lottery ticket and I had high hopes that Aunty Jenny's gift would not let me down.

On Saturday night I sat there with my ticket smoothed out beside me on the arm of my chair. When the numbers were called out I could hardly contain myself. There they were:

21, 31, 23, 43, 14, 24,

And the bonus ball; 11

I couldn't believe it! Oh, I had the bonus ball alright but all the other numbers were exactly reversed. 12 had become 21, 41 had become 14 and so on. I had the right numbers but in their mirror image.

Then it came to me! I remembered Aunty Jenny's words. "Dreams have to be interpreted." Of course! That was it! In my dream I'd seen the numbers in the mirror but I hadn't the sense to know I should have turned them round the right way. What a fool I was. Aunty Jenny would have known better. But then, Aunty Jenny wouldn't have bought a ticket in the first place. It serves me right for being so greedy as to try to exploit the gift of the second sight. So, that's it! I won't be buying another lottery ticket. Well, I don't think I will. But then again, I might just get into the habit of taking a little bit of cheese for my supper. Just in case, you understand. Just in case!

Conviviality

Fruit and wine,
Flowers,
And meat served in a pot
Made - and given me –
By a friend.
The domestic trappings
Of a simple meal,
But, for me,
Symbols
Of conviviality.

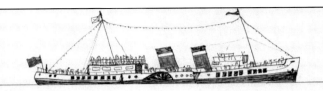

Slowly, softly, with red paint gleaming
The old ship Waverley comes steaming
Into the pier
Like a prodigal returning
From many a year
Of banishment.

The small crowd welcomes it.
On board, a few friendly souls
Raise hands in greeting
And on the pier uncertain arms
Wave feebly back.

The gang plank is lowered.
A child rushes forward
Only to be caught,
Safe in adult arms.

A would be poet calls:
"Pay a visit to Blairmore Halls
Pots of tea and lots of stalls.

Or join the friends of Blairmore Pier
To show you're happy to be here
On a sunny day in two thousand and five
When it's really good to be alive."

As they turn towards the village
The man's voice is heard again.
"My wife says the trouble with me
Is that I've never grown up.
It's true I suppose.
But why should I?
I have to grow old.
Do I need to grow up as well?"

As his voice fades in the distance
I look again at the grand old lady of the sea,
With her newly painted livery.
She looks much as she would in her youth
And still inspires the excitement of a child.
Maybe the man was right.
Like the Waverly, we must all grow old.
But as for growing up ----there, we still have a
choice.

Ma Man Likes Sailin

Ma man likes sailin in a wee oary boat
Wi the sun glinting on his ripplin muscles
An him as brave and sonsy as a Viking
Only no jist as big.

Ma man likes sailing in a wee speed boat
Skelping ower the waves
Like a stane ower a pond;
An him Bond – James Bond.

Ma man likes sailing in a yacht
Wi the wind in his hair
An him the captain in Moby Dick
Hunting the whale.
(Though there's no that mony whales
In the Holy Loch.)

Ma man likes sailing in the Guid Ship Waverley
We haund ower oor concession tickets
And we're aff
Tae Millport , Largs, Arran, Rothesay
Or the Kyles of Bute.

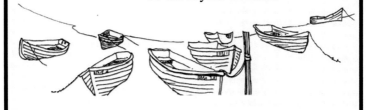

An come rain, wind or sun,
Ma man taks me up on the top deck
An he tells me a about the workings o the paddles
In *great* detail.

Then it's doon below
For a cup o tea an a scone
A look at the engines,
An a wee sermon
On the heyday
Of the steam ships on the Clyde.

Aye Ma man fairly likes sailing.

A don't like sailing.

But a really love ma man!

The Witch

Auld Granny Stoker was a witch. Everyone said so. Even Alice Thomson's Ma, and she was always telling us how it was wrong to speak ill of our fellow mortals. Yet she had Granny Stoker summed up alright. I heard her talking to my Ma one day.

"That old witch leads a charmed life. You can't deny that."

And, right enough, the evidence was there, plain for all to see. She lived in the end house on our

street. Well, it was only half a house really because a German bomb had sliced off the other half during the war. You could still see the fireplaces, one on the ground floor and another one half way up the wall where the bedroom would have been. There were big pink roses on the bedroom wallpaper and you could just make out the words of a text that had been stencilled above the mantlepiece. "Thou God see-est ..." The rest of the text was gone along with the wallpaper.

They say that when the bomb started to fall it was on a direct course for Granny Stoker's house, but she ran out into the middle of the road and shook her fist at it and shouted curses and spells. Whereupon, the bomb shifted it's course slightly and landed on the house next door instead. One of the Miss Patersons was killed outright. The other was so badly injured she had to go into a home somewhere. Granny Stoker was flung to the ground by the blast. But, when she came round, she just picked herself up and walked back into her own house, closing and bolting the door behind her.

Everyone says the heat in her front room must have been fierce and the neighbours tried to coax her out, but she was having none of it. They could see her moving around and drinking from a bottle that she kept on a shelf beside her chair. She wouldn't let anyone in, and she never came out for five days. But they say that in the middle of the night you could hear her singing and mumbling curses like the ones she'd used on the German bomb. Everyone was a bit wary of her after that because those who knew about such things assured us that that she was indeed a witch.

Of course none of us children knew what it was like in the witch's house. We couldn't see in the front windows because of the heavy net curtains, and the back of the house was hidden by the hawthorns that had grown up over the years. But we had seen her. And her cat! A lean black devil that stalked the pigeons through the yards and sent them squawking over the fences. Sometimes it was lucky and caught one, and you'd hear the men complaining about how the auld witch's cat had stalked it's last. But they never did anything about it.

Sometimes it sat on the front door step "like a demon guarding the portals of hell" Alice Thomson said. Other times it perched on the wall at the side of the house, ready to arch and hiss at anyone foolhardy enough to pass there. That's when we'd try to get the better of it. We'd wait till it was sitting on the wall then we'd creep round to the back and throw tin cans into the garden. The cat would leap and pounce on the cans and we'd race round to the front and bang on the witch's door. Then we'd hide, shivering and giggling, behind the wall across the road.

It was on these occasions that we'd see the witch herslf. She'd open the door and peer out, shaking her fist and mumbling curses. At least we took them to be curses. We never waited to make sure. At the first sight of that small black figure we'd take fright and run like fury over the yards and down to the burn where we knew we were safe.

We knew we were safe there because witches can't stand running water. We'd read that in a book at school so we knew it was true. In fact, it was the book that gave us our idea. That and Smithy Johnson's father.

Smithy's Da had something wrong with his chest. You always knew if he was anywhere around. You'd hear him hawking and spitting, and he'd have this terrible grey look on his face that'd make you think he was going to die on the spot. But then he'd straighten up and spit out a great glob of muck and you'd know he'd live awhile yet.

Smithy's Da didn't go to work. He had a plot of land over the fence and he used to grow potatoes and cabbages and swedes and things. He'd sell these to our Mas and they'd always give him a bit extra above what he'd asked because they'd be sorry for Smithy's Ma - her not having a regular wage, only the money she got from the wellfare.

Anyway, that summer it was very hot. "A scorcher" everybody said. We spent most of our time playing with the mud that was all that was left of the burn, and trailing sticks through the melted tar on the road so we could write things with them on the walls.

It was so hot that the vegetables in Smithy's Da's lot turned yellow and fell over to lie like thin old rags against the dried up earth. Smithy's Da used to get us to carry buckets of water from the sink and sluice them over the plot. At first it was fun, but it was real hard work and it didn't seem to help much so we took to throwing the buckets of water over each other which, needless to say, did not go down well with Smithy's Da. Even though Smithy had to help, the rest of us soon learned to make ourselves scarce when we saw the sun going down and knew it was time for the watering.

One Friday when the milkman came round, he stoppped his van outside Smithy's door and went round the back. We thought Smithy 's Ma hadn't paid again and he was trying to collect, but then he came back with Smithy's Da and the pair of them dragged this great coiled hose out of the van and left it in the yard.

The hose was old and leaked in half a dozen places but when Smithy's Da had patched it up it worked a treat. We took it in turns to hold it, sending the spray high up into the sky and trying to create rainbows like the boys sometimes did with their pee in the school playground when the teachers weren't looking. Then we watched the water slowing turning the parched earth from grey to black and then silver. And we could smell the soft wet scent of it rising.

We drenched each other with it too and that's how our idea finally crystallised into a plan - a brilliantly, stupendously clever plan. A plan that would prove once and for all and beyond a shadow of a doubt ("conclusively," Alice said) that Granny Stoker was a witch. We sat down by the dried out burn and worked it all out.

The next night, after we'd finished watering the plot, we dragged the hose round the front. Smithy stayed behind to man the tap and Dennis and I held the hose. Katie Smith was the fastest runner so she had the hardest job. At first she said she wouldn't do it but we called her "cowardy custard" and that made her mad, so she had to do it just to prove she wasn't scared. She tiptoe'd up to the witch's house and banged hard on the door with her fist. Then she ran round the back to tell Smithy it was time.

It worked perfectly! Just as auld Granny Stoker opened her door a thin hard jet spurted from the hose and caught her smack in the face. She let out a yell and we watched, fascinated, waiting to see her de-materialise. (That's what the book says happens to witches when they come in contact with running water. They de-materialise.)

Only she didn't de-materialise. She just sank down under the onslaught of the water, hugging her knees and crying and moaning as the water soaked into her hair and dripped down her face and onto her black jumper. The hose slipped out of our hands and water collected in puddles at our feet but still she didn't de-materialise - just sat there on the wet doorstep, rocking and moaning.

Smithy's Ma said we should "think black burning shame of ourselves for tormenting a pair auld body". And Smithy's Da said he'd "like tae tak a belt tae the lot o ye". And suddenly it didn't seem like such a great idea any more. We just stood there looking at her and saying nothing.

We didn't talk about it much afterwards either, just compared notes on what our parents had done to punish us. From time to time we still threw cans for the cat, but the fun had gone out of it. We only did it to show we didn't care. Eventually we stopped. We found a haunted house down by the river and we made that our den for the rest of the summer. Nobody mentioned Granny Stoker. Then one day Alice, who had obviously been giving the subject a lot of thought, gave us some comfort.

"I mean," she said in that affected voice of hers "I mean we didn't prove conclusively that she isn't a witch. It stands to reason that any old water isn't going to make her de-materialise. We should have realised that it obviously has to be Holy Water. And I for one am absolutely certain that she is a witch."

The rest of us were certain too. Maybe not quite so absolutely certain as Alice, but certain enough. Granny Stoker was a witch. Everyone had always said so!

Tempus Fugit

There may yet be
A plan
For man.
We know nought of it.

We may yet see
The dove
Of love.
We have not sought it.

Man may yet free
His mind
From time.
When he has stopped –
And caught it!

When I Was A Child

When I was a child I spoke as a child.
(Rock-a-bye baby on the tree top.)
    I understood as a child.
    (Bye baby bunting
    Daddy's gone a hunting.)

    Three blind mice
    And the wicked witch
    Who cut off their tails with a
        carving knife;
     And the good fairy who could
     Put Humpty together again.

But when I became woman
(Rock-a-bye baby on the tree top)
I put away childish things.

The wind blows
(Rock a bye baby on the tree top)

The wind blows
And the mice are merely
Another pattering irritation
In the kitchen

The wind blows
And
(pat-a-cake, pat-a-cake)
Daddy's gone a hunting
With the wicked witch.

The wind blows.
And there is no good fairy
To put back the pieces
Of the broken bough.

27

FORSYTHIA

There is,
There has to be,
An excuse for them.
Those foolish children
Who, I suppose,
Did not know any better
When they killed the tree.

I painted the stumps
And lifted the broken boughs
To place in water.
To watch their flowering
Only for me.
Those springtime flowers,
Whose branches you do not prune,
In springtime.

The yellow flowers
Grow only on the wood
Of last year's green

They bloomed for a time, these flowers
Before they fell,
Replaced by green, green leaves.
The green, green leaves
which grow only after the flowers
On the boughs
Of last year's wood.

And now they are but a memory
A memory kept alive
By the sound of passing children.

Last year's children
   Who, I suppose,
      Did not know any better
         When they killed the tree.

THE EASTER BUNNY

I heard the back door bang shut and waited for the inevitable long drawn out

"Mumeee."

"In here," I called.

There were another two bangs which I took to be discarded wellies, and a small figure appeared in the doorway, pulling off hat, anorak and scarf as she came.

"Mummy, we're doing a play tomorrow and I'm the Easter Bunny. And Mary's the Mummy rabbit and Miss Anderson says have you any white fur and empty cornflake packets or earmuffs and ..."

"Hey, slow down, " I laughed. "How about a glass of milk and a biscuit and you can tell me all about it?"

I looked fondly at my little daughter. Her fine brown hair lay in wispy tendrils which kept falling over her eyes. Blue eyes, that looked at me out of a pale, thin face, so like her father's. I sighed. I didn't want to forget, but I did wish I could somehow dull the pain I still felt after nearly a year. Ian's eyes used to light up like that, too, when he was excited. He was so full of life. There was something obscene about the way his body had lain after the crash, with only his face untouched. I could feel the familiar guilt and anger rising in me. Why hadn't he taken a taxi? Why had he insisted on driving home from the party?

I knew the answer, of course. Ian couldn't bear to lose face in front of his mates. He wouldn't want them to think he couldn't handle a drink. Stupid, macho attitude!   Maybe, if I'd been with him it wouldn't have happened.   If the baby sitter hadn't cancelled?   If I hadn't insisted that he go along without me? It was *his* friend's birthday, after all, not mine. If the other guy had been driving a bit more carefully? If........if, if if.

I pushed back the thoughts that crowded in on me and forced myself to listen to Dawn. She was still chatting excitedly, determined to make the most of her news.

"....and so will you Mummy? Pleeeeese!"

I looked at her eager little face and smiled.

"Come on, let's see what's in my bag. There might be some fur, but I can't guarantee that it'll be white."

The 'bag' was a large polythene laundry bag which held all the bits and pieces left over from the days when dressmaking had been a favourite hobby of mine. I had kept them in the hope that they might come in handy some day. They seldom did, and I hadn't looked into it properly in ages. We fished it out from the cupboard under the stairs. It was nearly full and everthing was jumbled together.

"Well," I said, "we'll be lucky to find anything in here. I've no idea what's at the bottom of this lot."

"Empty it out, Mummy. Please."

She was already delving in and rummaging about.

"Just a minute. Let's get this into the living room first, so we can see what we're doing."

The pile of cloth flowed over the living room carpet. Bits of lace, wool, soft filmy nylon, grey terelyne left over from an office skirt, bright summer cottons, some of the pieces so small as to make me wonder why on earth I'd kept them. And a piece of white fur fabric from a teddy bear I'd once made for a friend's new baby.

Dawn went into raptures over it, stroking it and digging her fingers into the pile.

"Will it be big enough," she asked anxiously?

"Oh, I think so." I reassured her. "Rabbit's tails aren't very big.   Just sort of round and fluffy, like this."

I rolled the fur into a ball and gave it to her. She rubbed it gently against her cheek.

"I bet this is the best tail in the whole class. Better than Mary's anyway. Her Mum said she'd use cotton wool.   I heard her say it when we were coming back in her car."

I left her sorting the cloth into piles and went to make the tea.

Later, when she'd finally fallen asleep, the white fur carefully packed in a plastic bag and tucked into her satchel, beside the earmuffs - which I'd kept since my skating days - and the ubiquitous cereal packet, I looked at the piles of material on the living room floor, and, in a fit of righteousness, decided to tackle "the bag". It was ridiculous to keep all those tiny bits! I spent most of the evening on it, being as ruthless as I could. Some of the bits brought back memories. Remnants of red satin from the dress I'd made in an evening because we'd been invited to a surprise party and I'd nothing to wear. It looked fine until I decided to press it with a hot iron and shrivelled the material at the front of the neckline. No-one was rude enought to ask why I'd pinned a large artificial rose across my cleavage. I guess they thought it was a fashion statement.

Then there were the bits of towelling I'd kept from a beach robe to make matching face flannels, only to find that the beautiful blue colour ran when it was wet! I was surprised to find myself smiling over them. I suddenly felt as if Ian was very close to me; as if he was laughing with me, in that infuriating teasing way of his.

I pushed the bag quickly into the cupboard and went to make a cup of tea.

"Oh, God!" I sighed. "Let me sleep tonight. Just one night without waking at 4am and finding myself caught in the same jumble of pointless thoughts. Just one night!"

I didn't expect my prayer - if that's what it was - to be answered. And I was right. Four o'clock found me as usual, wide-eyed and exhausted. I got up and made yet another cup of tea, took a couple of asprins and went wearily back to our big double bed.

The next day I discovered that I needn't have rushed to get the stuff together for the play. Miss Anderson explained that she was planning to start rehearsing the children that day but that the play itself would take place in a couple of weeks - just before the Easter Break - and that parents would, of course, be invited to come along if they could make it.

The next couple of weeks passed in much the same way as usual. I worked from nine to three, which gave me time to get home for Dawn and take my turn with the other mothers in the school run. Occasionally I'd invite one of the other mothers in for coffee, or I'd stop for a cuppa with one of them and we'd swap stories about our respective children.

. Dawn was very excited about her part in the play and talked non-stop about it. I was happy to hear her chattering away and glad that she finally seemed to have regained the spontanaeity that she had lost for a while after Ian's death.

It was in the evenings, after Dawn had gone down for the night, that I felt the loneliness most. Ocasionally an old friend would drop in, but, on the whole, our married friends hardly ever called or invited me out now. I suppose they felt they had to be so careful of what they said and this made them awkward and somehow embarrassed in my presence.

One day Dawn presented me with an invitation to the play. It read

> CLASS 2A INVITES YOU TO A
> PERFORMANCE OF
> THE EASTER BUNNY
> In the school hall on Fri. 4th April at 2pm
> **RSVP**

On the back she had painstakingly signed it in her best writing and drawn a picture of a rather lopsided rabbit alongside her signature. On the front there was a smudge at the bottom and then some wobbly letters which read RSVP.

"Do I have to write a note to say I'm coming, " I asked, pointing to the letters, "or do I just say I'm coming?"

Dawn wrinkled her brow.

"I'm not sure. Miss Anderson said it was short for French. She said we didn't need to put it in but we could if we wanted to. Is it wrong?" she asked anxiously.

"No it's certainly not wrong. In fact, all the important invitations have these letters. And Miss Anderson is right. The letters are short for words in French which mean 'please reply to this letter'. Come on upstairs and I'll show you something."

Her brow cleared and she bounded ahead of me up the stairs, taking them two at a time. I fished some old invitations out of the bureau drawer and showed her the tiny letters in the corner.

"Can I take them," she asked "to show Miss Anderson and Mary?"

"No darling" I started, "Mummy..."

Her face fell and the light died out of her eyes.

"Did you go to these places with Daddy?" she whispered.

I hugged her close and wondered at the insight of this small person who was a part of us both. I realised I wasn't being fair to her. She was just starting out. It wasn't fair to saddle her with my problems. I held her out at arm's length and tried to smile.

"Yes, " I said, as brightly as I could "Mummy and Daddy had a lovely time at some of these parties. We were very happy."

She nodded solemnly.

"And now you're sad?   Because Daddy isn't here any more?"

I nodded. "Yes, I'm a little bit sad. But..."

Before I could finish, she slipped her small soft fingers between mine and said

"But Daddy wasn't a sad person. He wouldn't have wanted you to be sad. He always made us laugh, didn't he?"

I looked down at her face, so like Ian's.   It was as if he was talking to me through his child.

With a sudden change in tone, she said "he would tickle you if you were sad. I've seen him."

She reached up impishly and tickled me under the arms. Unable to resist, I found myself laughing with her and, suddenly, a feeling of relief surged through me. She was going to be alright. And I would be too. Hovering somewhere between laughter and tears, I looked down at the sheaf of invitations in my hand.

"Here," I said, "you take these. You can show them to Miss Anderson and Mary and then bring them back and keep them for yourself. Mummy doesn't need them now and Daddy would want you to have them."

Her eyes widened.   "To keep?"

I nodded.

"For ever and ever?"

"Yes," I laughed, "for ever and ever."

"Oh boy. I bet Mary's Mummy doesn't have proper French invitations."

She jumped up and hugged me vigorously.

"You're the best Mummy in the world."

"And you're the best little girl. Now, Bed!"

She made a face at me - so very like her Father's when he was in one of his joking moods - and ran off towards the bathroom.

That night, for the first time in months, I slept right through till the morning.

37

On the Loss of a Goldfish from a Garden Pool

Look at the gulls" called Myra,
"look at the gulls".

Wingtip to fluttering wingtip
Beating time to a mad cacophony of sound.
Melancholy music out of time and key
Like a passage from a symphony
       Half-remembered,
       Distorted,
       In the fragment of a dream.
       Powerful yet elusive!
       Swooping and hovering just out of reach
       But within sight and sound.
       Their collective greed
       Forces attention. And -

"Look at the gulls
Called Myra
"Look at the gulls."

One, greedier than the rest perhaps,
        Or bolder,
        Or in greater need,
        Swoops, seizes a fish
        And soars upwards,
        It's strong wings
        harnessing the wind,
Shearing the surface of the pool
Into a myriad spray of rainbows.

        The small fish struggles,
        Powerless in that cruel beak.
        For a moment it glistens
        Golden in the sun
        And then is gone.

A small crock of gold,
Swallowed by the predator
Who can make rainbows!

SUN-DAPPLED

Florida landscape - flat and green.
A landscape peppered with hyphens.
Wall-to-wall hamburgers
Jostle
Disney-sloganned tee-shirts.
Designer-chosen flowers
In silk-dyed colours
Bloom confined
In man-made beds
Within leisure-inspired
Theme-parks.
Air-conditioned shopping-malls
Are ice-cold protectors
From the white-hot Florida sunshine.

Florida sunshine –
strong and dazzling.
It's spontanaeity cannot be
confined.

It bursts it's way through the planned
foliage
To dapple grass and flowers
With random patterns of light.

In this man-made environment
It defies man's design.

Gentleman John

The train wasn't busy when I boarded it at Plymouth but I knew from experience that it would be standing room only by the time we got to Glasgow. So, being of a naturally selfish disposition, I set about taking precautions to preserve my space from intruders for as long as possible.

I spread out my magazines, books, coats and other accoutrements in what I hoped looked like a convincing display of multiple occupancy. Alas, it was not to be. Immediately I heard a voice.

"Excuse me, is this seat taken?" Apparently absorbed in the view of an empty crisp packet on the grey platform, I feigned deafness.

"Excuse me," said the voice a shade more loudly, "Is this seat taken?"

Reluctantly, I transferred my gaze to the speaker, gave a bleak smile and resigned myself to the inevitable. "No, it's not taken. I'll just move these things."

As he made himself comfortable in the seat opposite I studied his reflection in the window. He was a small man, not much over five foot two and in his early seventies I'd have said. And he looked....I searched my mind for the right adjective. He looked...dapper. That was it! Dapper! It's not a word that springs readily to my mind but it was the only word to describe him. A dapper little gentleman!

He was wearing a suit of some expensive looking dark material. It was beautifully cut but of a style fashionable some twenty years before. Just visible across his waistcoat was a chunky gold Albert watch chain. He carried a black walking stick with a monogrammed gold handle, and a dark felt hat, both of which he placed carefully on the seat beside him.

As I watched he pulled a paperback book out of an inside pocket. The book was old and dog eared, curiously out of place in the hands of such a dapper man. Indeed the hands themselves seemed out of place. Lined and calloused with dirty cracked nails, they seemed to belong to someone else entirely. As he seemed intent on his reading, I judged that it might be safe to reach for my own book. Perhaps, after all, he would not prove to be the talkative travelling companion I'd dreaded.

Looking back on it now it seems odd that I went to such lengths to avoid human contact. Even more odd that, when he finally leant across and offered me a cigarette from a lovely gold case, I found myself falling quite naturally into conversation with him; a conversation which lasted throughout almost the entire journey and with not a hint of boredom.

By the time we reached Edinburgh we'd exchanged addresses. I'd promised to look him up if I was ever in his part of town. He'd promised to send me a leather bookmark like the one he had, which I'd admired and which he confided that he made as a hobby. And that was that! He left the train at Edinburgh and I continued on alone to Glasgow.

Several weeks passed. It was almost Christmas. I had practically forgotten the encounter on the train, when, one morning, the postman delivered a small package. Inside was a beautifully tooled navy leather bookmark and a Christmas card bearing the words, "As promised. With sincere good wishes for the festive season, John Paterson".

Touched that he'd remembered me, I dug out the slip of paper bearing the address of the cousin with whom he stayed. Major Johnson, 22 Aberdale Avenue. By way of thanks I sent him one of the small watercolours I liked to paint when I had some spare time and added a note on a Christmas card, telling him a little about the latest exploits of my son, whom we'd talked about on the train.

The following Christmas his card was one of the first to arrive. This time, he too had added a note about his brother in Plymouth and his niece, who was doing very well as a doctor in the local hospital down there. I responded in kind and over the following years we continued to exchange cards every

Christmas, always enclosing a note about our latest news as if we were old friends.

Then, last year, there was no card from him. I sent one as usual and wondered, briefly, if he was ill. But I was busy with other things and didn't pursue it. In fact, I'd completely forgotten about him when, in February, I received a note from his cousin, Major Johnson. John, it seemed had died of pneumonia just before Christmas. He'd left a number of items which the Major thought I might like to have as mementoes if I'd care to come and collect them.

Intrigued, touched and a little saddened, I set off for Edinburgh the first chance I had. I didn't phone first. I don't know why. Just didn't think of it I suppose. So it was only when I reached Edinburgh that I realised that I hadn't a clue where Aberdale Avenue was. I consulted a map. Aberdale Avenue was not, as I had imagined, one of the fine Georgian terraces but a small, bleak street in a run down quarter of the East End. I rolled down the car window and tried to look for Number 22. When this proved impossible, I finally found a parking space and continued on foot, checking the numbers as I went. 16, 18, 20, 22. Number 22 was a Salvation Army Hostel for down and outs! I checked again, but there was no mistake. 22 Aberdale Avenue was a hostel.

There was no-one at the desk in the foyer. I ran the bell and gazed around as I waited. My attention was caught by a small framed watercolour on the wall behind the desk. It looked vaguely familiar. Then I realised why. It was the one I had sent to John all these years ago. Puzzled by its presence here, I turned to speak to the man who'd just come to the desk.

"Hello. I'm Major Johnson. Can I help you?"

"Ah, Major Johnson. John told me about you. He said you were his cousin and that he stayed with you. But somehow I had the impression that you were a military man and that this was your home rather than your work address."

"I'm sorry." The Major looked confused. "I'm not sure what you mean."

"Oh no, I'm sorry. I should have introduced myself. I'm Linda Marshall."

"Linda Marshall? I.."

"Yes, you sent me a letter about your cousin John's death and asked me to come and collect some mementoes when I had the chance. I hope you don't mind me turning up out of the blue like this. I realise I should have let you know I was coming. But I just happened to have a free day and took off on the spur of the moment. It was very rude of me, especially bothering you at work like this."

"Oh, it's no bother. I don't mind in the least. Did you know John well?"

"No, not at all. Actually, I only met him once. On a train. But we kept in touch every Christmas and we became friendly. I liked him a lot and I was quite upset when you wrote and told me he'd died."

The Major nodded sadly. "Yes, we were all fond of John. We'll miss him. But I'm afraid he was a terrible liar."

"A liar," I stammered. "What do you mean?"
The Major smiled. "Look let's not stand here in this draughty foyer. Better come through to the office and I'll explain."

He led me through to the dingy office behind the foyer and pointed to a row of steel lockers on one wall.

"Do you see those lockers? Well, we use them to keep safe any items that our guests regard as precious. To avoid them being stolen. You understand?"
I nodded dumbly, but I didn't really understand. Not yet.
The major went on.

"John first started coming here about fifteen years ago. He was an alcoholic. He'd disappear on binges for weeks at a time. He'd come back here to dry out then he'd be off again. Often as not he'd end up in the hospital before coming back here."

"But," I interrupted, "his clothes….he looked so…"
I paused remembering the hands that had seemed so out of place. Somehow the "dapper" seemed out of place now too.

"He looked" I said, "such a gentleman."
The major chuckled.

"Yes. Gentleman John. We christened him that when the lady from Morningside gave him the clothes. I'm not sure where he got hold of the other things but he was so proud of them. That's why we agreed to keep them locked up for him permanently in the locker."

"But he was wearing them when I met him."

"Yes. Now that's a curious thing. Once a year at about the same time he came in quite sober and got all dressed up. Then off he went to Plymouth to pay his respects to his brother. Goodness only knows where he got the money for the fare."

"Then that part of his story at least was true. He told me he stayed with his brother in Plymouth and about his niece, Jennifer. She's a doctor. He was really proud of her."

Again the Major smiled sadly.

"Yes, Jennifer is a doctor – at the Royal Edinburgh Hospital, where John went to dry out – but she's no more his niece than I am his cousin. And I'm afraid that wherever he lived in Plymouth it wasn't with his brother. His brother died in the war; blown up in his ship in Plymouth docks."

It was with a heavy heart that I took my leave of the Major and walked back to the car. As I turned towards it I caught sight of a small antique shop tucked between two tenements. In the front of the window was a collection of bookmarks tooled in fine leather. I looked at the card. "Handmade in Edinburgh by Vera McGinn". I smiled wryly. So, even the bookmark was a lie. I'd really liked him, but my poor dapper little gentleman had been a complete fraud.

I tossed the gold topped cane, the cigarette case and the watch chain into the back seat of the car. In the cold light of day it was obvious that they were relatively cheap, gold plated imitations of the real thing. Like John himself.

And yet, he had honoured his brother's sacrifice. He had kept his promise and sent me a bookmark. He had kept in touch faithfully year on year. And now, he had left me his most precious possessions.

I glanced up at the leaden Edinburgh sky and felt a tear rolling down my cheek. Requiescat In Pace, John. Rest In Peace. I'll remember you as my dapper little gentleman – whatever the truth of it.

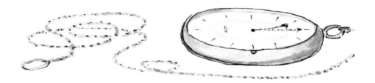

The Artist's Dilemma

I want to paint….
What? A giant-sized picture of Andy Warhol hidden under a mound of coca-cola cans?
No. I want to paint…….
Lady Gaga as Picasso would have painted her in his blue period?
No…..
A life-sized portrait of the little mermaid in the bay at Copenhagen?
No……
With red painted fingernails……
No….
And with ships in full sail behind her?
No….I want to paint….
The Mona Lisa in a thunderstorm with shutters of The Louvre flapping in the breeze behind her?
Or a thousand matadors charging into the bullring of a Spanish city - capes flying and picadors ready to hold up the ears of the bull to cheering and calling –
OLE! OLE! OLE?
No.
Well what do you want to paint then?
I want to paint….
Yes…?
I want to paint …..
I don't know what I want to paint
But I want to paint …………….

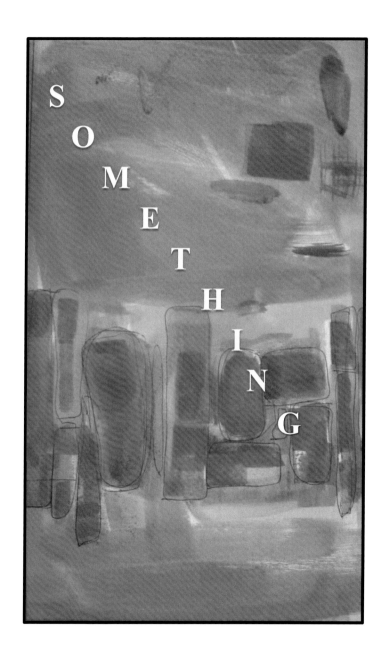

SOMETHING

The Artist

The old man stands before his easel,
In his mind he can see it now -
His canvas, glowing with the multivaried hues
Of a spring dawn.
He pauses, brush in hand, before
Making that first and telling stroke.
The placing is all important.
A failure now and the vision is ruined.
He breathes.
He considers.
He lifts the brush once more
Then slowly turns away.
Perhaps, after all, today is not the day
To make
Or break
A vision.
Tomorrow he will create a masterpiece!

As the door closes behind him
The canvas leers,
Untouched, pristine
And virginal,
As it has stood for years,
Waiting for each tomorrow.

Jimmy

I don't know whether Jimmy loved me. He never said he did. But I loved him - absolutely, totally, unconditionally. I loved the way he didn't seem to care that his socks were always puddling round his ankles. I loved the way he was able to time a sniff so that the green snot that slowly travelled down till it looked like it must go in his mouth was suddenly sniffed right back up and disappeared into his nose, ready for another excursion. Some of my friends thought it was disgusting. I loved it. I tried to copy that sniff but with nothing to sniff up it seemed pretty pointless.

Jimmy always had a cold. I hardly ever had one. When I did, it was the kind of bunged-up nose, sinus headache, sore ears and antibiotics kind of cold that made me miserable without the compensation of lots of snot to experiment with.

Most of all I loved Jimmy's smell. At the time I couldn't think what it reminded me of. Now, all those years later, I go down the steps to the Glasgow Underground and immediately I'm right back there in Primary Six with Jimmy.

Jimmy and I didn't see each other after school. He lived in "the scheme", the new houses built as overflow for Glasgow people cleared out of the tenements. I lived in The Avenue. The two weren't that far apart actually, but as far as my mother was concerned they existed in different universes.

A few months into the autumn term I did so badly in my spelling test that I was demoted from the back row right down near the front of the class, with the admonishment

"and you, young lady, will have a note to take back to your parents if you don't buck up your ideas. Laziness, " and she leaned right into my face as she said this. "Laziness will not be tolerated in this classroom. So what do you have to say to that?"

I wasn't quite sure whether she wanted an answer or not, so I tried to look contrite without actually making eye-contact with the twitch that always developed in her left eye when she was annoyed. Inside I was rejoicing. I'd done it! I'd managed to get a seat close enough to Jimmy to smell his smell and pass him secret notes with the right answers so she didn't shout at him all the time.

It didn't last, of course. I knew it wouldn't. I couldn't risk doing so badly that she'd carry out her threat and send the wretched note. Then I'd have been forced to spend hours in my room pretending to learn a lot of stuff that I already knew perfectly well. Even though I loved Jimmy dreadfully, and would have done almost anything for him, this was a sacrifice too far.

I was moved up to the back row again with a pat on the head for having "taken a tumble to myself". I was a bit upset, but before long I realised that Jimmy didn't seem to mind too much when he got the answers wrong and she shouted at him. In fact, he didn't seem to mind anything much. It made him, in my eyes, incredibly brave and strong.

Round about this time my mother began to make her annual noises about my birthday party. Until I was about eight or so I loved my birthday parties; the games, the cake with its candles, jellies, trifle, and dumpling with twenty pences in it, wrapped up in greaseproof paper. The trouble is my mother had never noticed that I was now nine, due to be ten in a few weeks, and that a ten year old does not - definitely not - want to play musical chairs or pin the tail on the donkey. Nor does she want an all girls do at three o'clock on a Saturday afternoon.

"Mum, couldn't I have my party in the evening this time?"

"Don't be absurd. It'll be dark in the evening."

"But that's the point. We could have candles to make it all nice and partyish. Or we could put the lights out and play murder in the dark and things."

"Murder in the dark! Next you'll be telling me you want to play kissing games and dirty dancing. Anyway candles are a health hazard when there's kids around. Except for the cake, of course" she added hastily. "No, we'll just have the party in the afternoon like we always do and you can have ten people at it - including yourself. That's about as many as I can manage single-handed."

"Why single handed?"

. "Oh don't be so dense, Emily. You know what I mean. Gran's getting too old to be much help. She just likes to sit and watch you all enjoying yourselves."

I felt a little guilty. I loved my Gran. But Mum's mentioning her had given me an idea. I knew, beyond a shadow of a doubt, that I wanted Jimmy to be at this party. I also knew that my mother would have a hairy fit if I even suggested it. She didn't know anything about Jimmy, or the fact that I loved him, but I knew, instinctively, that the sight of him, or even a vague mention of where he lived, would immediately relegate him to the X Zone. He would be so far out of her orbit that I wouldn't just be forbidden to have anything to do with him, she'd have him exorcised out of existence. But if I enlisted Gran's help? Mn. She was, after all, my mother's mother and, although she'd never have admitted it in a hundred years, my mother was still a little in awe of her.

Next day found me down at Gran's house, telling her all about my love for Jimmy and my need to have a more grown up party this year, with cheese cubes on sticks and pickled onions and little sausages and murder in the dark instead of musical chairs. Gran listened. Gran always listened. She handed me a freshly baked scone with raspberry jam on it, and poked at a seed that had got stuck down behind her dentures.

"Hm," she said "I can see your problem. But I'm not sure I can help much this time, love."
She paused and patted my knee reassuringly when she saw my look of dismay. I waited. She poured herself another cup of tea. Then she said

"Leave it with me, love. I'll try to sort something out. Though I warn you, it's not going to be easy."

"Oh, Gran."
I was so excited that I even forgot to say thank you, but the hug I gave her probably said it well enough.

A few days later my mother informed me of the arrangements for my party. It could start at six o'clock and everyone should be ready for collection by nine o'clock. No later! I could have about twelve or fourteen people, including myself. If I wanted to I could ask some of the girls and boys from my class as well as my friends from The Avenue.

I looked at her in astonishment.

"And I can invite people from my class? Boys?"
My mother nodded and smiled at me.

"You're growing up, Emily. I keep forgetting that. It was your Gran that reminded me about what I wanted at my parties when I was your age. And I suppose you're no different to me. So, yes, boys as well if that's what you want."

"Thanks Mum. Thanks. That's great!"
I hugged her and thought, "Good old Gran!"

When I gave Jimmy his invitation he just said "thanks" and tucked it into the back of his jotter.

"You will come, won't you, " I asked anxiously.

"Yeah, I'll try. If we get back from my Nan's in time. We always go over there on a Saturday."

"But surely if you tell your mother you've been invited to a party she'll make sure you're back in time to get ready and everything."
He stared at me for a moment then gave a funny snorty kind of laugh.

Yeah. You're right. She'll make sure I'm on time and all dressed up and ready to go"

"Oh good, because....." and Miss McDonald chose that moment to rap on her desk.

"Emily Parker, get back to your seat this minute. And Jimmy Carson, if I catch you slacking again I will not be responsible for the consequences. Do you hear?"
The last three words were accompnied by three sharp pokes in the general direction of Jimmy's chest. I sighed. Why was she always picking on him? She was just plain mean.

The Saturday of the party was drizzly and overcast and my mother was having second thoughts about the whole thing.

"I just don't know how I'm going to manage everything. I've only got one pair of hands."

"It's okay Mum, don't worry. I'm here. I can help. After all it's my party. It's the least I can do."

My mother looked somewhat dazed and wandered back into the kitchen and said something to Dad. I didn't catch what it was she said, but I heard Dad saying "what?" and then both of them laughing.

Poor old Dad! He still hates parties and social events. He doesn't mind helping - loading the dishwasher and that kind of thing, but he hates having to make polite conversation. I can understand that. I think I take after Dad more than my mother. Anyway, on that day I was determined to do my bit to make sure everything about this party was as perfect as it could be, even if it meant I wouldn't have as much time to get myself ready. And the main thing, the very best thing, was that Jimmy was coming.

By six fifteen everyone had arrived except Jimmy. By six thirty he still hadn't shown up and I was beginning to get anxious. We'd done the "stick a note on your forehead and try to guess who you are by asking other people questions" game. We'd put Gran in charge of the music for "statues". (Well, it was better than musical chairs.) We'd worked our way through two whole oranges covered with cheese and pickled onions on sticks, and we were just about to begin a game of forfeits when the doorbell rang.

I flew to anwer it.

" Jimmy I'm so glad you......"

It wasn't Jimmy. It was Kevin Paterson. He was wearing a smart suit with a white shirt and his school tie. He actually looked quite nice; different from how he normally looked. Even his hair looked different, slicked down and lying flat on the top of his head.

"Kevin, what on earth are you doing here?"

"Well it was Jimmy. He said he'd got to go to his Nan's and he doesn't much like parties anyhow. So he gave me his ticket so I could come instead. So it wouldn't be wasted like."

"His ticket?"

Kevin held out the invitation. It was still clean and uncrumpled in its crisp white envelope.

"He said you wouldn't mind. Would probably want to keep the numbers up like."

He looked at me expectantly.   So what could I do? My mother would have a fit if I turned him away, especially with him so clean and respectable looking. And she wouldn't mind his Geordie accent like she'd mind Jimmy's Glasgow one.   I shrugged.

"Well you'd better come in, Kevin.   You're a bit late though. It's almost time for the cake and dumpling.

"Ay well, yes, you see I only got the ticket at half past five when Jimmy got back from his Nan's and then I......"

He stopped, and his face turned a deep red as he realised what he'd said.

"Did you say he came back from his Nan's? He came back from his Nan's at half past five?   And gave you his invitation?"

"Yeah well ....he hadn't anything to wear you see. He meant to come but his Nan's tumble dryer broke down and he hasn't anything to wear. I mean his Mam'll have to go down the laundrette in the morning and see if she can get everything dry for Monday."

"I see."

I didn't really see, but it seemed that Kevin's lie was designed to protect Jimmy and make me feel not so bad about his non appearance. If that was the case, it hadn't worked. I liked Kevin well enough. But he wasn't Jimmy and I was devastated.

"Emily? What's the matter, Emily?"

My mother's foosteps were approaching at a fast click.

"Why are you standing there in the hall? There's a terrible draught.   You'll freeze us all to death. Bring your friend in.   And this is Jimmy? Am I right?"

Without waiting for an answer, my mother gave him her bright social smile, closed the door and shooed him into the lounge where the game of forfeits was in full swing. I gave Kevin an apologetic look, shunted him into a chair and fled to the bathroom where I sat for what seemed like ages.

When I'd finally stopped crying, and I thought about what Kevin had said, it gradually dawned on me that Jimmy must be poor. It's funny. I'd never given that a thought before. He was just Jimmy. Okay, he did wear the same clothes every week, but so did a lot of people in the class. And okay, he didn't seem to bring a snack with him for playtime. But that didn't matter because I always gave him some of mine and he said he wasn't that hungry anyway.

And I remebered that, whenever we went on a school trip, Miss McDonald always seemed to send him on an errand for her, and then give him a reward for having done it right; fifty pence to spend on whatever he wanted for himself.

As I sat there in our pine-scented, fluffy bathroom I realised something else. Something that made me feel a bit cheap and guilty. I realised that, in a funny sort of way, I was relieved that it was Kevin standing there all spruced up, and not Jimmy in his smelly school clothes. It dawned on me that Jimmy was being kind to me by sending Kevin in his place. And that made me feel a little better. He probably did love me, after all.

I dried my eyes and went back to blow out the candles on the cake. I don't really remember very much about the rest of the party, but it seems to have been a roaring success.

The following week at school I looked at Jimmy with new eyes. I still loved him. Of course I did. But now that love was kind of different from what it had been like before. It was mixed in with guilt and a feeling of pity. I didn't want Jimmy to be poor and different from me. "Unsuitable" as my mother would have put it. I didn't want to compare him to Kevin Paterson. But I did! I began to notice that Jimmy's hair was oily and greasy, there was a red patch above his lip where the snot ran down and his clothes were the kind you wear when you haven't anything else. I still loved him. But now I felt uncomfortable with him and I didn't like that. It made me feel smaller somehow, and a bit mean.

And then Miss McDonald did something which took us all by surprise. She came in one morning with a piece of paper in her hand and read out a list of names. My name was read out, and so were those of my friends, Beatrice and Hannah, and Kevin Paterson and Len Barbour and some others I didn't know so well. Jimmy's name was missing.

"Right, " said Miss McDonald, " the people whose names I've just read out will start clearing out their desks. Take all your jotters and pens and pencils, but leave your textbooks and anything else that dosen't belong to you. You're moving next door into Mr. Lawson's class and you'll take your exams this year instead of next. It's high time you lot were challenged. You've had it far too easy this year so far. Right get on with it and NO talking."

And so I moved out of Jimmy's class and, when I started at secondary school, out of Jimmy's life. I don't know what happened to him. I never really tried to find out. I do know that he was my first love. And every time I go down the steps into the Glasgow Underground, I remember him and wonder how he's doing. For all I know, he might be a millionaire by now. I'd like to think so.

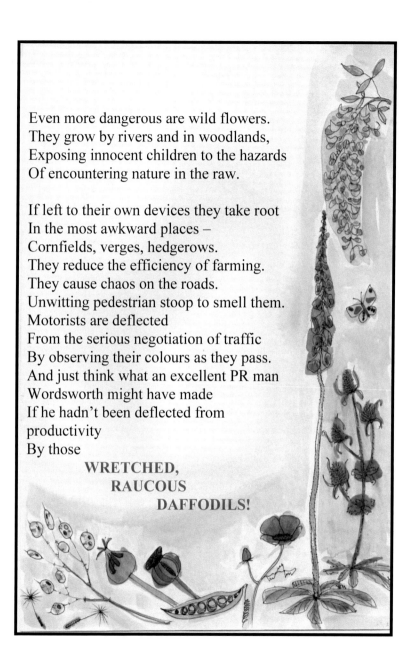

Even more dangerous are wild flowers.
They grow by rivers and in woodlands,
Exposing innocent children to the hazards
Of encountering nature in the raw.

If left to their own devices they take root
In the most awkward places –
Cornfields, verges, hedgerows.
They reduce the efficiency of farming.
They cause chaos on the roads.
Unwitting pedestrian stoop to smell them.
Motorists are deflected
From the serious negotiation of traffic
By observing their colours as they pass.
And just think what an excellent PR man
Wordsworth might have made
If he hadn't been deflected from
productivity
By those
      WRETCHED,
         RAUCOUS
            DAFFODILS!

We therefore call upon farmers,
Local authorities and
All right-minded people
To join together in a campaign
To step up the use of
Herbicides, pesticides
And much more besides.

If we all work together in this way
We can eliminate, once and for all,
The growth of flowers in our land.

Therefore, henceforth all flowers
Will be required to carry
This warning –

**FLOWERS CAN
SERIOUSLY DAMAGE
YOUR HEALTH!**

THE CLOCK

Margaret looked again at the big grandfather clock. The pendulum was swinging away as though it had never been stopped.

"You know," she said, smiling at Colin, "I've no idea how that hypnotist guy can possibly affect inanimate objects but he's done it! The guy's marvellous. That's the first time that clock's worked in years."

She switched off the television.

"How do you think he does it?"

Colin shrugged his shoulders.

"Probably just a coincidence." He yawned widely "You should phone Channel Four and tell them about it. They'll no doubt add it to the list of miracles he's supposed to have performed already."

Margaret laughed and shook her head.

"No. The switchboard's probably jammed as it is."

"Oh, well, you can always tweet about it."

"No way! You know I hate facebook and twitter and all that stuff."

Colin laughed then yawned again.

"Well, I'm off to bed. Coming?"

"No. Not just yet. You go on. I won't be too long behind you."

Margaret sat for a time gazing into the fire. She could hear Colin clumping about upstairs, and then there was silence. She shivered a little in spite of the blaze and glanced once more at the clock. In the silence the ticking seemed to grow until it filled the room. There was something vaguely menacing about it as though a living presence had been released.

Margaret shook her head quickly, smiling a little at her own foolishness. She damped down the last of the blaze and settled the fireguard firmly in place. The sound of the clock followed her out of the room and, as she turned to put out the light, the pendulum flashed as it swung, to and fro, to and fro, hypnotic in its rhythm.

With a quick nervous movement she pressed down the switch, closed the door firmly and ran upstairs; glad, for once, that Colin was so little troubled by imagination. She snuggled into him, reassured by his warmth and the comfortable bulk of his familiar body. She could feel the tension draining from her as she slowly relaxed into sleep.

Suddenly, she was awake. She peered at the alarm by the bedside. Two o'clock. What on earth had wakened her? Then she heard the last of the chimes dying away downstairs.

"Oh, no," she thought, "that wretched clock is making enough noise to wake the dead."

For some reason the thought make her uneasy. She sat up and listened. Nothing. No….there was something. Not a sound….a smell. A smell like….She leaped out of bed and ran downstairs. The smell was unmistakeable now. She hesitated in front of the door, then quickly turned and ran back to the bedroom.

"Colin! Colin! Wake up!"

"What's that?"

He sat up, rubbing sleep from his eyes.

"What's wrong?"

"There's a fire," she gasped. "Downstairs. In the living room."

The fireguard had fallen to one side. Beside it, Margaret's small, antique nursing chair was in flames, and little tongues of fire were licking at the base of the clock.

Colin grabbed a rug and smothered the flames. Within minutes, the blaze had died down to a thick, acrid smoke which caught at their eyes and throats. Colin dragged the chair out into the garden and poured buckets of water over it.

"How on earth did that happen?"

"I've no idea. I know I put the guard on."

"Oh, you probably thought you did. But…" and there was a hint of accusation in his tone, "fires don't just start by themselves."

Margaret gazed at him.

"Like clocks," she said quietly.

69

"What? Oh, for goodness sake. I wish we'd never seen that blasted programme. You've been obsessed with it all night. That's probably why you forgot to check that the fireguard was secure."

"I didn't forg…..oh, never mind," said Margaret wearily.

"Well, at least there wasn't too much damage done. It could have been a lot worse if you hadn't wakened in time."

He paused for a moment, puzzled.

"What was it that wakened you anyway? Did you smell the smoke?"

"No," she replied evenly. "I heard the clock chime."

She turned and walked back into the living room. Everything seemed normal, or as normal as it could be after what had happened. She looked up at Colin as he followed her into the room.

"I was very fond of that chair," she said. "Do you remember when we bought it?"

Colin put his arm round her shoulders, pulling her towards him. He still marvelled at how small and slight she felt. He traced the few grey hairs on her crown with his finger.

"I remember," he said softly. He could feel her body shaking.

"Don't cry," he whispered. "It all happened a long time ago."

Margaret looked up, dry eyed and with a tight, hard expression on her face.

"Yes," she said harshly, "a long time ago. Nine years to be precise. Do you remember what we did?" She wrenched herself free. "We stopped the clock. Do you understand? Oh, my god." She began to laugh hysterically. "We killed her. Isn't that funny? Our own little girl. And we killed her."

She dropped to her knees and rocked backwards and forwards, keeping time to the pendulum.

"Tick tock." She chanted. "Tick tock."

"Margaret stop it. Do you hear me. Stop it." He pulled her to her feet and shook her roughly. She stopped laughing then and the tears ran slowly down her cheeks.

"You think I'm mad, don't you?"

"Of course not. You've had a shock. That's all. Come on. Come to bed. You'll feel better in the morning."

"No! You must listen. Now! Don't you see? We killed her. As surely as if we'd taken a knife and cut her throat."

"Oh for god's sake, Margaret, I…"

"No. Don't go. You must listen. Why can't you see it? She was restless all night. We blamed the noise of the clock chiming. We said it was the noise that was keeping her awake. You wouldn't wind it up the next day. And," she moved over to the window and stood looking out into the darkness of the garden, "and that night she seemed to sleep so peacefully. Do you remember? You said that proved it. And in the morning when I went to wake her, she, she….."

"Hush. Don't torture yourself. There was nothing we could have done. The doctor explained it all at the time. Cot death. It just happens sometimes. We couldn't have saved her."

"We killed her," she said stubbornly. "We stopped the clock. And later, when we tried to wind it up, it wouldn't go. It's stood there like an ornament ever since."

"Oh, for god's sake, Margaret," he said brutally. "Stop all this nonsense about the clock. She died because of cot death. There isn't a day goes by when I don't think of her, wonder if we could have done anything, torture myself imagining what she'd be like now. If I could do anything in this world to bring her back I'd do it. But I can't." He leant on the mantelpiece and passed his hand wearily over his brow. "I'm sorry, Margaret, but you must try to accept it. There was nothing we could have done."

She moved from him then and stood in front of the clock.

"We might have wakened in time to save her," she whispered, "if we'd heard the clock chiming."

Colin could feel the rage that threatened to erupt with even breath.

"We never wanted the damn clock in the first place," he muttered between clenched teeth. "We only took it because the nursing chair and the clock were being sold as a set. The auctioneer practically paid us to take the bloody thing away. And it wasn't going then either, if you remember!"

"No," she agreed. "It only started after we moved it in here into that corner. I thought it was such a friendly thing to have beside me when I was feeding Rosie. Something big and comforting for her to look at, even if it never worked. And then, when it started to go, do you know what you said? You said the jolt it got coming off the van must have shocked it into life. That's what you said," she repeated tonelessly, "into life."

"Oh, don't be so melodramatic. It's a clock, that's all. A bloody clock."

"No," she insisted. "No, it's more than that. Don't ask me how I know. I just know, that's all." She looked up at him almost triumphantly. "That's why the set couldn't be broken up. That's why the will said the clock must go with the chair."

He stared at her for a moment, seeing a stranger. Then the clock began to chime the hour. The sound seemed to rob him of his wits. He reached down and picked up the heavy brass poker from the hearth and, turning away from her, struck savagely at the front of the clock, striking it again and again. Glass and wood splintered but the chiming continued.

She leapt forward, clutching his arm.

"No," she sobbed. "No, don't kill it. Don't kill it!"

Suddenly there was silence. The front of the clock was in pieces, the wood crushed and bent, the pendulum still. Only the hands remained untouched, still pointing to three.

She stood, gazing in horror at him as he sank slowly to his knees. He was crying, his whole body wracked with sobs. And yet, he made no sound.

It was as if something in her snapped. Colin! Strong, dependable, rugby playing Colin. Colin was crying!

She reached forward and gently withdrew the poker from his clenched hands.

"You did the right thing," she murmured softly, pressing him to her and holding him as one would a child. "You did the right thing. We'll get someone to take it away in the morning. It has too many memories for both of us." She raised him gently to his feet and led him unprotesting from the room. "Come to bed now. It'll be alright in the morning."

They slept late the next day. Missing breakfast altogether, neither of them referred to what had happened till after lunch.

"Margaret, I'm sorry, "he started, "I don't know what…"
She leaned over and placed a finger on his lips.

"Sh," she said almost gaily, "there's work to be done." She stood and surveyed the mess around the fireside. "Look, you tidy up here and I'll nip down to the village and see the insurance people. Then I'll see about getting all this rubbish uplifted."

"Thanks," he answered simply. "Yes, you do that. That would be the best thing.

They smiled at each other, then she reached up and kissed him softly. "See you later," she whispered.

It was one of those fine autumn days. The sun seemed like a pale reflection of the trees and there was just a hint of frost to come. Margaret

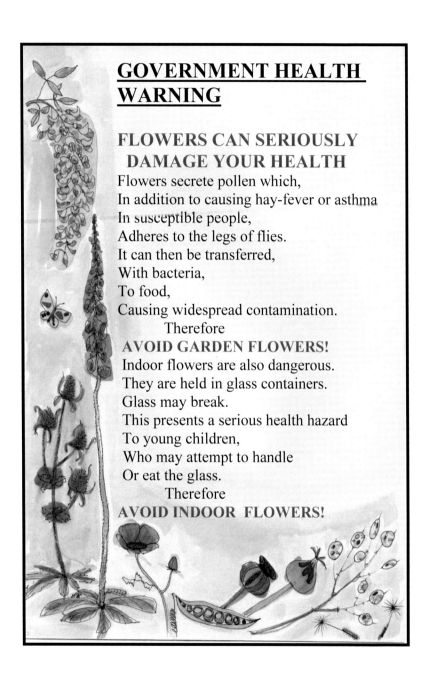

GOVERNMENT HEALTH WARNING

FLOWERS CAN SERIOUSLY DAMAGE YOUR HEALTH

Flowers secrete pollen which,
In addition to causing hay-fever or asthma
In susceptible people,
Adheres to the legs of flies.
It can then be transferred,
With bacteria,
To food,
Causing widespread contamination.
　　　Therefore
AVOID GARDEN FLOWERS!
Indoor flowers are also dangerous.
They are held in glass containers.
Glass may break.
This presents a serious health hazard
To young children,
Who may attempt to handle
Or eat the glass.
　　　Therefore
AVOID INDOOR FLOWERS!

locked the car and walked briskly down the High Street. She felt strangely light hearted.

"Too little sleep, I suppose," she thought, as she composed her face into an expression doleful enough to suit the insurance company.

On her way back to the car she lingered in front of the flower beds in the square. On a sudden impulse, she turned and nipped into the little pub on the corner.

"Hello, Harry. How's business then?"

"Hello Mrs. Morrison. I haven't seen you or your husband in here in ages. Everything alright, is it?"

"Yes. How about you?"

"Me? Oh there's never much wrong with me. Well now, what can I do for you?"

"Any chance of a table for two tonight? About eightish?"

"Yes, of course, Mrs. Morrison. We're never too busy on weeknights. Celebrating?"

She smiled at him. "You could put it that way. Perhaps we're just laying a few ghosts."

"Ghosts?"

Margaret laughed. "Forget it, Harry. Just a rather bad private joke." She looked over his shoulder to the clock above the bar. "Heavens! Is that the time? Ten to three?"

"No. That clocks about ten minutes fast." He winked at her. "Gives me time to chuck people out, eh?"

She left him chuckling at his own joke and made her way back to the car. The light heartedness she had felt was gone now and she almost regretted the impulse to book a meal. All she wanted was to be home.

As she rounded the bend at the foot of the hill, she felt a sudden stabbing pain in her chest. It was so severe that she wrenched at the wheel and the car slewed half across the road before she managed to control it.

She drew to a shuddering halt and sat gasping as wave after wave of pain hit her and was gone. She tensed herself against the next one but it never came. She shivered slightly and lifted her wrist from the wheel. The hands of her watch were pointing to three. With a sudden cold certainty, she knew!

She started the car and drove swiftly home. The charred remains of the chair lay on the lawn and the front door was open. She stepped into the hall and pushed open the door of the living room.

Colin lay face down on the floor with the heavy clock on top of him. She rushed forward and, with a huge effort, heaved it off him and turned him over.

Piercing his chest like an arrow was the solid brass pendulum. The hands of the clock still pointed to three. And the clock was ticking.

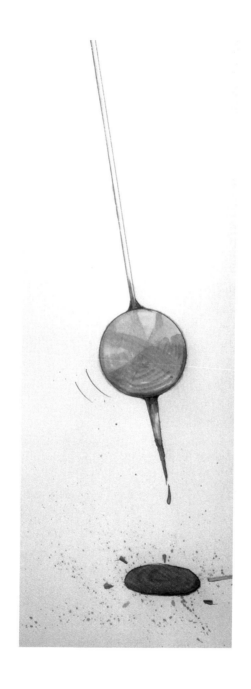

PEACE IN THE SILENCE

There is no such thing as silence.
Noise is everywhere.
In the small ticking of the clock,
In the loud bark of the dog,
In the tiny creaks and grumblings
That tell of a house,
A home,
Settling into its allotted place
In time and space;

In the flutter and chirp
Of songbirds in summer,
In the roar of traffic
Muted by snow in winter.

Even the tiniest sound
Can loom large
In the vacuum created
By ever-circling thoughts
That crowd and rob the brain
Of sense and feeling.
And finally stop.

In this vacuum
There is no such thing as silence.
Yet there may be,
Of a kind,
Peace.

<u>Acknowledgements</u>

Ann would like to thank the following people for all their help and encouragement and, without whom, this book would never have seen the light of day:
Liz, not only for her illustrations but also for her help in proof reading and her patience throughout; my husband Andy for his love, encouragement, support and especially for his remedial actions when my computer refused to co-operate! Thanks also to Eliot whose help during the printing process was invaluable.